The Way of the Gadfly

The Way of the Gadfly

A Study of Coherency
in Socratic Thought

Ryszard Legutko

St. Augustine's Press

South Bend, Indiana

Manufactured in the United States of America.

1 2 3 4 5 6 29 28 27 26 25 24

Library of Congress Control Number: 2024939380

Paperback ISBN: 978-1-58731-593-0
ebook ISBN: 978-1-58731-594-7

∞ The paper used in this publication meets the minimum requirements of the American National Standard for Information Sciences – Permanence of Paper for Printed Materials, ANSI Z39.48-1984.

St. Augustine's Press
www.staugustine.net

Table of Contents

Introduction

A historian of philosophy writing a book about Socrates is akin to an actor playing Hamlet. For both, it is a great temptation and a great challenge. Socrates is the focus of everything that matters most in philosophy: from rigorous arguments to the art of living, from abstract speculations to riveting personal experience. He is famous for his incessantly critical spirit, paradoxical arguments, and irony inherent in logical aporia. Yet notwithstanding what is conventionally thought to be true about him, doubts abound. Socrates leaves us no definitive interpretation of his thought, which grants much room—perhaps too much—for interpretation.

This book is the fruit of several decades of research. Ancient texts, particularly those written by Plato, reveal their meaning gradually. Every close reading uncovers new content and, with it, a possibility for a new interpretation. Yet, neither does one have the feeling that the ultimate meaning has been grasped nor that the content has been exhausted. Classic texts invite a lifetime of study. If I were to write a book summarizing Socrates' thought after ten more years of study, the end result might not be identical.

Synthesizing Socrates' philosophy in a single monograph is risky for yet another reason. Scholars over the centuries have already dedicated themselves to the arduous interpretive work. Dozens of first-class minds have produced scores of scholarly and popular volumes. Whoever still sets about writing a book about Socrates must have a good reason to do so.

My reason was simple. Returning to the texts about Socrates by Plato, Xenophon, Aristophanes, Aristotle, Plutarch, and others led me to certain interpretative ideas, initially vague but becoming increasingly clear. They were interesting enough to examine in-depth and to attempt to organize into one interpretative construction. And after several years of work, I managed to gather various threads of Socratic thought into a coherent whole. The image of this whole, although including familiar elements, does not always remain within the boundaries of accepted interpretations.

Every deliberate act of interpretation requires an initial impulse to determine its direction. Sometimes more than one impulse conspire to plot the scholar's course. Three intuitions emerged in my mind not long after beginning my Socratic trek. None of them is truly original, but neither are they terribly obvious. They nevertheless set the course for further research, helping me first to shape more detailed hypotheses.

My first intuition concerns Socrates' moral impact on the people around him. To my surprise, quite possibly the most illustrious teacher of morality, famous for his miraculous ability to open the minds of his interlocutors, suffered a stunning defeat in educational terms. Much has been written about his influence on others, yet that is not the picture painted by the ancient authors. Those surrounding Socrates, those who considered themselves his students or disciples or were regarded as such by others, seemed to understand precious little of his teachings. It is difficult to identify a single character in Plato's dialogues, who could be said to have taken Socrates' teachings to heart and changed his life accordingly. It is more likely that his interlocutors' approval of his ethical guidelines in no way influenced their conduct. Even those in the closest and longest-standing relation to the philosopher failed to draw any conclusions from their master's and friend's teachings. His intellectual impact on the philosophers who came after him was immense; his impact on the actions and lifestyle of those who surrounded him—negligible.

My second intuition relates to Socrates' intellectual stance, which has been usually contrasted with that of his greatest student, Plato. Plato has the reputation of an authoritarian philosopher, one who, in the dialogues, openly imposes his views on the interlocutors, himself being the sole authoritative commentator, interpreter, and sometimes critic of the philosophical arguments. In his later works, Plato often uses the form of mock dialogue—mock, because the person leading the conversation does not expect his participants to respond, only to acknowledge his reasoning. The Socrates of Plato's early dialogues usually argues, sometimes backs down, demonstrates instances of aporia, and sometimes distances himself from his own words. His was truly an image of fertility: the philosopher who not so much talks to others as stimulates them to think, arouses their interest in certain problems, induces them to examine their own views, and introduces an intellectual ferment.

It all looks very attractive, but—and this was my second discovery—it has little to do with reality. A closer reading reveals that Socrates was neither particularly dialogue-oriented nor especially committed to inspiring his interlocutors to undertake the intellectual effort. His was consistently *the* dominant mind, even as (or *especially* when) he was wearing a simpleton's mask. At all times, he tightly controls the course of the exchange, its design, and its end. His conversations, as related by Plato, offer insight into the workings of an extraordinary mind, for which the interlocutors turn out to be a reflective background. When examined in some depth, the question-and-answer format turns out to be an overt display of Socrates' intellectual virtuosity. The basic premises of his reasoning do not come forth from the minds of the interlocutors as a result of Socrates' intellectual stirring or midwifery. They have, rather, been planted there by Socrates himself so as to lead an argument to its predefined or anticipated conclusion.

My third intuition concerns Socrates' attitude toward democracy. At present, there is a tendency to dilute the philosopher's criticisms of it. Close reading of Plato's dialogues strengthened my initial view that Socrates' disapproval of democracy was both profound and principled. His particular experience in Athens was a life lived in a democratic society among democratic citizens, who were shaped by the very political system that they were busy shaping. The human soul that provoked his theoretical reflection was the soul of the democratic man. What he discovered was not encouraging, either for philosophy or for the health of the soul. Socrates disapproves of the democratic man because he discovers in him a deep-seated dislike of both philosophical reflection and of self-reflection and, in general, of the pursuit of truth. For those and other reasons, deferring to the expectations of the *demos* constituted a deadly threat to the soul. The democratic man, after refusing to subject his views to critical reflection, henceforth felt no need to justify them.

The philosopher's deeply critical attitude toward democracy reveals a more puzzling question. Socrates passionately interacted with other people. He never tired of interrogating them, often overcoming their resistance, and he did all this because, as he believed, the god expected him to. Putting divine command aside, why ever engage so deeply in conversation with a democratic man if one views him so negatively? Why put such effort into a philosophical project that seems to already possess a foregone conclusion?

These intuitions were the points of departure when I began construct-ing my interpretation of Socratic philosophy. The initial picture of the philosopher was somewhat perplexing: one of the greatest moralists in his-tory, who did not manage to educate anyone in his periphery; a master of philosophical dialogue whose interlocutors served as background for his carefully choreographed monologue; a philosopher who—to quote Cic-ero—"was the first to call philosophy down from the heavens and to place it in cities, and even to introduce it into homes," but who simultaneously shows how badly it is always going to be treated in those cities and homes.

Socrates' philosophy is, therefore, full of pitfalls and traps from the out-set. Describing Socratic thought as full of paradoxes is tantamount to pos-ing the problem anew, not finding a solution. A better approach is to ask and attempt to answer whether Socratic paradoxes might be explained or even resolved. The book puts forward a thesis that Socrates' thinking is sys-temic rather than paradoxical or aporetic. He might have been a gadfly—after all, the metaphor he uses about himself accurately captures his inquisitive mind that irritated so many of his contemporaries—but what he was after were not occasional intellectual disputes or intermittent logical victories, rather a coherent moral philosophy that could, potentially, have a larger ramification in a system of knowledge.

The book is about Socrates as depicted in Plato's dialogues, with only a few references to Aristophanes and Xenophon. As it happens, Plato's account gained a dominant position at some point. This is no surprise since there are two kinds of good reasons—literary and philosophical—behind it. Still, nei-ther is free of problems. It is true that Plato was a great artist, and it was his art of writing that produced the Socrates who has shaped the European mind in the last twenty-five centuries. But there is also a flipside to it. If Plato is a literary genius, then his "Socrates" is easily an artistic creation, not the real historical figure. The myth of Socrates, its power, and the moral paradigms that originated from it, can therefore be interpreted as belonging to the realm of imagination. Perhaps, as some argue, for centuries we have dealt (almost) exclusively with the Socratic legend rooted solely in Plato's literary and artistic creation.[1] When reconstructing Socrates' thoughts from the works of others,

1   Serious doubts about the truthfulness of these accounts were already raised by scholars in the 19th century (Georg Anton Friedrich Ast and Martinus

we are confronted with the extremely difficult task of separating the real from the imaginary. The actual Socrates, who existed and taught in Athens, constantly eludes our direct perception. He is seen only through a glass darkly.

The philosophical rationale that makes Plato the principal authority is no less tricky. Socrates appears in most of his dialogues, and it is clear that in many of them he is not related in any way to the historical figure but rather communicates Plato's views and arguments. In these works, he is deprived of his characteristic personal qualities and becomes solely a vehicle for certain philosophical points of view (e.g., *Republic*, except Book I). Thus, it is prudent to conclude that the surest way to proceed would be to separate the Socratic dialogues from the Platonic ones, those that seem to recount the views expressed by the historical Socrates from those in which Plato presents his own ideas. Such a conclusion may be supplemented with an extra common-sense rule, which maintains that Socratic dialogues belong to Plato's early works, whereas strictly Platonic dialogues are written later. This approach is common, although not universally accepted.

Schanz). The best-known examples of this approach in the first half of the 20th century are Dupréel (1922) and Gigon (1947). The former treated everything about Socrates as a legend, whereas the latter attempted to demonstrate that the real Socrates was an insignificant individual and became what he did thanks to literature; therefore, one must not rely on any information about the supposedly real person because the extant texts contain different or even contradictory information; hence any attempt to establish the hard facts beyond the basics related to his biography represents "a fruitless effort" (1947:64). DeVogel (1970a) wrote polemically about the ideas of Gigon and of other authors who doubted the presence of any important truths in Socrates' philosophy or even questioned his existence. Another author who emphasised the literary nature of writings about Socrates was Chroust, who argued that "since the whole of the ancient Socratic literature seems to be primarily intentional legend, ... we know practically nothing about him" (1957:225). Later authors representing this line of thinking include Mario Montuori, who, as he himself writes, goes even further than Gigon: "The Swiss scholar insisted that the sources were literary, removed from reality and not historical. ... The present investigation has found that Plato, quite simply, has not told us the truth. He profoundly altered the character of Socrates' personality ... and he gives us in point of fact the fictitious and literary image ... that has nothing whatsoever to do with the Socrates indicted, tried and condemned" (1981:142).

Analyzing them chronologically, the views of Plato's Socrates appear to become increasingly complex; sometimes they even cease to be directly related to those presented in the earliest dialogues. Yet the later dialogues belonging to the middle period, such as the *Gorgias*, depict a Socrates that predates the Socrates of the earliest works, such as the *Apology* and the *Crito*. In other words, the chronology of Socrates' life does not correspond with the order in which Plato's dialogues are composed. As a result, it may be presumed that Socrates' thought grows in complexity not so much because subsequent strands of his ideas are gradually revealed, rather due to Plato's maturation as a philosopher, who may have begun to notice certain aspects of his teacher's views he had not formerly seen. Plato may also have slowly begun to present his own reflections using the same engaging literary formula of the Socratic *logos*.

The above remarks touch upon only a handful of the most important questions behind the "Socrates problem." With the necessarily limited historical material, it cannot be fully resolved. The relation between the historical figure and the literary character will remain forever uncertain. Notwithstanding trifles, studying it, formulating new arguments, and analyzing the old ones is not an exercise in futility. Certain partial findings are acceptable—at least provisionally. Any project aimed at interpreting Socrates' thought in its entirety must begin either with making specific decisions about the assumptions concerning the "Socrates problem," or with an initial qualitative analysis of the available material. Or both.

With regard to Plato, the literature seeking to establish which dialogues are more Socratic and which more Platonic—in other words, which ones represent at least an approximation of truth about Socrates and which ones use his character to convey Plato's philosophical views—is enormous and inconclusive. A number of appealing hypotheses have been formulated to justify one or another choice of dialogues on one or the other side. Even the most popular and common-sense interpretation, which associates earlier dialogues with Socrates and later ones with Plato, is controversial. There are authors who completely reject it—and their arguments are hard to ignore or dismiss as completely groundless. Eminent experts on Plato have proposed that almost all the dialogues, apart from the last ones, convey Socrates' views. Conversely, other likewise outstanding scholars attribute all views to Plato and place Socrates himself beyond the reach of our historical horizon. Even the *Apology*, frequently named the most documentary of Plato's texts, is sometimes interpreted as a work of literary fiction.[2]

2   The history of theories devoted to the sources of knowledge about Socrates' views is long and complex. The argument that Socrates' views should be sought in Plato's dialogues was advanced in the early 20th century primarily by Burnet and Taylor, distinguished British scholars ranking among the foremost experts on the subject (Burnet 1928:126–28; 1998: xii–xxiii, xxxviii, li–liii Taylor, 1911; 1953:34). Naturally, it did not settle the issue of which dialogues should be regarded as presenting Socrates' ideas, and which ones advanced Plato's own views. Burnet and Taylor greatly expanded the number of Socratic dialogues and reduced the number of Platonic ones; for example, the theory of ideas was considered to be a Socratic concept. Previously, Paul Shorey, a prominent American scholar, published a work on the unity of Plato's philosophy (Shorey 1903), deliberately rejecting the chronology of the dialogues as a criterion for identifying Plato's actual views; thus, Socrates as a historical figure merged with "Plato's Socrates." A similar position was taken by Diès according to whom Socratism and Platonism were "le dehors et le dedans d'une même unité vivante" (Diès I:169). Xenophon's works as a source of knowledge about Socrates were not entirely discredited either. But the adoption of Plato's work by Burnet and Taylor as a primary source of knowledge about Socrates was not universally accepted. Soon after the publications of the fundamental works by both British scholars, Robin, an eminent French expert on Greek philosophy, published a critical analysis of Burnet's and Taylor's ideas (1942a). De Magalhães-Vilhena took a rather obscure position on these questions (1952 passim). Approximately at the same time, in the mid-1950s, Hackforth stated that Burnet's and Taylor's opinions were "almost universally rejected" (Hackforth 1992:128), and several years later Guthrie wrote that these views "find little support today, if any at all" (Guthrie 1977:31). But these declarations were only justified in part. It is true that analysts ceased to attribute Plato's theory of ideas and other related concepts to Socrates. Still, Plato's authority as the main source of knowledge about Socrates was upheld. Gregory Vlastos reduced the number of Socratic dialogues and increased the number of Platonic ones, arguing confidently that Socrates' ideas can be clearly identified and isolated, and that the philosophy of the historical Socrates can be found in the early dialogues but also what he called "transitional dialogues" which include, among others, *Meno, Lysis, Euthydemus, Greater Hippias* (Vlastos 1991:45–80). This does not mean that Vlastos' verdict was universally accepted. The best-known opponent of the view that Plato was the source of knowledge about Socrates is Charles Kahn, who suggested a modified chronology of the dialogues and changed the starting point: he claimed that we should

Some of these disputes arise from the different opinions pertaining to the chronology of the dialogues. Sometimes it is impossible to classify certain dialogues as belonging to the middle or to the early periods. The most difficult to position are the *Gorgias*, *Meno*, and *Phaedo*. For example, the concept of *anamnesis* appears both in the *Meno* and in the *Phaedo*, but in distinctly different versions. Is one of them Socratic, and if so, which one? Or perhaps none of them is? One might also justifiably argue that *anamnesis* does not belong at all in Socrates' philosophical inventory.

Problems are also caused by those dialogues that can be said with reasonable certainty to teach Plato's philosophy yet still contain Socratic elements. Socrates as a character is depicted in them so vividly and with such a sense of psychological insight that it is difficult to dismiss them as works of complete fiction. This is the case with the *Phaedo*, the *Phaedrus*, and the *Theaetetus*. The *Phaedo* appears to have been written before the *Republic* (which is considered to belong to the middle period and, hence, Platonic), whereas the *Phaedrus* and the *Theaetetus* were written afterward. Moreover, in all these works, Socrates does much more than fascinates as a character; certain views expressed are indeed attributable to him. The *Phaedrus* features an episode devoted to the *daimonion*, which is one of Socrates' distinguishing features. In the *Theaetetus*, Socrates mentions his maieutic art and his mother, who was a midwife, which suggests an authentic reference rather than a literary device. Next, in the *Phaedo*, Socrates discusses the development of his philosophy. For a number of reasons, the *Symposium* is quite accurately regarded as a Platonic dialogue but it also contains biographical information about Socrates' relationship with Alcibiades, as well as the problem of irony, another important distinguishing feature of Socrates' philosophy.

Whatever, then, the division between the early Socratic and later Platonic dialogues is assumed to be, conclusions are never simple. Socratic elements are present in numerous dialogues, including the later and very late

seek an anticipation of the views held by the mature Plato in his earlier dialogues, rather than regard them as a chronicle of his teacher's actions (Kahn 1992:35–52 and 1988, cf. also Halper 1992:81–87; Prior 1997:109–24). For a critique of the purported difference between the two Socrateses in Plato's works see Rowe 2006.

ones. In the *Parmenides*, the eponymous philosopher meets the young Socrates. The details of the conversation certainly come from Plato, yet the mere mention of such a meeting should make us wonder not only about its historical authenticity, but also about its possible philosophical consequences.

Scholars writing about Socrates usually make use of all these sources. In this respect, my approach is not very restrictive. I am not involved in the debate as to whether Socrates was a historical figure. I have assumed that the basic sources of our knowledge about Socrates are Plato's early dialogues as well as certain early-middle and middle dialogues. I confront the *Phaedo* selectively, as is done with the *Theaetetus* and the *Symposium*. I also consider Book I of the *Republic* to be Socratic, which is not an uncommon position amongst scholars.

I therefore assume that the information presented in later dialogues can be utilized if a good reason is offered. This demands that one address whether it can be shown to be consistent with what is said in the Socratic dialogues and with the information handed down to us by Aristophanes and Xenophon. This approach permits a certain evolution of Socrates' views but rejects the possibility of any contradiction in them. For him, contradiction was always tantamount to error. I cannot claim to be certain that my reconstruction and interpretation refer entirely to the philosopher who existed and lived in Athens and that no literary element has slipped in. But neither can any other scholars, for that matter. This does not entail that the views presented and analyzed here refer only to a certain personal-*cum*-philosophical construct created by Plato, which has been developed for dozens of generations and has become rooted in our imagination so strongly that we consider it real. Despite Plato's genius, I do not think that he was capable of creating one of the greatest heroes of Western culture without a living prototype. In the words of a prominent scholar of Plato, I believe that "authentic Socratic thought survives in Plato's recreation of it."[3]

3   Vlastos 1988:111.

Chapter I - Knowledge

1. In search of knowledge

The thesis of this chapter is that for Socrates, knowledge was a system of logically connected propositions and that his philosophical activity was largely an attempt to discover parts of such a system. This means that we can attribute to Socrates a very early version—somewhat naïve, to be sure—of the coherence theory according to which justification of the propositions is, in fact, the criterion of truth, and the propositions cannot be justified but by other propositions. This does not mean that Socrates weakened the concept of truth. On the contrary, some of his statements he thought unquestionably true, and in his search for consistency, he used them as the pillars of the system.

1.1 Socrates' criteria of knowledge (SCK)

To have a theory of knowledge presupposes a well-developed epistemological awareness. Indeed, Socrates is probably the first philosopher with such a quality and to a high degree. This can be indirectly confirmed by the constant insistence of his own ignorance, which could not have happened without being aware of what he lacked in knowledge and longed to have. He may have been ignorant—which he was not, not literally, that is—but he certainly could identify which statements he was able to justify and where justification failed, which statements could and which could not be reconciled. The problem of what does and what does not count as knowledge absorbs him from the beginning.

There is no better illustration of this than a well-known passage in the *Apology*. Socrates cited the prophecy of the Delphic oracle, according to which none was wiser than himself (21a3–8). He disagreed with those who called him a sage—after all, he is capable of finding glaring ignorance in himself—and tried to undermine the prevailing opinion to that effect.

The easiest way to do so was to find someone wiser. With this in mind, he questions the representatives of the three important groups constituting Athenian society: the politicians, the poets, and the craftsmen. The effects of these conversations proved disappointing: it turned out that none of the interlocutors was wise, although they themselves thought the opposite.

Exerting great effort to uncover ignorance in his interlocutors, Socrates must have presupposed his possession of positive criteria of knowledge. Without these criteria, his assertion that this or that group lacked knowledge would have been arbitrary, especially since in none of the crafts he examined—politics, poetry, and artisanship—did he have any competence. The only way to prove he could legitimately detect ignorance in these fields was to claim he had the epistemological tools—formal, not substantive—with which he could assess his interlocutors' statements. This was an extremely bold move, though not an entirely new one in Greek philosophy. Before him, Parmenides had discredited the entirety Ionian philosophy by introducing the conceptual distinction between 'is' and 'is not,' without refuting any specific arguments and conceptions of his predecessors. Socrates' move was likewise bold: he admitted not having knowledge in the disciplines represented by his interlocutors and yet, with complete self-assurance, he made himself the supreme judge in deciding whether what they said did or did not qualify as knowledge.

Socrates did not specify on what grounds he made his harsh judgments about the ignorance of the politicians, poets, and artisans, but when one examines what he said, one can quite easily discover how he identified knowledge and how he distinguished it from ignorance.

About the politicians, he made the following statements:

(i) they were not wise but considered themselves to be so, as did others;
(ii) they knew nothing about "the most important things" (*kalon kagathon*—21d4), although they believed otherwise;
(iii) those politicians who enjoyed a particularly good reputation were the least deserving; whereas others, generally considered inferior, were "more knowledgeable" (22a5–6).

Next, he characterized the poets:

11

(i) they said "many fine things," but they "knew none of the things they [said]" (22c3);
(ii) they did not create their works on the merit of knowledge, but "by nature and by inspiration" (22c1–2), as did the prophets and soothsayers;
(iii) thanks to their creative output, they considered themselves to be wise in other matters, whereas, in fact, they were not.

And finally, Socrates described the craftsmen:

(i)   they knew matters in which Socrates himself lacked competence;
(ii) they believed that by virtue of their "success at their craft" (22d6–7), they were also wise "in other most important matters" (22d7);
(iii) such a belief constituted a "folly" and "obscure[d] that wisdom" (Grube trans.)

When talking about knowing, Socrates used three words—wisdom (*sophia*), craft (*technē*), knowledge. "Wisdom" recurs throughout the passages but remains undefined. "Knowledge" was expressed by the verb *oida* in various forms. Thus, after talking to a certain Athenian, Socrates said, "I am likely to be wiser than he to this small extent, that I do not think I know (*oida*) what I do not know (*eidenai*)" (21d6–7, Grube trans.). In other dialogues, the meaning was conveyed by the noun *epistēmē* and by the verb *epistamai*. *Technē* must have also overlapped with wisdom. When Socrates criticized the craftsmen for having illegitimately extended the scope of their craft, he said it was a "folly" that "obscure[d] that wisdom."

It is safe to assume that in the passage, the three concepts have roughly the same meaning and Socrates used them, in most contexts, interchangeably.[1] Whatever the difference between wisdom, knowledge, and *technē*, he did not think it sufficiently important to reflect upon it in formulating his argument about the Athenians' collective ignorance.

1 In this, I disagree with Brickhouse and Smith, who distinguish between "the kind of knowledge that is constitutive of wisdom and a kind (or some kinds) that is (are) not" (1994:38). Nothing in Socrates' critique of the three groups suggests that he assumed such a distinction. Nor do I think that Socrates linked *sophia* with *sōphrosynē*, and not with knowledge (King 2008).

The conversation with the three groups is the first attempt in Plato's Socratic dialogues to indicate, though somewhat indirectly, the conditions that knowledge must fulfill. Let us call them Socrates' criteria of knowledge (SCK).

The first of these is the correct identification of its proper object (IO). This can be seen in Socrates' criticism of the poets and the craftsmen. Their fundamental mistake consisted in exceeding their shared area of expertise: the poets considered themselves to be wise in other respects as well, while the craftsmen were eager to express their opinions on "other most important matters." Whatever good things they managed to convey in their respective fields of competence, they lost any credibility they may have accrued once they ventured beyond it. This was particularly evident in the case of the craftsmen, whom Socrates rated the highest of all the groups under consideration. Indeed, he accused them of only one thing—namely, that they tended to go beyond the object of their craft. Yet this error alone sufficed to discredit them.

The second criterion is a hierarchy of the objects of cognition (HO). A relatively favorable opinion about craftsmen is somewhat misleading insofar as they violated the principle that the objects of cognition are arranged in a hierarchical order, and for Socrates, knowledge only properly applies to those objects that occupy the highest tiers in this hierarchy. This can be easily discerned in Socrates' criticism of politicians who were unable to discern the proper object of the political craft, which, according to Socrates, was *kalon kagathon*, or "the most important things."[2] The craftsmen had this ability but the objects of their *technai* were inferior to those of the politicians.

Socrates did not explicitly describe the nature of this hierarchy, but it seems clear enough. The craftsmen produce things that are important for human life but not as important as those that the politicians are expected to provide. Elsewhere Socrates said that politics is a *technē* that has as its

---

2   This epistemological hierarchy was not a controversial idea. Some of Socrates' interlocutors promoted it themselves, though, of course, not necessarily in accordance with his philosophy. In the *Gorgias*, the eponymous sophist described rhetoric as the supreme skill of "the greatest and the best of human concerns" (451d7). Plato followed in Socrates' footsteps and formulated his own hierarchy. In the *Republic*, he mentioned "the most important subjects" of cognition (503e4), and that "the greatest thing to learn is the idea of good" (505a2).

object the human soul (*Gorgias* 464d4), and the soul is more important than the human body. Politics then was more important than gymnastics and medicine, the *technai* that take care of the physical condition of the body (464d6–7), and, as we can guess, this should likewise be superior to other *technai* such as carpentry or masonry.

The third criterion—the hierarchy of expertise (HEX)—is the consequence of the second. The *Apology* alludes to the hierarchy of expertise in the quoted passage and elsewhere (20a–c), but we find this explicitly stated in the *Crito*: "[W]hen a man is in training … he [does not] pay heed to the praise or censure or opinion of each and every man … only to those of the individual who happens to be his doctor or trainer" (47b1–3, Gallop trans.). The criterion allowed Socrates to reject the political/democratic claims to truth. The fact that he thought he should include this rejection in the concept of knowledge means there was a widespread conviction—not surprising in a democratic society—concerning the close connection between the truth and the opinion of the majority. But the criterion expressed something more, namely, that knowledge is established by the individual mind and follows only its rules. And if the individual mind succeeds in discovering the truth, it is no longer individual but represents the truth itself (*Crito* 48a6–7). The higher the object in the hierarchy of knowledge, the more difficult it is to achieve expertise. Hence, ideally, at the top of this hierarchy, there is the supreme expert or master of the *technē*, who represents the power of truth.

The fourth criterion one can detect in certain evocative words that Socrates used. When he recounted his search for men wiser than himself, he said he had tried to refute (*elenxon*) the oracle, but it turned out to be irrefutable (*anelenktos*—22a7–8), thereby introducing a crucial notion for his concept of knowledge—namely, that of *elenchus*. In short, knowledge must be subjected to critical analysis (CA). The crucial aspect of this analysis is consistency: the *elenchus* served primarily—though not exclusively and, as will be argued, not ultimately—to detect all inconsistencies and contradictions.

This leads to the fifth criterion. Socrates judged the knowledge of the three groups not on what they did but on what they said. Knowledge had to be expressed in speech. This was most unusual. The politicians were (and still are) judged on how well they ruled their society, not on how well they talked about it; the poets were (and still are) judged on the quality of their works, not on talking about them; the craftsmen—on what they produced, not on their reflections on their craft. Yet Socrates examined their theoretical competence rather than practical performance and concluded that his interlocutors failed to meet the criterion according to which whoever possesses knowledge must be able to give a theoretical account (TA)—*didonai logon*.[3]

This means that what constituted knowledge was *logos*—not simply a practical skill or an ability to give correct answers—but *logos* in the sense of a proposition, but rather a chain of propositions forming an argument and a theory. The *Apology* does not say explicitly that a good craftsman, a good poet, and a good politician, just as any person who aspires to knowledge, should be able to have a clear awareness of a theory that explains and justifies their respective activity, but he blames them for not having it. From the entire episode with the politicians, poets, and craftsmen, one can infer three reasons why the theoretical *logoi* are indispensable for knowledge. Having such a theory would prevent the representatives of those groups from mistaking the object of their knowledge for the object of another type of knowledge and from exceeding the limits of their respective competence. This would also reveal to them the vastness of their ignorance. And finally, it will also make it possible to meet the previous criterion: the *elenchus* is based on *logoi*, and so without them no critical analysis of one's knowledge would be possible.

But we can look at the problem from the other side. If Socrates tends to identify *epistēmē* with *technē*[4], then he must have assumed that theory

3   "Giving a reason" is a formula familiar to all students of Plato's dialogues. The original Greek expression *didonai logon* may have been used for the first time by Socrates; and even if it was not, it nevertheless reflected his intentions very well. It is used by his interlocutors, for example, by Crito in the *Charmides* (165b3), by Lysimachus in the *Laches* (187c2), and by Alcibiades in the *Protagoras* (336d1). The expression also appeared in later dialogues: the *Cratylus* (426a2), the *Theaetetus* (169a7), and the *Republic* (533c2). Socrates used it several times in the *Phaedo* (76b8, 95d7, 101d6)—a dialogue in which the problems of knowledge and theory played a major role. There, the phrase could be best translated as "offering a rational account" or as "justification using arguments."

4   We already know that it is difficult—if at all possible—to distinguish, with sufficient accuracy, between *epistēmē* and *technē* in Socrates' thought. Initially,

should in some way influence practice, and, especially, directly related to human conduct is the highest object of knowledge—namely, *kalon kagathon*. The analogy to a craft such as carpentry and a theory of *kalon kagathon* need not be interpreted too literally. It is enough to say that whoever masters this theory is internally compelled to live by the standards of *kalon kagathon*, just as whoever masters carpentry is internally compelled to follow the best standards of carpentry. "Internally compelled" means being obliged by the requirements of the skill (a good carpenter will not produce a bad artifact by a deliberately unskillful execution) and by an unwritten ethical code of the craft (a good carpenter would be ashamed to fall to the level of inferior carpenters). In other words, the theoretical *logoi* can and should have considerable power over human behavior.[5]

Of the five criteria, one, IO, is obvious and possible to meet, at least for those with a sufficient degree of epistemological sensibility. Two of the criteria—(CA) presenting philosophy as a combination of theoretical construction and theoretical criticism, and (TA) creating theoretical justifications by arguments and testing those justifications also by arguments—are

technē was deemed to be the principal concept, as it included both practical and theoretical knowledge. In the *Gorgias*, Socrates divided the *technai* into two categories: the first included crafts that did not necessarily employ *logos* and were based on physical work (*ergon, ergasia*); whereas the second referred to crafts where *logos* was indispensable and where the element of physical effort was absent. The fine arts belonged to the former; arithmetic and geometry were representative of the latter category (450c7–e2). In the *Meno*, virtue was considered an *epistēmē* (87c5); the same term was also used in the context of geometry (85c9–12). Similar distinctions were drawn in other dialogues, including the later ones (*Euthydemus* 288d–290d, *Sophist* 218e–219d, *Statesman* 258b–260b, *Philebus* 55d-58a), which further contributed to the blurring of this distinction. There are scholars who argue against the theoretical aspect of *technē*; for instance, Roochnik who called Socrates' knowledge "non-technical," that is, "the Doric harmony of word and deed … that can be lived," "not an abstract *technē* like mathematics or a productive one like shipbuilding" (1996:107).

5   The most elaborate argument about the role of power (*dynamis*) in Socrates' theory of knowledge we find in Benson. He argued that for Socrates, knowledge was a power (*dynamis*) "associated with a particular object or subject matter that is necessary and sufficient for the production of an interrelated, coherent system of true cognitive states involving that object" (2000:190).

certainly not easy, but one can say that they mark the direction taken by philosophy in the centuries that followed. The two remaining criteria, HO and HEX, also find continuation in subsequent philosophy, but Socrates presents them in such a way that his entire concept of knowledge seems to be beyond the reach of any human being.

Everything depends on how high these hierarchies should reach. Socrates gave examples of two such theories or potential theories that arguably met the highest standards.[6] They covered everything—from the entire nature to the soul and moral problems. How much expertise could one acquire in them? The persistent emphasis on ignorance—Socrates' own and that of others—excluded the possibility of attaining that goal. The goal was too high in the hierarchy, and the ignorance too great, especially that HEX disqualified almost everyone, with the exception of very few experts—perhaps only one—who were purely hypothetical beings, and no concrete person could even approach this position.

The "most important things" from HO that interested Socrates relate to the problems of virtue. But even here, the results of inquiries did not satisfy Socrates. Reaching higher and aspiring to supra-human knowledge made little practical sense, given that what human beings are capable of knowing is negligible in comparison to divine knowledge (23a5–7). All in all, both the highest object of and the expertise in knowledge in the full sense of the word are unattainable.

This should have perplexed Socrates but did not. Nowhere do we find the statements that undermine the determination to pursue knowledge or lower its position in the hierarchy of human concerns. There are several reasons why Socrates did not intend to adjust his concept of knowledge according to human limitations, of which he was well aware, and never stopped urging others to pursue knowledge. Some of the reasons will be discussed in subsequent chapters. But one of them has already revealed itself in the passages discussed above. Socrates had a strong notion of what knowledge should be and what criteria it should fulfill, and was able—with great precision—to identify and refute unfounded aspirations to knowledge. He readily admitted his lack of knowledge but never doubted his possession of the knowledge of what knowledge is.

6   See 6.3 below.

1.2 Knowledge of knowledge

The statement that Socrates held meta-knowledge, a knowledge of knowledge, meets with a serious difficulty. He himself analyzed this concept (*epistēmē epistēmēs*) in one of his dialogues (*Charmides* 169b1,6, c1, d4 &ff.), but the result is rather negative. In his view, the notion is "strange" (167c4) and has deep flaws. He reserves discussion of it for another occasion (169d4–5) but never properly returns to it.[7]

The term "knowledge of knowledge" in the *Charmides* is introduced when discussing a definition of *sōphrosynē*, one of the cardinal virtues. At the moment, however, we are not concerned with the *definiens* of a specific virtue but an epistemological idea.[8] Socrates' basic thrust against the concept of knowledge of knowledge is that cognitive, volitional, and emotional acts are other-directed, not self-directed. We see objects but do not see seeing itself; we desire wealth or fame but not desire itself; we love somebody but not love itself; we fear unhappiness or death but not fear itself. Similarly, we know mathematics which deals with numbers, or architecture which deals with building houses, but not knowledge as such.

To strengthen his argument, Socrates points out some absurd consequences of the concept in question. The expert epistemologist—considering that he can distinguish between knowledge and non-knowledge—could tell a good doctor from a bad doctor, without knowing anything about the object of medicine, which is health. There are more absurdities. One might

7   Socrates' knowledge of knowledge from the *Charmides* may resemble Aristotle's *peirastikē*, that is, the art of examination from the *Sophistical Refutations* (172a21–b1): "for neither is *peirastikē* of the same nature as geometry but it is an art which a man could possess even without any scientific knowledge. For, even a man without knowledge of the subject can examine another who is without knowledge ..." (Forster trans.). My point is, however, that Socrates' knowledge of knowledge as we see it in most dialogues is not solely an art of examination or refutation but something like a theory of knowledge.

8   These are, of course, not two separate problems. Knowledge of knowledge may define not only *sōphrosynē* but virtue as such. Since Socrates had knowledge of knowledge, did it mean he was virtuous in the full sense of the word? Rejection of knowledge of knowledge as the *eidos* of virtue meant, among other things, that Socrates did not claim virtue on account of having this meta-knowledge. See also McKim 1985.

even imagine a society ruled by the experts in knowledge of knowledge overseeing all other sciences and *technai*—from medicine and shoemaking to the mantic art—the result of which may be that everybody is better off and happy (173b).

Socrates' argument provokes a reply. While one might be inclined to think that we do not see seeing, the cases of fear, desire, and love are different. Certainly, we might be afraid of being afraid, for example, when we are about to sit for an important examination, and we become afraid of becoming paralyzed by exam nerves, or when we are about to fight a battle, and we fear that its critical moment will see us overcome by fear. It is easy to imagine someone desiring the state of desire, for example, or a person who envies others their passions.

To this, Socrates could have replied as follows. Surely it is possible to desire desires, to be afraid of fear, etc., but the point is that what we then experience is not a fear of fear as such, but a fear of failing an exam or of coming across as a coward. Likewise, if someone desires desire, it is not a real desire in the sense of strong emotions since the person does not feel real desire unless accompanied by the object of this desire, that is, a woman, fame, satisfying one's pride, etc. In short, the fear we fear, the desire we desire, etc., ultimately point to objects beyond themselves.

We indeed see objects and not seeing as such, and in this sense seeing is other-directed, not self-directed. But one might imagine the following reflection on what one sees: just as when we see a painting, we pay particular attention to the colors, or composition, or something else, we seem to observe the process of seeing and pay particular attention to how we see, how clear is our vision, whether we are short-sighted or far-sighted, etc.

When Socrates indicates the criteria of knowledge, it is not self-directedness but a particular kind of knowledge that we may call meta-knowledge, and meta-knowledge can scale successive meta-levels. The knowledge that Socrates is a philosopher is indeed other-directed, but there is nothing impossible about reflecting upon the truth and validity of this statement, and then on the notion of truth and validity that justifies this statement, etc. Socrates used the criteria of knowledge quite skillfully, and, if we are to believe the *Apology*, never had the slightest doubt that he successfully unmasked the ignorance of the politicians, poets, and craftsmen. But this might provoke one to wonder whether his ability to separate knowledge from ignorance makes him sufficiently competent to be an authority in particular kinds of knowledge—politics, poetry, shoemaking, etc. In other words, this would create a situation that Socrates warns against in the *Charmides*—namely, that having the knowledge of knowledge will ultimately lead to objects other than itself and, consequently, to claims of competency in medicine, house-building, and other *technai*.

Somebody like Socrates, who declares his ignorance, would then feel tempted to tell the representatives of every craft what and how to perform and might eventually hope to oversee all *technai* in order to make everyone better off and happy. This is, of course, a caricatural exaggeration, but the fact that Socrates resorted to it is significant. However loud the declarations of ignorance might sound, someone who has acquired the intellectual instruments to unmask other people's lack of knowledge is bound to develop a sense of superiority, and his ignorance, instead of being a mitigating factor, might turn into the opposite. Indeed, it is not difficult to detect Socrates' sense of superiority.

Socrates in the *Charmides* solves this problem. He reconciles his professed ignorance with the ability to unmask other people's lack of knowledge and does this with a simple move. The knowledge of knowledge—he makes his interlocutors believe—is not knowledge at all. The solution is simple, but Socrates does not seem to express it with particular emphasis. In the subsequent parts of the chapter, we will see why not. It will turn out that he is not consistent and that the elements of meta-knowledge sometimes appear as parts of knowledge or are used to justify it.

2. Definitions

The propositions which Socrates finds crucial for his philosophizing are definitions. In fact, he is the first philosopher to address the problem of defining concepts as a prerequisite for meaningful argumentation. Aristotle makes this point on three occasions in his *Metaphysics* (987b1–6; 1078b17–32; 1086a37–b5) and in *On the Parts of Animals* (642a24–31). Aristotle wrote that Socrates had been the first to look for "the universal" and to "concentrate upon definitions." He added that to Socrates two things were attributed—namely, "generalizations and general definitions."

As we know, most of Plato's Socratic dialogues are built around the definitional problem "What is X?": What is piety? (*Euthyphro*) ... courage? (*Laches*) ... *sōphrosynē*? (*Charmides*) ... justice? (*Republic I*). Socrates starts with moral concepts—in fact, he never really goes beyond them—but it is not only the definitions of those concepts that engages him, rather also a theory of definition or a sketch of such a theory. As previously noted, while searching for knowledge, Socrates supplies the elements of meta-knowledge.

The outline of his theory of definitions appears in the *Euthyphro*, and the contexts for this is the question of piety. What Socrates proposes we might call an eidetic interpretation of definition (EID): to define the concept is to define its essence. For this, he uses two words: *eidos* and *idea*, which would later play a major role in Plato's metaphysics.[9] There is no reason, however, to suppose that Socrates' remarks in the *Euthyphro* go beyond the field of epistemology.[10]

The first question that arises regarding EID is how we discover the essence of the meaning of a given concept. The simplest way is to apply inductive reasoning: for example, collate all the meanings of the word "pious" as normally used and identify a common element in them to be treated as the form. This was probably the source of the "generalizing propositions" mentioned by Aristotle when he discusses Socrates' contribution to epistemology. While Socrates might have found such an inductive procedure acceptable as an auxiliary instrument, there is little evidence that he ever applies it since he values neither induction nor experience.

9   Sometimes, Socrates used the word *ousia,* as in *Protagoras* 349b4, but its meaning in this context is not clear. Clark translates it as "a distinct essence" (2015:449), Taylor as "some separate thing" (1976), and Denyer sees in it "a metaphor drawn from finance" (2008:172).

10   Robinson (1953:58) points out that the Socratic concept of definition arises from several previously adopted assumptions: (i) the defined concept is unambiguous; (ii) the defined concept has an essence; (iii) the essence is real; and (iv) the essence has a structure which can be described. The most problematic is (iii). Most commentators tend to agree that Socrates had in mind "real definitions" as contrasted with "nominal definition" (Gulley 1968:12; Penner 1992; Crombie 1994; Irwin 1995:25–27) (Wolfsdorf 2003). However, one can have some reservations. If *real* means denoting reality, then Socrates' definitions meet this criterion, except that the ontological status of "essence" was never discussed (Wolfsdorf 2003:304–05).

The more plausible interpretation is that, according to Socrates, the mind grasps the essence or visualizes it, as it were, which then gives an impulse to intellectual reflection leading to the formulation of the logos. Such an interpretation is confirmed by a passage from the *Charmides*, where Socrates urges the eponymous character to make an attempt to define *sōphrosynē*. He says,

> "Now it is clear that if *sōphrosynē* is present in you, you have some opinion about it. Because it is necessary, I suppose, that if it really resides in you, it provides a sense of its presence (*aisthēsin tina*), by means of which you would form an opinion not only that you have it but of what sort it is." (158e7–159a3, Sprague trans.)

In other words, we gain an insight into the *eidos* not so much by adopting a broad perspective on individual cases and identifying a common element in them as by careful reflection on the "sense of its presence" or "a perception of it" in ourselves.

The EID—that is, the claim that the *definiendum* of the concept is its *eidos*—contains three additional propositions. Socrates' example is the *eidos* of piety, but what he says undoubtedly also refers to all other concepts, particularly the moral ones on which he focuses his attention.[11]

The first proposition explains what the *eidos* is. We are told that the *eidos* of piety is the absolute and exact opposite of impiety and is identical with itself or, as Socrates puts it, is "in itself similar to itself" (5d3–4, 7a8–9). The *eidos* of piety is then a pure abstraction—rather grasped by the mind in an intellectual perception than distilled from the concretes—not mixed with any physical object or quality. Nor is it in any degree mixed, or reconciled, or united with its opposite; just like in arithmetic, the oddness of a number cannot be mixed with the evenness.

This proposition excludes the erroneous tendencies that Socrates notices among his interlocutors when they attempt to define a concept.

---

11 Robinson correctly points out that not all Socrates' definitions are eidetic. Some are more modest and serve simply to designate or to identify things or their qualities (1953:54–55). A good example comes from the *Meno* (75b9–10): "shape is that which alone of existing things always follows color" (Grube trans.)

Sometimes they pointed to a concrete fact or to a current situation that they generalized ad hoc to justify their self-serving actions, and sometimes, instead of providing the *eidos*, they enumerated various concretes that are characterized by the same quality (pious, just, etc.). Euthyphro exemplified both tendencies. He said piety is "to do what I am doing now" (5d7), and he also noted that piety—besides the situations he described—covers "many other things" (6d5–8).

The EID includes another proposition—namely, that the *eidos* makes the concrete what it is: the *eidos* of piety "makes all pious actions pious" (6d11–12). This means that when we call something or somebody pious, we refer the adjective to the *eidos* as the only source of the meaning of the word "pious."[12] Consequently, correctly formulated definitions of piety, justice, etc., are independent—either generically or semantically—of any political or other external pressure. The actions are pious, just, etc., only if they comply with the *eidos* of piety, justice, etc.

To understand the importance of this proposition, we must contrast it with the opposite ones. If the meaning of the concept and the thing itself do not come from the *eidos*, where do they come from? There was an influential and time-honored Greek tradition according to which victory, fame, and remarkable deeds are the source from which one could learn moral lessons and strive to act (or desire to act) accordingly. Hector, Achilles, Odysseus, Penelope, and other extraordinary characters were building people's moral imaginations. What was victorious, outstanding, and even excessive deserved respect and appreciation but also acquired a normative character. The norms were not conceptualized, so one cannot excogitate the meanings of the concepts, let alone their *eidē*, but the heroes could teach the Greeks by their behavior what it means in practice to be brave, wise, loyal, or pious.

There is another possibility. The moral meanings and models of conduct may come from the polis and its institutions. This is more or less the

---

12 Let us note of Geach's well-known article in which he criticized Socrates in the *Euthyphro* and called his argument a fallacy: "We know heaps of things without being able to define the terms in which we express our knowledge. Formal definitions are only one way of elucidating terms; a set of examples may in a given case be more useful than a formal definition" (1966:371).

position argued for by Protagoras in his conversation with Socrates (*Protagoras* 325c–326e). The parents, teachers, laws, all these educate the citizens from childhood when each of them is told, "This is just, that is unjust, this is noble, that is ugly, this is pious, that is impious, he should do this, he should not do that" (325d3–40).

The proposition that the *eidos* is independent of and prior to any human or divine decision, emotion, or preference, means its function is potentially critical or subversive of concrete moral traditions, political institutions, laws, and social practices. It does not mean that whoever accepts the eidetic definition of piety or justice, as Socrates did, is immediately hostile to the polis, laws, Homeric tradition, and Athenian religion as forces that tend to appropriate and adapt the meanings of the moral concepts to their own interests. But such a person will not call something or somebody just or pious only because they have been so called on the basis of some custom, tradition, consensus, or a political decision.

There is also a third proposition that directly follows the second. Strictly speaking, it should not be included in EID because it depicts the moral function of the definitions and does not refer to the definitions themselves. But in Socrates, as we know, epistemology and ethics are often indistinguishable. Socrates says, this time applying the term *idea*, that he could "look upon [the *idea* of the concept], using it as a model (*paradeigma*)" to assess one's own and other people's actions (6e3–6).

In other statements, Socrates makes a more radical step. He seems to imply that not only can we use the defined concepts as paradigms, but that we in fact do it, even when the definitions we take for granted are erroneous. In the final part of the dialogue, he says to Euthyphro: "If you had no clear knowledge of piety and impiety, you would never have ventured to prosecute your old father for murder on behalf of a servant" (15d3–5). Socrates apparently held the view that whenever we assess our own or someone else's actions, we always presuppose a certain interpretation of the concept in question, even if this presupposition is only intuitive, unexamined, and often not admitted. This view eventually led him to one of the main tenets of his philosophy—namely, that moral knowledge is a prerequisite of moral action.

The propositions that constitute EID have an important consequence: they simplify and unify the information that has been coming from without and from within. The perspective this theory imposes on the human mind is that of unity. In its pursuit of knowledge, the mind seeks to find one *eidos*, "the same or alike in every action" (5d4–5). When in the *Meno*, Socrates asks his interlocutor what virtue is, he responds by answering that there are different virtues—men's virtue, women's virtue, but also those of children, elderly people, free men, and slaves. "There is virtue"—he concludes—"for every action and every age, for every task of ours and every one of us ... [and] the same is true for wickedness" (72a2–4). To this, Socrates replies: "[W]hile I am looking for one virtue, I have found you to have a whole swarm of them" (72a5–6, Grube trans.).

In the light of EID, Socrates' answer was predictable—obviously, there is one *eidos* that covers all concrete manifestations. But the answer is also troublesome. One can legitimately ask if there is such a thing as male virtue or female virtue and if there is, what is its *eidos*? The dismissive remark about "a whole swarm" of virtues clearly indicates that Socrates was rather uncompromising on this point. The unity of the *eidos* is absolute, not partial. Whatever eidetic element one could find in male virtue or female virtue, it did not interest Socrates.

His silence on the virtues enumerated by Meno has a deeper reason that is not difficult to point out. Let us recall SCK's two criteria—the hierarchy of objects (HO) and the hierarchy of expertise (HEX). Both of them seem to favor absolute unity. Virtue as such is a worthier object than that of men or women because it comprises the entire human character, whereas male virtue or female virtue only a part. No wonder Socrates never talked about them. Also, mastering virtue as such is a higher form of expertise than mastering the *technē* of war or management. Socrates was a good soldier but never brought up his military virtues.

All in all, occupying oneself with male or female virtue instead of virtue as such would mean disregarding HO and HEX, and this means putting oneself in the position of someone who studies carpentry and various forms of woodworking without reflecting on the concept of *technē*. And this would lead to the errors that the craftsmen from the *Apology* commit—namely, that they are unaware of how limited their skills and their object of knowledge are.

But the unity that EID induces creates a problem, or rather two problems, related to the two propositions. If the unity is absolute, then the *eidos* becomes a pure abstraction, too pure, cleansed of all identifiable properties, and the mind will no longer be able to grasp it. And if the *eidos* is too elusive, then it can no longer function as a paradigm to assess people's actions and motivate their behavior. Socrates faces both these problems when he attempts to give an account of the unity of virtue.

3. *Elenchus*

Equipped with the epistemological propositions, Socrates proceeds to conduct his relentless scrutiny of what one knows and what one does not know. His method of probing people's views—ascertaining whether they could resist critical analysis—has been referred to as *elenchus* and the activity itself rendered by the verb *elenchō*. Whether the procedure is ultimately aimed at discovering the truth or only detecting inconsistencies is still a matter of dispute.[13] Let us look at the two important examples of the *elenchus* in the Apology, when Socrates questions Meletus, one of his accusers, about the allegations that led to the trial.

As regards the allegation that Socrates corrupted the young, his argument can be summarized as follows:

(i)   Meletus claimed that no one in Athens corrupted the young except Socrates;
(ii) Meletus did not deny and therefore implicitly assumed that corrupters constituted a majority, whereas good educators remained in the minority, just as was the case "with horses and all other animals" (25b5–6);

---

13   The reader will immediately recognize that my interpretation of the *elenchus* is taken from Vlastos' important article (1994a). I agree with his reconstruction of the elenctic structure, but the further use I make of his argument is clearly at odds with his general interpretation of Socrates' philosophy. Vlastos' interpretation provoked some critical comments (Kraut 1983; Davidson 1992; Brickhouse, Smith 1994; Benson 2000; Tarrant 2006). Let us emphasize, however, that in the truth-consistency controversy, the point was not whether Socrates had been searching for the truth—most agreed he had—but whether the *elenchus* was an instrument to achieve this goal. Vlastos argued it was; Benson—it was not.

(iii) Socrates belonged to the minority, so he did not corrupt the young;

(iv) ergo, Meletus claimed that Socrates corrupted the young, yet at the same time implicitly acknowledged that he did not.

In the case of the allegation concerning impiety (or failure to respect the gods of the polis), the argument reveals a similar structure:

(i) Meletus claimed that Socrates did not recognize any gods "at all" (26c7), but some other new spirits;

(ii) Meletus did not deny that the spirits are believed to be "either gods or children of gods" (27d1) and that they were gods "of some sort" (27d4–5), so he must have implicitly assumed that this was the case;

(iii) Socrates recognized the existence of spirits and thus recognized the existence of gods;

(iv) ergo, Meletus claimed that Socrates denied the existence of the gods yet implicitly assumed that they existed.[14]

The two examples show that Socrates intended to prove that Meletus' allegations elicited contradictions. In other words, it was the inconsistency rather than falsehood that refuted both allegations. On the other hand, it would be rational to expect that Socrates' intention must have been to prove his innocence or at least to prove the falsity of the accusers' allegations. Considering that in his speech Socrates presented himself as a defender of virtue who was carrying out the god's mission, he could not satisfy himself by indicating the confused state of his accuser's mind and not disproving the charge of his spreading moral corruption and impiety.

The structure of the *elenchus* is simple:

(i) Meletus formulates proposition A;

(ii) Socrates make Q propositions and conducts a series of inferences;

(iii) on the basis of these propositions, Socrates refutes A.

The crucial problem is, of course, the status of the Q propositions because it will determine the nature of the refutation and the status of 'not

---

14 Both arguments in full are more complex and include extra layers, but this had little relevance to my point.

A.' Here are several examples of the *elenchus* that follow this pattern.

Apology (24c4–25c4):
>   (A) Socrates corrupts young people (while others educate them well).
>   (Q_1) Corrupters are in the majority, whereas good educators are in the minority.
>   (Not-A) A is refuted because Socrates was in the minority.

Apology (26b3–28a1):
>   (B) Socrates does not recognize the gods but new spirits.
>   (Q_2) The spirits are gods of some sort.
>   (Not-B) B is refuted because Socrates recognizes the spirits.

Euthyphro (6e10–8e9):
>   (C) What pleases the gods is pious.
>   (Q_3) Conflicts—whether among the gods or the people—always refer to such questions as justice, goodness, etc., and their opposites.
>   (Not-C) C is refuted because what might please one god need not please another.

Euthyphro (9a1–11b5):
>   (D) The pious is what all the gods love, and the opposite, what all the gods hate, is the impious.
>   (Q_4) There are two categories of things: those that are loved because someone loves them, and those that are in themselves loveable.
>   (Not-D) D is refuted because the definition is about the *eidos* of the concept, not about someone's—whether a man's or a god's—attitude or preference.

Euthyphro (14a11–16a4):
>   (E) Piety is a kind of knowledge of how to sacrifice and how to pray.
>   (Q_5) To sacrifice means to make a gift to the gods, whereas to pray is to beg from the gods.
>   (Not-E) E is refuted because by making piety a *technē* of mutual trading between gods and men (14e5–6), it commits the same error as the previous definition—it does not grasp the *eidos* but an attitude or a preference.

Charmides (160e5–161b2):
>   (F) *Sōphrosynē* is modesty (*aidōs*).
>   (Q_6) Modesty may be good or bad.

(Not-F) F is refuted because *sōphrosynē* is a virtue and must be good.
Charmides (165b4–166b6):

(G) *Sōphrosynē* is knowing oneself, that is, knowing what one knows and what one does not know.

(Q7) Every knowledge is knowledge of something distinct from itself.

(Not-G) G is refuted because *sōphrosynē* as knowledge must also have an object different from itself.

Laches (198a1–199e5):

(H) Courage is a part of virtue.

(Q8) Courage is "the knowledge of practically all goods and evils put together," and whoever has this knowledge is not lacking in virtue.

(Not-H) H is refuted because courage is "not a part of virtue but rather virtue entire."

The first thing to be observed about the Q propositions is that they are stated by Socrates and not by his interlocutors. Socrates is, therefore, the author of the whole argument, its direction and structure, and very little comes from the interlocutors who usually have to agree—sometimes reluctantly—with each step of reasoning.

The Q propositions provide a larger context of the initial statements A, B, etc. For instance, in reaction to A, proposition Q_1 introduces a non-democratic view that education is essentially hierarchic and that the majority cannot educate well. In reaction to B, the proposition Q_2 introduces the problem of the relation between gods and spirits. In reaction to C, proposition Q_3 points out that the moral concepts by their nature generate conflicting interpretations. In reaction to D, proposition Q_4 distinguishes two senses of the adjective *theophiles*. In reaction to E, proposition Q_5 explains what sacrifice and pray mean. In reaction to F, proposition Q_6 points out the ambiguity inherent in the concept of *aidōs*. In reaction to G, proposition Q_7 raises a theoretical question about knowledge and its object. In reaction to H, proposition Q_8 suggests a tentative definition of courage.

It is easy to see that some Q propositions are more general and of a higher order than A, B, C, etc. The statement about the educational qualities of minorities and majorities is more general than that about Socrates as the only Athenian to corrupt the young. The statement about the relations between spirits and gods is more general than that about Socrates being an atheist worshiping new spirits. The statement about the essentially divisive character of moral concepts is of a higher order than that about piety as pleasing the gods. The statement about the two senses of *theophiles* is of a higher order than that about piety defined as being *theophiles*. The statement about knowledge having an object distinct from itself is of a higher order than that about *sōphrosynē* being the knowledge of oneself. Propositions Q_5, Q_6, and Q_8 do not follow that pattern: they define or provide additional information about the concepts which were either undefined or not sufficiently explained in E, F, and H.

In all these cases, however, we see a similar strategy. To evaluate a statement, Socrates had to find for it a set of logically connected propositions to which it seemed to be related, and then he examined whether this was really the case or whether this set and the statement contradicted each other. This connection could be horizontal as Q_5 and Q_6 or vertical as in the other examples where the statement was related to the propositions more general or of a higher order. The vertical structure appears to be more interesting as it could potentially lead—in a chain of logically connected propositions—to the basic statement, most general or of the highest order, from which other statements would follow.

The described strategy suggests that the *elenchus* was aimed not to discover the truth but to detect inconsistencies in the interlocutors' views: one could not hold both Q_1 and A, both Q_2 and B, etc., to be true. If one wanted to be consistent, one would have to replace A by not-A, B by not-B, etc. This is a rational interpretation of the *elenchus*, but I think it does not give justice to Socrates' intentions. It would imply that the propositions Q_1 ... Q_n have nothing in common but are separate clusters of arguments, some true, some false, but their truth and falsehood do not depend on the elenctic arguments in which they are used.

It would be impossible to deny that in Plato's dialogues, there are several examples that indicate consistency rather than truth. Q_2 is a case in point. Meletus made himself an easy object of criticism when he ascribed atheism to Socrates—not believing in gods "at all." Then it was enough to find one case to the contrary to refute the claim. If the *daimonia* were divine signals, Meletus could not argue that Socrates accepting the *daimonia* did not believe in the divinities which sent those signals. Of course, Socrates could find a more tangible example to contradict Meletus' claim, such as his devotion to Apollo, but for some reason, he did not seek material proof but only inconsistency on the part of his accuser. He explicitly stated that Meletus contradicted himself (27a1–6).

The example F and Q_6 is also primarily about inconsistency. *Sōphrosynē* was unconditionally good because it was a virtue, and for the Greeks the virtue was by definition unconditionally good, being the opposite of vice. Socrates would have said that its being good was in the *eidos* of the concept of virtue. Modesty, on the other hand, did not, by definition, entail goodness. Socrates quotes Homer about modesty being no good for a needy man, to which his interlocutor does not object. If there are exceptions to the goodness of modesty, then *sōphrosynē* cannot be modesty.

These two examples are about inconsistency, but this does not mean that Q_5 and Q_6 are not believed to be true statements but arbitrary ad hoc propositions that Socrates slyly makes his interlocutors accept without giving them time to reflect. Their respective truth value is not questioned, and probably both Socrates and his interlocutors find them persuasive. But it is easy to notice that they convey things of fairly little importance, and their truthfulness is not crucial to Socrates' philosophy. Socrates is not keen on discovering the origin of his *daimonion*, nor is he much bothered about the ambiguity of *aidōs*.

But there are examples where, though inconsistencies also occur, truth is the key. If we look at the other Q statements from the above list, we see that some of them are not taken out of the blue and do not function as *ad hoc* hypotheses to test the consistency of the interlocutors' views. They either belong to or are the consequences of Socrates' basic philosophical inventory, mostly from his concept of knowledge.

Q_1 about corrupters being in the majority and good educators in the minority is, on the one hand, a common-sense observation based on a rather simple process of induction: as Socrates told Meletus, the good trainers of horses and other animals are always few. On the other hand, one can see in it a variant of HEX, Socrates' expertise criterion of knowledge. HEX had its ramification in his criticism of the democratic opinion that a large number of supporters all holding a certain view decides or suggests its truthfulness. All this is a recurrent theme in Socrates' epistemology, ethics, and theory of politics.

Similarly we see this with other examples. Q_3 is certainly not a theological inquiry into the gods' minds but rather a statement about how the subjective understandings of justice, piety, and suchlike affect the conduct of people and gods and why the divergent interpretations of those concepts can create conflicts and hostility. The proof, as before, is partly empirical, and the examples were easy to find. Euthyphro's arbitrary definition of piety justified the moral action for which the Athenians considered him "insane" (4a1), although he defended himself by pointing out how brutally the Greek gods treated their fathers (5d–6a). People, or the Athenians at any rate, as Socrates was explaining to Euthyphro, did not like when somebody clever tried to teach them "his own wisdom" (3c7). Socrates was himself an object of hatred (*Apology* 21e4).

Yet primarily Q_3 is a statement that Socrates could legitimately derive from EID. This theory stipulates that if one defines the concepts of justice, piety, etc., by subjective desires, preferences, or interests rather than by *eidē*, or confuses them with certain customs or popular views, then such definitions are bound to become arbitrary and will necessarily lead to conflicts. A search for the *eidos* of justice, piety, etc., require a high degree of disinterestedness on the part of the searcher where the questions of pleasing, displeasing, or convenience could not matter. Otherwise, a difference of opinion is likely to develop into a conflict over which point of view would prevail.

Q_4 can also be derived from EID on roughly the same grounds. The difference between a thing that is loved because someone loves it and a thing that is in itself loveable is a difference between a thing that is perceived and valued according to subjective criteria and a thing that is perceived and valued by what it is in itself, that is, by its *eidos*. Again, this is not a theological contention about the gods and their preferences and shortcomings but a statement about the objective and subjective qualities: there are things loved because they are intrinsically good, and the god's love for them cannot add anything to their intrinsic quality, and those that are not intrinsically good and then even the god's love for them cannot make them intrinsically good.

Q_5 follows the same track. Ultimately, it leads to Euthyphro's previous claims and commits the same error. The definition of piety that Socrates introduces—sacrificing (giving) and praying (begging)—is certainly not his, but apparently convincing to an average Athenian. To the question of what we give the gods, Euthyphro answers: honor, reverence and *charis*

(15a9–10). But since *charis* means what the gods find gratifying, we are back to the previous argument about the gods finding something pleasing or loveable. This, as we know, violates the eidetic character of the definition.

Q7 also relates to Socrates' concept of knowledge. As we remember, this *elenchus* enabled him to formulate an important proposition about the limited validity of knowledge of knowledge. At the background, though not explicitly stated, we can find a solution to one of the Socratic problems—namely, how to reconcile the strong opinions about what is and what is not knowledge with the declaration of ignorance.

The line of inferences that goes to Q8 is long and somewhat tortuous, starting with fear and confidence and then taking the question of knowledge of past, present, and future. Finally, Socrates spells out Q8 rather nonchalantly, but the proposition stems from EID and, in particular, from its consequence—namely, the unity of the *eidos*. H is, therefore, unacceptable because it contradicts the concept of the unity of virtue and of the virtuous man. The oneness of *eidos* and its non-contradictory nature implies the oneness of virtue and the oneness and non-contradictory nature of the moral character.

To sum up, Socrates' *elenchus* detected inconsistencies in his interlocutors' opinions but did not stop at that. Among the propositions that led to discover the inconsistencies, some were indeed true. In a few cases, Socrates supplied quasi-empirical evidence in their support, but the main argument for their truthfulness was their grounding in the essential constituents or the consequences of Socrates' philosophy. Without the hierarchic character of knowledge (HO and HEX), without EID and its notion of the unity of the *eidos*, the *elenchus* would have been solely an instrument used to discover inconsistencies, and Socrates' philosophy would have lost much of its ambition.

In the subsequent parts of the chapter, it will turn out that Socrates does not lose sight of much more comprehensive theoretical systems that extend to the entire universe. Since he imagined the system of knowledge to be one and all-encompassing, he must have assumed that this system must be true and not just coherent. And true, not only coherent, had to be its parts, such as in his theory of virtue and the soul.

4. True opinion

There is yet another concept that supplements Socrates' theory of knowledge—"right/true opinion" (*orthē doxa* or *alēthēs doxa*). The name would suggest that true opinions are simply isolated statements that happen to be true. After all, everyone might occasionally say something true, those educated and those uneducated, the elite as well as the *demos*. But this is not what Socrates had in mind.

Two different accounts in the *Meno* give us crucial information about the concept. The more elaborate and fairly detailed description occurs at the end of the dialogue. The context is practical and is concerned with the conditions guaranteeing that "men do things well and rightly" (96e3). The obvious requirement of such conduct is knowledge in the sense outlined above, but the requirement, as we know, is seldom met. If it were the only requirement—which Socrates calls "ridiculous" (96e2)—no one's conduct could be described as right and good. One should therefore introduce—in the absence of knowledge—yet another condition that will explain how people could, and in fact sometimes do, act in a right and good manner. This condition is the "true opinion." And here is Socrates' explanation.

> "If someone who knew the road to Larissa, or wherever else you like, went there and guided others, would he not guide them rightly and well, wouldn't he?... And what if it were someone who had a right opinion as to what the road was, but had never been there and did not know? Wouldn't he, too, guide aright?... And so long as he has right opinion about what the other person has knowledge of, presumably he will be no worse as a guide through supposing (*oiomenos*) what is the truth, but without being wise on the matter, than someone who is wise on it." (97a9–b7, Day trans. modified)

The passage is far from easy to interpret. The first difficulty arises because the language is metaphorical rather than literal. Indeed, a guide who knows the way to a given city because he has acquired the requisite skill and traveled it several times does not possess knowledge in the Socratic sense: whatever he knows does not meet the above criteria of knowledge.

The central point is that Socrates was talking about a *hēgemōn*—a guide, a commander, and a leader. How can a leader bring people to attain the right ends? Socrates mentioned three possibilities: the first is "things which come out by mere chance," and the remaining two are "through human guidance"—that is, by true opinion and by knowledge (99a1–5). Since Socrates talked about guides and guiding, the first possibility does not seem relevant.

Guiding or leading people to good ends through knowledge in the full sense of the word must have been extremely rare, considering the hierarchy of expertise (HEX) and other almost impossible-to-fulfill standards. Whether Socrates thought such political leadership feasible will be discussed in due course. So, what is left is the third possibility—namely, human guidance based on true opinion.

The problem is that Socrates is not eager to exemplify what he has in mind. The statement that there are people who "have many great successes in what they do and say, all without thought" (99c6–8) may sound ironic, considering the last phrase (*noun mē echontes*). However, one can understand it in a more serious sense as "not paying sufficient intellectual attention to the problem." The serious rather than ironic interpretation seems more plausible. The point Socrates made earlier, that having knowledge as he understands it as the only condition of acting "well and rightly" would be "ridiculous," is legitimate.

Socrates apparently admits that some people have been successful in some respects and that their respective success should be accounted for. A successful man without knowledge differed from the person with knowledge in that he was not sure about truth and made only suppositions (*oiomenos*); the probable reason why he is not sure is that he did not give it enough thought (*noun mē echontes*). Speaking in Socratic terms, we can say that his suppositions are not justified by other *logoi*. What verifies them is practice, that is, his "many great successes." The "true" refers to those practical effects rather than to the supposition.

Obviously, such successes could not occur regularly but are occasional. Suppositions may be correct or incorrect, and whoever makes a correct one does not have a guarantee that in the future he will not err. If the guide from the above quotation correctly indicated the road to Larissa without having any knowledge of it, it does not mean that he would have been equally fortunate in guessing the road to another town.

So, there appears to be an element of chance here, which brings us back to the first possibility we rejected at the outset as irrelevant. But whatever Socrates had in mind when he mentioned the first possibility, it might cover, at least partly, the situation when a politician happens to have a correct supposition about something and then acts upon it with much success. All this implies that we should relate true opinion to what already happened in the past and thereby explain this or that success, but never to the future. The unpredictability of hitting upon the right supposition does not allow us to think of some long-term strategy or have too much faith in the correctness of particular opinions, nor in the continuity of past successes.

This certainly would be the case with politicians. Socrates did not indicate politicians as the only ones who use true opinions, but he mentioned them alongside two other groups—poets and soothsayers (prophets, seers). Their case was different. The poets say things that may always be true, and the soothsayers tell us about the future. Socrates frequently cited poets, especially Homer, apparently believing that their works conveyed important truths. In the *Apology*, he refers to Homer, who had Achilles argue that death should not be feared if something just was to be done (28c–d). In the *Gorgias*, Homer's statement—"just people love strangers and fear the gods"[15]—provides Socrates with an argument against the politicians, specifically against Pericles (516c3). Are these true opinions, as Socrates elucidates in the *Meno*? Possibly. Socrates chose not to invoke the soothsayers but often interpreted dreams and visions as signs that allowed one to gain an insight into the future, though usually only his own (*Crito* 44a10–b4). But perhaps a true opinion would be Delphi's oracle about which we read in the *Apology*, and which inspires Socrates' elenctic activity and enables him to diagnose the degree of ignorance among his fellow citizens.

To a possible question of where the true opinions of those three groups came from if they did not come from knowledge and from chance, Socrates suggested divine inspiration (99c11–d5, 99e6). The answer is somewhat unexpected, considering that Socrates criticized the first two groups in the *Apology*, and nothing indicates that he had anything favorable to say about them. One can hear an echo of this criticism in the *Meno* where Socrates says that the politicians, like the soothsayers and poets, "speak successfully

15   *Odyssey* 6.120, 9.175, 13.201.

on many great issues without knowing what they are talking about" (99d4–5).

The problem with Socrates' view about divine inspiration is that it is not easily reconcilable with what he said before about true opinion as a form of human guidance. Divine inspiration and human guidance are not, strictly speaking, contradictory, but they certainly point to different agencies. This makes the entire concept even less intelligible. What we can make of it so far amounts to the following. There could be some unique men—politicians, poets, soothsayers—who do not have the knowledge (that is, were not able to provide theoretical justification for what they said), but managed to be successful guides and leaders to other people; thanks to those guides and leaders some good things were achieved. The basis for their beneficial actions are true opinions, unjustified and unexamined, yet powerful. The fact that they occasionally appeared, that no argument supported them, and that they produced beneficial effects might indicate divine inspiration at the root of these true opinions.

It is easy to see that the last step of the reasoning is highly strained, and the conclusion does not follow. A more plausible explanation would be to invoke chance and, again, return to the first possibility. There would be nothing implausible in the claim that certain great and beneficial things happen by chance. Why Socrates introduces divine inspiration, we do not know. Perhaps he is not quite serious, or perhaps he could not really accept that great and beneficial things happen simply by chance, or that no guidance, human or divine, is necessary.[16]

---

16 Other commentators also noted the role of chance (*tyche*) in this argument. Weiss makes this point. The heart of her interpretation is that at a certain point, Socrates dropped "true opinion" and used *eudoxia* (99b11), which she translates as "good repute." "The good reputation, then, that some enjoy and that catapults them into positions of power for doing and saying the right thing that is the mark of politicians—without understanding both preserves and promotes the good reputation with which they were already blessed. The esteem in which they are held, therefore, like their political effectiveness, must be credited not to them but to the gods ... The only kind of 'guide' that *eudoxia* can then be is *tyche*" (2008:166–67). Whether Socrates really dropped the notion of true opinion and, in the case of politicians, replaced it with true reputation, I am not sure. *Eudoxia* can also mean "good judgment," which

The second information about true opinion appears earlier in the dialogue (85b11 et seq.). This time it is not about a *hēgemōn*, a leader or a commander, achieving many great things without knowledge. The object of the analysis is a slave boy whom Socrates helped solve a geometrical problem. Since the slave boy had no prior knowledge of geometry and only answered Socrates' questions, the fact that he finally found the solution meant that his correct answers were somehow latent in his mind, and the questions only activated them. This is at least what Socrates claimed. "So someone who doesn't know something, whatever it may be he doesn't know, has true opinions in him about the very thing he doesn't know" (85c6–7, Day trans.).

The concept of true opinions is thus a consequence of a theory according to which the human mind is equipped with some cognitive content, initially hidden and non-active, and which, therefore, requires an activating impulse, a sort of awakening (rendered by the verb *anakineō*)—for example, by questions such as those Socrates asked the slave boy. In fact, there are two phases of the activation, corresponding first to true opinions and then to knowledge. The slave boy reached only the first phase. "At present it's as though in a dream that these opinions have just been aroused in him. But if someone questions him many times and in many ways about the same things as now, you may be sure he will end up knowing them as precisely as anyone does" (85c9–d1, Day trans.).

The true opinions are thus the true statements that the mind retrieves or is made to retrieve from the latent content it contains. They are fairly isolated and limited to a concrete problem, as illustrated by the slave boy's incursion into geometry. The slave boy would have reached the level of knowledge if he had trained his mind, retrieved more latent information, and organized all pieces in a way that geometry requires, with theorems, arguments, axioms, chains of reasoning, etc.

It seems that the true opinions are also fairly elementary. Not only is no divine inspiration needed, but a simple uneducated slave boy is able to grasp some of them if properly guided. The slave-boy experiment suggests that Socrates must have thought it applies to all human beings: this is how

tallies well with "true opinion." Besides, at the root of true opinions are suppositions, and one cannot free them from chance.

the human mind works, he appears to be saying. It does not mean, of course, that every mind will attain the level of knowledge, although Socrates was pretty confident that the slave boy, if properly activated by questions, could learn geometry. Moreover, he added that the slave boy could make similar progress not only in geometry but in any other field of learning (86e2).

It is rather unlikely that Socrates implies here that any slave boy or any person could achieve knowledge in the full sense of the word. The expertise limitations (HEX), one of the epistemological conditions, precludes wide access to the most important objects of knowledge (HO). This would also clash with the widespread ignorance diagnosed in Athens. What we have here is rather a general indication of how the process of knowing things proceeds, and the word "knowing" does not necessarily denote knowledge in the full sense of the word, but primarily particular disciplines, such as geometry. In all these, we start with some true opinions that the mind retrieves and can make use of to master various fields of learning.

The two accounts in the *Meno* differ and point to two different interpretations of true opinions. The first account answers the question: how is it possible that knowledge is so rare and so difficult to attain, and yet there are quite a few people who act rightly and well? The second account answers the question: how do human beings leave the state of ignorance and begin to know things?

The first account saves Socrates' concept of knowledge from the *reductio ad absurdum* conclusion that people cannot act rightly. The concept of true opinion helps to offset this counterargument, but rather unsuccessfully. The number of people acting well and rightly is still quite small, being limited to *hēgemones*. Not only is it small, but the mere suggestion that the guides are divinely inspired leaves the initial charge practically untouched. The statement that Socrates himself calls "ridiculous" is eventually left unrefuted.

The second account is certainly closer to Socrates' concept of knowledge, and it identifies a certain state in the process of knowing at which a human being leaves the level of ignorance and is ready to continue this process, provided he makes good use of true opinions and on their basis builds a more solid and organized construction. Since they are precisely Socrates' elenctic pursuits that created the situation where the interlocutors

39

found themselves between the ignorance they were leaving and the knowledge they expected, the concept of true opinions should be pertinent.

Let it be noted that the interlocutors' ignorance is not the same as that of the slave boy. Whereas he knew nothing at all about geometry and at the start his mind was, in that respect, a clean slate, the interlocutors held a lot of strong views that Socrates considered false. The aim of the conversations was to refute the false propositions but also to find the true ones, and their truthfulness was sanctioned by a logical chain of other propositions.

It seems that what I called the Q propositions performed a similar function as true opinions in the slave-boy experiment. Admittedly, Socrates never said he retrieved them from the latent cognitive pool in his mind, but the interlocutors accepted them as true. He did not call them true opinions, but at least some of them he considered unquestionably true, primarily those that derive from his knowledge of knowledge. What is more important, however, is that they serve Socrates as a means to advance philosophical pursuits.

If we look at the above eight examples of *elenchus*, we can see that the conclusions are mostly negative. This, again, makes them different from the slave-boy experiment, where the conclusion is positive, and the pursuit of other problems in geometry would also be positive. But in Socrates' case, the Q propositions help him to remove some misleading notions that stood in the way of what he considered true. And indeed, he went out of his way to refute the claims that there are several virtues, that virtue can be divided into parts, and that the meaning of virtue is contextual and relative. This allows him to come up with his own positive proposition that virtue is one.

5. Midwifery, anamnesis, activation

It is sometimes said that Socrates employed another method aside from his elenctic probing, which he called the craft of midwifery. Both terms—craft (*technē*) and midwifery (*maieusis*)—appear in the *Theaetetus* (150b6–c3), which is a late, unambiguously Platonic work, conceptually distant and stylistically distinct from Plato's early Socratic dialogues. The passage, however, has been cited on numerous occasions as an example of a perfect insight into Socrates' thought. In this dialogue, Socrates compares his efforts to the activities of his mother, who had been a midwife (151b9–c2). He argues that he is not so much a teacher in the ordinary sense of the word but rather an assistant who oversaw the thinking process aimed at discovering the truth. However, such an opinion of himself is not well justified. I would argue that Socrates was no philosophical midwife.

5.1 Midwifery and intellectual activation

The analogy between Socrates' pursuit of philosophy and the craft of midwifery can be summarized in the following manner. Socrates made two claims regarding good midwives. First, they were women who had given birth in the past but later reached an age at which it was no longer possible. Second, the midwives were also eminently suited for matchmaking. Aware of the effects of procreation, they also knew, in Socrates' view, how to match the right men with the right women.

What interests us now is the first analogy. The parallel between the midwife and Socrates is by no means complete. The difference is that the midwives have given birth in the past, whereas Socrates admits that he had never delivered any wisdom (150c7–8). His variant of the craft of midwifery, as opposed to the skills of a genuine midwife, did not come from practice (for he said he had none) but was exclusively god-given. It constituted a kind of miraculous skill that he finds in himself, a skill so mysterious that it was impossible to account for it except by resorting to the will of the gods. Socrates himself, although he uses the word "craft" to describe his skill, must have considered himself to be something of a prodigy of nature (149a6–9), owing to the difference between what he did and midwifery proper.

He thus describes his craft of midwifery: "I watch over the labor of their souls, not of their bodies" (150b8–9), which probably means "distinguishing the true from the false offspring" (150b3). Further, he says, "the most important thing about my art is the ability to apply all possible tests to the offspring, to determine whether the young mind is being delivered of a phantom, that is, an error, or a fertile truth" (150b9–c3). Just like the fetus growing in a woman's body, the content of people's minds must be delivered when mature. After delivery, when the thought is true, the baby is kept, but when proved to be a phantom or an appearance, it is discarded (151c4).

The textual evidence to support Socrates' claim that he really acted in this way is scarce.[17] Perhaps the only passage in Plato's dialogues that might match the midwifery pattern is the slave-boy experiment from the *Meno*. This passage does not use the term midwifery, nor does it contain any reference to the metaphor of childbirth, but Socrates probably thought of this experiment that way. He says to Meno, "I am not teaching the boy anything, but all I do is question him" (82e4–5). He concluded that the slave did not express a single opinion that was not his own, that initially, he did not know the right answer, and hence he must have had these views in his mind (85b8–c4).

Socrates drew a square on the ground and then asked the slave what the length of its side should be in order to double the area. Let us first note the discrepancies between what we find in the *Theaetetus* and the *Meno*. The Socrates who discusses geometry with the slave does not resemble the intellectual midwife described in the *Theaetetus*. He is certainly not a prodigy of nature—helping others to bear thoughts, but himself, unlike real midwives, unable to give birth to any intellectual offspring. His demonstration in the *Meno* was based on a topic he knew very well:

17 Distinguished commentators attributed intellectual midwifery to Socrates. Burnet wrote: "we can prove this to be genuinely Socratic from the evidence of Aristophanes, who had made fun of it" (1929:161). Burnet had in mind the passage in the *Clouds* where one of Socrates' disciples said he miscarried the thought (137). Some scholars still find the evidence in the *Clouds* persuasive (Sider 1991). Guthrie also called midwifery "genuinely Socratic" (1977:124). The arguments to the contrary seem to have at least equal weight. Robinson argued that midwifery "is a purely Platonic invention, made long after Socrates' death: and it serves the unconscious purpose of enabling the *elenchus* to preserve the good standing in an otherwise very un-Socratic mind" (1953:84). Robinson was right, indicating that the metaphor appeared in a late dialogue and did not appear where it should have—in the early dialogues. Dover pointed out that the textual evidence in Aristophanes' *Clouds* is too scanty to be a mocking allusion to Socrates' midwifery (1968:xlii–xliii). A well-argued case against linking Socrates with midwifery was made by Burnyeat (1992). My point is simple: I do not exclude that Socrates might have played with the metaphor; in fact, it is quite probable he did since the metaphor is too personalized to be completely separated from his life; I deny, however, that it applies to Socrates' philosophy.

he knew how to double the area of the square, and he guided the conversation accordingly. The dialogue with the uneducated slave resembles a demonstration of the craft of teaching as staged by a competent professional.

It is true that Socrates did not give the slave a lecture on geometry but only asked him questions. But he also made the drawings on the ground and introduced at least one basic concept. Without those two additions, the questions would probably not have induced the solution to the geometrical problem. It is characteristic that when the boy was confronted only with the questions, his answers were largely erroneous. When asked how many times one should increase the two-foot length of the side to double the area of the square, he answers: "Clearly, it will be twice the length." Only after Socrates drew it on the ground, he realized that the area did not double but increased fourfold. And again, when led by Socrates to understand that the four-foot length is too big and the two-foot length too small, his reply was again incorrect—three feet.

It is mostly the drawings that opened his mind to the errors he committed. But not only that. Socrates did another thing: he introduced the concept of the diagonal, which made possible the solution to the problem. Without this concept, the slave would have either continued his guesses about the length of the sides or given up. It was an obvious intervention on the part of Socrates through which he reoriented the slave's thinking. Until that moment, the slave boy seemed unaware of this possibility, being focused on the length of the sides. Then Socrates resumed the drawing, and everything became clear: one doubles the area of the square by building a square on the diagonal.

How does this refer to the activating of the slave's mind, which Socrates mentioned (85c9–d1)? Socrates was right that the geometrical propositions that the slave boy learned are true opinions. Starting with them, one could indeed construct a logically connected system of propositions about the square, and possibly the slave boy, had he proceeded with the inquiries, would have been able to progress in the geometrical science. However, during the experiment, there was not much awakening in him, but, using Socrates' metaphor, he continued to find himself in a dream, only eliciting true opinions on the basis of what he saw drawn on the ground. In other words, a lot of information came to him from the outside, not from within.[18]

Socrates could not then say that he did not put anything in the boy's mind. The combination of perception and pure reasoning has been, for a long time, a well-known practice in teaching mathematics, especially at the early stages of education. Assuredly, it is possible for some minds to grasp the concept of the square with such clarity that all geometrical relations pertinent to the square reveal themselves deductively in an inferential order, with one proposition activating another. But the slave boy's mind did not belong to this category, nor did the experiment prove Socrates' midwifery.

The method used in this conversation had some elenctic elements, though it is different from the *elenchus* in the standard form. To be sure, there are questions and yes-or-no answers. As in the *elenchus*, it all starts with Socrates' specific question, to which the slave boy gives a wrong answer. But the contradictions and inconsistencies do not really matter because the problem is stated differently than usual (not about a definition of a moral concept). The problem had its graphic representation, which was never the case in the elenctic pursuits. Searching for the similarities, one might wonder whether the introduction of the diagonal was not a version of the Q propositions, at least as regards Socrates' intervention in the dialogue.

What is undoubtedly similar in the elenctic conversations and the slave-boy experiment is Socrates' dominating position. It is he who leads the

18 We have to distinguish between two problems—that of midwifery and that of recollection. I agree with those authors (Vlastos 1996b; Moravcsik 1994) who argue that Socrates' experiment was about the perception of logical relationships and that on the process of learning/recollection, the slave boy was on the way to discovering such relationships. The hand-drawn figures were simply teaching props. Whether the slave boy fully grasped the logical relationships is not certain. Contrary to Vlastos, I would not entirely dismiss Ross's claim (1953:18) about the importance of sense-perception in the slave boy's answer. The boy was still in a very early stage of education. His correct answers, as Socrates admits, were true beliefs, not knowledge, and the true beliefs need not be free from empirical content, though undoubtedly the slave's mind was opening to geometry as a non-empirical deductive science. But this interpretation of Socrates' experiment in no way gives credibility to the midwife metaphor unless, of course, we assert that every mathematics teacher resembles a midwife in the *Theaetetus* sense.

conversation, sets its tone, provides its theoretical context, and selects all the basic concepts. Without his participation, there is no progress in the conversation. The interlocutors all defer to his guidance, but in no way did they extract the truth from their own minds. It is Socrates who built the entire structure within which their minds operate, and it is not at all certain that they would be able to go through the whole reasoning process again. The slave-boy conversation is more demonstrative because the interlocutor is docile and laconic, but even if he had been more resistant, the steering wheel would still have been firmly in Socrates' hands.

5.2 Anamnesis

The fact that a person completely ignorant of geometry finally arrived at the correct solution to an abstract problem prompted Socrates to make the conclusions more ambitious than those in the remark about the activation of true opinions. Those conclusions related to what preceded the experiment and occasioned it—namely, a theory that Socrates outlined and attributed to "priests and priestesses," and also to "Pindar and other divinely inspired poets" (81a9–b2). The theory consists of the following theses: (i) the soul is immortal; (ii) it has been born many times; (iii) it has seen "both of what is here, and what is in Hades, and everything"; (iv) "there is nothing it has not learnt"; (v) "it's possible that it should recollect both virtue and other things, as after all it did know them previously"; (vi) what people call learning is recollection; (vii) since "the whole of nature is akin and the soul has learnt everything, there's nothing to prevent someone who recollects … just one thing, from discovering everything else" (81c–d).

The theory is so amazing that no wonder Socrates attributes it to divinely inspired people. It covers and promises to explain almost everything—the world and beyond, the human soul, nature, moral problems, and all this in one system in which all propositions are directly or indirectly interconnected so that whoever knows one piece can reconstruct the rest. One could plausibly associate it with divine wisdom from the *Apology*, as in both passages it is complete and has the stamp of divinity.

No doubt Socrates found this theory fascinating, and there is a lot in it that concurred with his philosophical interests and ambitions: the problem of the soul (whether immortal or not), virtue, latent knowledge, consistency, and interconnectedness of propositions. Hence, he proposed to do an experiment with the slave boy. What must strike everyone is an enormous contrast between the grandness of the theory and the exiguity of the experiment. The trouble someone might have with doubling the square and then finally solving the problem with the help of a teacher does not really shed much light on what the divinely inspired sages affirmed in their theory.

The main point Socrates aims to prove in the experiment is the thesis (iv) of the theory—that is, the thesis about anamnesis, that learning is recollection. This is a much stronger claim than that about activation, especially given that immediately after the statement about the slave's awakening to the true opinions, Socrates makes a swift transition to theses (iii), (iv), and (v) of the grand theory, and indirectly to theses (i) and (ii) about the immortal soul being born many times.

The difference between the activation argument and the recollection argument is obvious. One can legitimately suppose that the slave boy, after being exposed to thinking about geometry could himself discover the diagonal and make further attempts to solve the problem. Such a supposition does not necessarily stem from the assumption about the immortal soul being born many times and having seen the square and its diagonal in Hades. Finding connections between propositions and inferring new ones may generate the question about the functioning of the mind and its miraculous power to discover the irresistibility of logic, but the mind's inherent ability to formulate and prove geometrical theorems, and to arrange them in a deductive system, does not compel us to seek justification in the immortality of the soul and its recollections from the life outside the body.

In the grand theory, the immortality of the soul is the basic statement from which the rest follows. The argument starts with "since the soul is immortal" (81c5), and then all other theses ensue, the last being about a possibility of discovering "everything from one thing." This direction of the argument is correct. If the soul is really immortal, then a lot of important things might follow, including, perhaps, innate knowledge and learning as recollection.

The direction of Socrates' argument in the slave boy experiment is reverse: first comes the claim that the experiment proves that learning is recollection, and then from this he infers that the soul must have many lives: since the slave boy did not acquire the true opinions in geometry "in his present life, doesn't it clearly follow that he had them and had learnt them at some other time?" (85e9–86a1). Finally, Socrates arrives at the conclusion about the immortality of the soul: "If the truth about the things which are is in our souls always, the soul must be immortal, must it not?" (86b2, Day trans.).[19] To put it crudely, the slave boy's success in doubling the square enables Socrates to talk about the immortality of the soul.

The last sentence might sound somewhat unfair. The fact is, however, that Socrates could not resist re-introducing the sweeping claims of the grand theory into his own argument, apparently not being satisfied with the less ambitious conclusions. He develops his argument from the concrete to the abstract, from the small to the big, and from the minimalist to the maximalist. This direction was quite natural as Socrates always starts with the concrete, mostly with the opinions of people he meets, and examines their words to find a glimpse of the truth. The problem is, however, how far he could push the argument and how broad (maximalist) the conclusions he could risk.

In the above passage, after incorporating segments of the grand theory, he seems to have second thoughts and eventually backs down, admitting that he "wouldn't be absolutely adamant about the rest of the argument" (86b), probably meaning the theses about the immortal soul having many lives, and seeing the things in Hades. But is he also less adamant about the soul recollecting those things? If he is, then the whole concept of anamnesis, as expounded in the dialogue, would be superfluous; if he is not, then the question is what justifies recollection once the immortality of the soul and its many lives have been placed in doubt.

19 Vlastos introduces another variant of this view, namely the distinction between the concept of anamnesis in the minimalist sense, which entails the existence of non-empirical knowledge and the concept of anamnesis in the maximalist (full-strength) sense, according to which all knowledge is non-empirical, and the soul is subject to reincarnation (1996b: 158–65). Unlike Vlastos, I insist that the maximalist version is not important in the *Meno*. For, I do not subscribe to his opinion that, in this dialogue, the concept of anamnesis is the creation of "a profoundly religious spirit united with a powerful philosophical mind" (ibid., 165); This "profoundly religious spirit" is not overly apparent. Day is right when she indicates that Vlastos changes the direction of Socrates' argument. Socrates derives reincarnation (or rather immortality) from the concept of anamnesis; he does not derive the concept of anamnesis from the belief in reincarnation (1994:23–24).

When in his reverse argument, Socrates reintroduced the theses from the grand theory, he omitted the last one (vii) regarding the possibility of an all-encompassing system that could be constructed from one element. The omission may seem surprising as the thesis did not seem less broad (maximalist) than the previous ones, and furthermore its picture of knowledge Socrates would have found particularly attractive, considering his insistence on consistency and logical interconnectedness of propositions.

But he returned to the question of knowledge after admitting that he was not absolutely adamant about some parts of the argument. And this is what he says:

> "[T]hat we shall be better people, more manly and less slothful, by supposing that one should enquire about things one doesn't know, than if we suppose that when we don't know things we can't find them out either and needn't search for them—this is something for which I absolutely would fight, both in word and deed, to the limit of my powers." (86b6–c2, Day trans.)

This comment is disappointing and appears to be a withdrawal: no more ambitious claims, no recollection, no activation, just encouragement to pursue the truth. But despite the ambiguity, the withdrawal is only partial as Socrates attaches to his words additional weight. He presented a clear alternative: either we try to find what we do not know—and we thereby become better, more manly, and more dynamic—or we resign and become worse, cowardly and slothful. This looks like a forceful plea to choose a more ambitious road to the truth: too great a compromise would push us to the side of evil, cowardice, and sloth.

About the ultimate conclusions, we can only speculate. In this passage, Socrates mentioned different objects of inquiry: (a) "the whole of nature"; (b) "virtue and other things"; (c) geometry and "all other areas of knowledge" (85e2–3). Socrates' not being adamant about some of the claims may mean giving up on (a). After all, acquiring knowledge about the whole of nature in one grand theory is closer to divine than human capacity. On (b), Socrates could not have given up as it was his main preoccupation. On (c), he did not need to give up as he seemed to be quite competent in geometry, and whatever "all other areas of knowledge" might be, they should not be beyond human reach if they possess a similar status and degree of complexity.

The most difficult question is whether there is anything left of anamnesis after one rules out or suspends the immortality of the soul and its seeing the things in this world and in Hades. What is left would be perhaps closer to the concept of activation than to the recollection from the grand theory. The experiment showed the slave boy discovering the properties of the square, not only the obvious ones like four equal sides but also those that were latent—for instance, those that enabled him to double the area of the square. If we imagine that his soul had been in Hades before, it is not at all obvious what it could have seen there to help him now to see the length of the diagonal.

What Socrates probably found mysterious was that the mind might not only find the abstract properties of an abstract object but that to do it, no specific training is necessary. The mind somehow grasps them with inner certainty. To put it in a more graphic way: if a new-born baby could speak, it would also understand the properties of the square and their relations. The slave boy was such a substitute for a new-born baby. The use of the figures, however, seriously distorted the experiment as one could not tell for sure whether what triggered the mental process was a drawing or an abstract question. Socrates might have replied—though in the text, he does not use this argument—that once the slave boy discovered these properties, he knew that they were the properties of any square or the square as such, and not those of this particular square drawn on the ground.

If we call this type of cognitive ability a recollection, it would be in a very loose sense of the word. The grasping of a certain problem in deductive sciences, such as doubling the size of the square, is often accompanied by the strong conviction that this piece of knowledge does not come from outside, for instance, from experience like in empirical sciences, but from within. It is like bringing to light what was concealed or opening what was closed. Socrates' verb *anakineō*—to activate—would certainly be a more accurate rendering than recollection. But then activating does not need a midwife, only a skillful and inspiring teacher.

It would be instructive to compare the concept of anamnesis in the *Meno* to that in the *Phaedo*. It is generally acknowledged, and with good reasons, that what we learn about anamnesis in the former dialogue is

Socratic, while what we read in the latter is Platonic. Indeed, despite certain similarities, the two descriptions are different, and so are the problems to which they refer.[20] The *Phaedo*'s relevant excerpt is about how we arrive at general concepts, whereas the *Meno* is about how we arrive at true opinions and how we develop knowledge about something we do not know.

In the *Phaedo*, the main example of a general concept is equality. According to the empirical-inductive interpretation, the concept of equality originates from generalizing the experience of perception of equal objects, just as the concept of courage arises by generalizing certain kinds of behavior, which we then call courageous, and so on. According to Socrates (or rather to Plato), general concepts arise in a different way: when we see equal physical objects, we recollect the notion of equality inscribed in our souls, and this notion enables us to identify all the empirical instances of equality.

To demonstrate that the general concepts appear in our mind via recollection, Plato employed an analogy between two pairs of concepts, or rather, the correspondence between two experiences. The objects of the first one, let us call it E, are a specific person and his portrait, whereas the other, called F, refers to equality itself (its *eidos*) and to the sensory perception of equal objects. In the former case, when we see the portrait of a person, let us say, Simmias, we remember him. In the latter case, seeing equal or like objects, we recollect the innate concept of equality.

Experience E: "[W]henever one is reminded of something from similar things, mustn't one experience something further: mustn't one think whether or not the thing is lacking at all, in its similarity, in relation to what one is reminded of?" (74a5–7, Gallop trans.). The exemplification of this was Simmias and his portrait: we see the portrait of Simmias, we recall Simmias himself, but at the same time, we realize that the portrait differs from the original in that it is an inaccurate and very imperfect copy of the person.

Experience F: "[W]henever anyone, on seeing a thing, thinks to himself, 'this thing that I now see seeks to be like another of the things that are,

---

20 The most important difference—duly noted by the commentators—is that the *Meno*, unlike the *Phaedo*, demonstrates no relationship between *eidē* and anamnesis (Ross 1953:18; Crombie 1963:143–44; Gallop 1975:115). Dissenting opinions also occur: Hackforth claimed that in the *Meno*, this relationship was "only implicit" (1992:74).

but falls short, and cannot be like that object: it is inferior,' do we agree that the man who thinks this must previously have known the object he says it resembles but falls short of?" (74d9–e4, Gallop trans.). The exemplification was equality (the equal itself) and equal objects: when we see equal objects, we understand that they are not identical with equality as such, that they differ from it and constitute its very imperfect copy; hence we can say by analogy with E that those objects made us recollect the equal itself.[21]

The structure of the argument is clear. As before, Socrates reversed the direction of reasoning. In E, we start with a recollection—the portrait reminds us of Simmias—and then we notice that the copy is imperfect when we compare it to the original. In F, we start by noticing that the equal objects are imperfect in their equality; from this, we infer that there must be the perfect original and that therefore thinking about this original must be recollection. One may, of course, have doubts about whether the reversal is justified and proves what Plato says it proves.

Whatever the doubts, Plato/Socrates did not have second thoughts and did not back down, as he did in the *Meno*. On the contrary, he upheld the argument and led it to the ultimate objective, which was the immortality of the soul. It should be emphasized, however, that the anamnesis argument in the *Phaedo* is more modest than the grand theory from the *Meno*. What it says is that the soul acquired the knowledge of the concepts before the human body was born. It is silent on reincarnation and the soul's stay in Hades. It is also silent about the claim that the whole of nature is a unity and that there is one theory of interconnected propositions that describes it.

6. Ignorance and knowledge

It is time to address the perennial problem in Socrates' philosophy—namely a paradox of ignorance, also known as a disavowal of knowledge. How does one reconcile the paramount role he attributes to knowledge with a simultaneous emphasis on his own and other people's ignorance? At the outset,

21   The difference between these two statements has not been sufficiently emphasized. Friedländer is one of the few to have noticed it (1969:46–47).

let me reject two possibilities: that his statements are ironic,[22] and that they contain a contradiction.[23]

6.1 What Socrates did not know

Socrates' ignorance has different shades of meaning. Here are its main variants.

(A) In the *Gorgias*, Socrates says: "For the things I say I certainly don't say with any knowledge at all; no, I'm searching together with you" (506a3–4, Zeyl trans.). In the *Charmides*: "But Critias ... you are talking to me as though I professed to know the answers to my own questions and as though I could agree with you if I really wished. This is not the case—rather, because of my own ignorance, I am continually investigating in your company whatever is put forward. However, if I think it over, I am willing to say whether I agree or not. Just wait while I consider" (165b4–c2, Sprague trans.).

(B) In the *Theaetetus*, we have Socrates saying: "I am not at all wise myself, and there hasn't been any discovery of that kind born to me as the offspring of my mind" (150c8–d2, McDowell's trans.). Socrates asserted that he had helped people to formulate various opinions, deciding whether they were true or false, but that he himself did not "deliver"

---

22 There are exceptions to this, for instance, the *Lesser Hippias* 372b3–e1.

23 Numerous interpretations of this problem can be found in the literature. For Zeller, ignorance meant that Socrates "had no developed theory and no positive dogmatic principles" (1877:123). Gulley argues that Socrates' ignorance was largely a mask (1968:62–74). Irwin believes that ignorance concerns knowledge, whereas the positive views are true opinions (1991:39–40). Reeve and Woodruff discriminate between expert knowledge, which Socrates does not possess, and non-expert knowledge, which he does (Reeve 1989:53–62; Woodruff 1992:86–106). Vlastos identifies two kinds of knowledge—absolutely certain and elenctic—and argues that ignorance refers to the former (1994:39–66). According to Brickhouse and Smith, Socrates disclaims the knowledge of virtue and is not able "to judge all bona fide cases of a given moral quality" (1994:36). In Benson's view, Socrates sincerely professes his ignorance, which he believes to be "the inevitable condition of mortals," but "he repeatedly expresses his design to seek out and acquire the knowledge he lacks" (2000:188). Of all these interpretations I find the last one most persuasive.

any such views (150d2–8). He admitted that together with the god he was responsible for people's thoughts (150d8–e1), but whatever was true in these thoughts did not arise in his mind but in the minds of other people.

(C) In the *Apology* there is another testimony, already been cited above: "But in fact, gentlemen, it would appear that it is only the god who is truly wise; and that he is saying to us, thorough this oracle, that human wisdom is worth little or nothing. It seems that when he says *Socrates*, he makes use of my name, merely taking me as an example—as if to say, *the wisest amongst you, human beings, is anyone like Socrates who has recognized that with respect to wisdom he is truly worthless*" (*Apology* 23a5–b4, Gallop trans.).

(D) Finally in the *Laches* Socrates admits: "I myself, on the other hand, am unable to discover the art even now" (186c5, Sprague trans.), where the word "art" refers to the formation of the soul. Socrates declared that since he had not managed to master such an art, he could not consider himself an expert in properly disciplining the soul.

One might simplify these four variants of ignorance to the following four statements:

(A_1) Socrates did not know the answer to many questions, but he was trying to find them.

(B_1) Socrates helped other people to contribute to knowledge but never contributed to knowledge himself.

(C_1) Socrates understood that his knowledge when compared to the god's was worthless.

(D_1) Socrates did not manage to master the skill of teaching other people moral excellence.

In each of the statements, ignorance denotes something else, and they also vary as regards their plausibility. There is nothing controversial—or Socratic, for that matter—about A_1. Socrates presented himself here as a truth-seeker, which usually ruled out formulating initial dogmatic propositions—these were yet to be determined. A similar statement could be made by any serious student or scholar. After all, Socrates did leave a number of problems unresolved or deferred their examination to another occasion (*Charmides* 169d4–5).

It is true that some of his conversations end without a final answer: the *Euthyphro* does not give us the authoritative definition of piety, the *Charmides* the authoritative definition of *sōphrosynē*, etc. There have been controversies among commentators as to what extent those dialogues provide positive answers and to what extent they are aporetic. Regardless of the interpretation, it would be absurd to claim that those dialogues are manifestations of Socrates' ignorance. In the *Euthyphro*—to give an example—we learn quite a lot about Socrates' views not only on the definition but also on piety.

B and B_1, on the other hand, are demonstrably false. It is not true that Socrates never said anything that he himself would qualify as wise—the statement about injustice as the greatest evil is the obvious example to the contrary. The falseness of B, and consequently of B_1, results from the misleading metaphor of midwifery, which, as I argued earlier, does not really correspond to what Socrates was undertaking.

What is patently false in this description is a contrast between, on the one hand, Socrates not having any wisdom and not being able to deliver it, and, on the other, his associates who successfully gave birth to "many admirable" (*polla kai kala*) ideas. It does not matter how we define knowledge or wisdom, but obviously the criteria must be the same for both Socrates and his associates. It is difficult to imagine or to find the smallest shred of textual evidence that there is a criterion that allows us to consider Socrates inferior in wisdom/knowledge to his associates.

C and C_1 are unmistakably Socratic. The distinction between divine and human knowledge is like that between a whole and its tiny fragment. The god's knowledge must be complete; otherwise, we would have to assume that there is a part of knowledge not accessible to the god, a conclusion Socrates would not have accepted. If so, the distance between what Socrates knew and what the god knew must be really immense, and from that perspective, Socrates' knowledge might have indeed seemed "worthless." Let us repeat: on the basis of the Socratic notion of definition, the criteria that constitute knowledge are the same in the divine and the human domains.

We have a glimpse of what Socrates may have meant by divine wisdom from the grand theory that he described in the *Meno* and attributed to priests, priestesses, Pindar, and other divinely inspired poets. The theory is complete in that it covers everything from nature and the gods to the soul, ethics, and mathematics. It is also a unified theory, logically structured in such a way that from one piece all other pieces could be reconstructed. Certainly, this grand theory, if it ever came into being, should potentially meet all the criteria of knowledge that Socrates elaborated. Therefore, one need not be surprised that anyone's knowledge is miniature compared to the grand theory or divine wisdom.

Much of this sense of ignorance that Socrates experienced came from his knowledge of knowledge. As we remember, he criticized this concept because he imagined it could lead to a completely illusory conviction of being a supreme authority on other branches of knowledge, even if one did not have any particular competence in these. With Socrates, the situation is reversed: the knowledge of knowledge that he had, made him acutely, perhaps even excessively aware of what he did not know and how vast his ignorance was.

With D and D_1, the problem is different. They refer to a selected area of knowledge, that is, to a skill of teaching virtue. We may assume that such an exemplary teacher of moral excellence, a moral expert, as Socrates interpreted him, had to be himself a highly virtuous and knowledgeable person. In Socrates' words, it should be someone who is "the expert on matters of justice and injustice" (*Crito* 48a7). The concept of such a moral expert appears several times in Socrates' conversations.[24]

The problem he indicated is a real one. If justice is a craft like medicine or shoemaking, then there should be those who mastered this craft and those who benefited from it. But in justice or virtue, no masters could be identified, and likewise no beneficiaries of such craft. Socrates certainly did not consider himself a moral master or a moral expert, and his successes in the field of making people more virtuous were rather scant. It does not mean that his influence on his associates was destructive—far from it—but certainly, he could not be proud of the moral progress they made. And even if we dismiss Socrates' self-evaluation and think of him as a moral giant,

---

24 Socrates talked about an expert in the craft of justice, using the terms *technikos* (*Laches* 185a1, b11, d9, e4; *Charmides* 173c1; *Gorgias* 500a6, 504d6) or *epaiōn* (*Crito* 47b10, 48a7; *Protagoras* 314a6).

the problem will not disappear; his craft must have been deficient, judging by the fruit.

Perhaps the mistake was in the very use of the craft analogy. The criteria that Socrates established for knowledge are so stringent that in the field of morality, one could not expect the practical results to match those of medicine and shoemaking. Once the craft analogy emerged and Socrates put the *technē* of justice alongside other crafts, he was bound to lose.

Those four cases show that there is not much of a paradox in Socrates' ignorance. In A and C, the concept of ignorance does not exclude the possibility that Socrates could have acquired some scraps of knowledge—that is, a set of propositions that are consistent, well-tested, having as its object the most important matters such as virtue and the soul, and undeniably true. The fact that he did not know all the answers and the pursuit of truth had to continue (as stated in A) and that what he knew was very little in comparison to, say, the grand theory (as stated in C), did not render him ignorant in the standard sense of the word. But Socrates' constant insistence on his ignorance was serious and sincere. The awareness of ignorance prevented him from falling into cognitive hubris, which happened quite often among the people he knew, and provided a stimulus to continue his elenctic inquiries.

B and B$_1$ should be simply rejected as implausible, being elements of a rhetorical device to embellish the image of Socrates as an intellectual midwife. As an image, it is captivating, but as a piece of information about his philosophy, it makes no sense and cannot be reconciled with what we read elsewhere. Suffice it to say, Socrates could not have practiced *elenchus* if he had had this type of ignorance unless, of course, as the *Theaetetus* passage suggests, his activity resulted from the god's intervention or he himself was a prodigy of nature. But on this, no philosophical interpretation can be built.

Perhaps the closest to a paradox are D and D$_1$. If we define moral ignorance as a failure to achieve the status of a moral teacher and to educate morally one's disciples to a noticeable degree, then some kind of ignorance might be ascribed to Socrates. Considering that he denied being a teacher of virtue and that the people around him did not improve under the influence of his *logoi*, one would expect at least occasional reactions of disappointment, frustration, or the lowering of expectations. But this never happens; instead, we have a continuous, uncompromising, and unrelenting elenctic activity as if the purpose was finally achievable. This is one of the intriguing aspects of Socrates' philosophy, to which we will return later.

6.2 What Socrates knew

His disavowals notwithstanding, Socrates made quite a few statements that, undoubtedly, he considered true. These are the statements that are crucial for his philosophy, and any doubt sustained about them or their validity would ruin this philosophy. We could call them true opinions, as those mentioned in the slave-boy experiment, except they are more than that, being coordinated with other propositions and as such, approximating the status of knowledge. Let us select some of those statements and arrange them in distinct groups.

(E) In the first group there are the following statements and prohibitions that refer to injustice.
"If I really were to claim to be wiser than anyone in any respect, it would consist simply in this: just as I do not possess adequate knowledge of life in Hades, so I also realize that I do not possess it ... I shall never fear or flee from something which may indeed be a good for all I know, rather than from things I know to be evils" (*Apology* 29b4–9, Gallop trans.).
"The greatest evil is *adikein* (commit injustice)" (*Gorgias* 469b8–9).
"*Adikein* is worse than *adikeisthai* (suffer injustice)" (*Gorgias* 473a5).
"One must not *adikein* at all" (*Crito* 49b8).
"One shouldn't return injustice or ill-treatment to any human being, no matter how one may by treated by that person" (*Crito* 49c10–11, Gallop trans.).

(F) The second group are those that refer to justice, virtue, goodness, etc.
We do not "consider the element to which justice or injustice belongs, whichever part of us it is, to be of less value than the body" (*Crito* 47e7–48a1, Gallop trans.).
"Living well is the same as living honorably or justly" (*Crito* 48b8, Gallop trans.).
"We should attach the highest value ... not to living, but to living well" (*Crito* 48b5–6, Gallop trans.).

"The good are not unjust" (*Euthydemus* 296e8).

"[A]ll I do is to go about persuading you, young and old alike, not to care for your bodies or for your wealth so intensely as for the greatest possible well-being of your souls (*hōs aristē estai*). It is not wealth, I tell you, that produces goodness (*aretē*); rather, it is from goodness (*aretēs*) that wealth, and all other benefits for human beings, accrue to them in their private and public life" (*Apology* 30a7–b4, Gallop trans.).

(G) In the third group there are the statements about epistemological hierarchy and how it affects the hierarchy of opinions.

"[A]cting unjustly in disobedience to one's betters, whether god or human being, is something I know to be evil and shameful" (*Apology* 29b6–7, Gallop trans.).

"[W]e shouldn't care all that much about what the populace will say of us, but about what the expert on matters of justice and injustice will say, the individual authority, or Truth" (*Crito* 48a5–7, Gallop trans.).

"[D]on't you think it a good principle, that one shouldn't respect all human opinions, but only some and not others, but those of some people, and not those of others? … And one should respect the good ones, but not the bad ones? And good ones are those of people with understanding, whereas bad ones are those of people without it? … Consider, then, do you not think it a sound statement that one must not value all the opinions of men, but some and not others, nor the opinions of all men, but those of some and not of others?" (*Crito* 47a2–11, Gallop trans.). The answers to the questions are, of course, affirmative.

These three blocks of statements constitute what we may call Socrates' Basic Theory, or in case they do not amount to a proper theory, Socrates' Basic Theses (SBT). Whether they really form a theory may be debatable, but now let us examine them. The simplest and easiest to justify is the E group. It amounts to the statement that wrongdoing is inadmissible, and that inadmissibility generates a categorical prohibition—namely, one must never do wrong. When we compare the F statements with other statements from the remaining groups, we will see that they stand out in their unequivocal simplicity, clarity, and intransigence. If there is anything Socrates was absolutely and unmistakably sure of, it was the forceful condemnation and prohibition of *adikein*.

The verb *adikein* has two major meanings—a narrow one: to harm others; and a more abstract one: to violate a *nomos*, human or divine. The same goes for the nouns that are etymologically related—namely, *adikia* and *adikēma*, meaning acts of harming someone and acts of violating *nomoi*. This, of course, creates a problem of whether Socrates would have accepted harming people whenever it would accord with the *nomos*. And the answer is he would not. He accepted punishment, even severe, provided its intention was to help the wrongdoer to liberate himself from evil and not just to make him suffer. This problem will reappear in the next chapter.

With this proviso in mind, we can say that for Socrates the ban on *adikein* was absolute and that the ban also covered retaliation: the person who was wronged must not do wrong in return. *Adikein*, whatever the circumstances, was so bad that Socrates called it not only evil but the greatest evil. The last phrase suggests that there were other kinds of evil, lesser ones. And this is, indeed, what Socrates stated explicitly in the *Gorgias*, where he made the distinction between the greatest evil and lesser evils, and in the latter category, he included poverty or sickness (477b), and also—to use Polus' examples—being put on the rack, having the eyes burnt out, being crucified, burnt in a pitch coat, etc. (473c).

This distinction complicates the problem because under one concept of evil, we have essentially different things: *adikein* was evil in the moral sense, whereas sickness and poverty were not. It is similar with being a victim of *adikein*—that is, with *adikeisthai*: being exposed to all those tortures with which Polus tried to impress Socrates was horrible, painful, etc., but was not morally evil; what was morally evil was to perpetrate those horrendous acts. There is no good explanation of why Socrates subsumed all those things under the same concept, but whatever his reasons, the crucial point remained intact—all moral wrongdoing is the greatest evil.

It is now clear why the verb *adikein* denoting the greatest evil does not and cannot distinguish between various degrees of this evil. "The greatest" does not allow gradation. All forms of *adikein* in the moral sense, whether extreme or seemingly less harmful, fall under the category of the greatest evil. Even if an action is not a drastic violation of the rule, its less drastic character does not make it right, if only in part, and does not condone committing it. Socrates had to be aware of the difference between being a cruel tyrant and escaping from prison, having been justly condemned to death, but he preferred to die rather than escape and, by escaping, risk committing an act of wrong-doing.

The statement that *adikein* is worse than *adikeisthai* is irrefutable and unshakable on purely conceptual grounds. Let us repeat: *adikein* is worse than *adikeisthai* because the former involves doing the greatest evil, whereas the latter does not. No wonder that in the later part of the *Gorgias*, Socrates, after repeating the former proposition "any injustice against me and mine is both worse and more shameful for the man who does the injustice than for me who suffer it," made the memorable assertion: "these things ... are held firm and bound down ... by iron and adamantine arguments.... For my argument is always the same that I myself don't know who these things are, but no one I've ever met, just as now, is able to speak otherwise without being ridiculous" (508e4–509a6, Irwin trans.).[25]

The E-statements are analytical propositions, at least close to tautologies that unfold what inheres in the concepts themselves. They owe a lot to EID, particularly to the complete separation between good and evil, justice and injustice, each being contained within and determined by its own essence. The absolute ban on *adikein* is a direct consequence of this, and so is the statement about committing wrong-doing being worse than suffering it. Since injustice is essentially distinct from justice, there cannot be any excuse, nor any exemption to inflict it on others: wrong-doing, even in a small dose, contaminates the action and the actor because whoever decides to commit it agrees to do the greatest evil, and the greatest evil is categorically prohibited.

25 The tension between the two parts in the passage—on the one hand, (i) "iron and adamantine," and on the other, (ii) "I don't know how things are"—provoked comments. Irwin claims that (i) is dogmatic and Platonic, while (ii)— "a concession to Socratic modesty" and refers to "stable beliefs supported by argument without knowledge" (1979:228–29). According to Brickhouse and Smith, "Socrates is saying that he does not know how it is that the claim for which he has such good arguments is true" 1994:38–39. Vlastos argues that the two phrases refer to two kinds of knowledge—knowledge whose hallmark was "infallible certainty" and elenctic knowledge (1994:55, 59). Benson claims that (i) testifies to the stability and consistency of Socrates' beliefs, while (ii) states that (i) is not knowledge (2000:84–85). I would say that (i) is part of knowledge, self-evident on Socrates' terms and derived from the criteria of knowledge; (ii) may be about lack of "infallible certainty" but only in the sense that Socrates' system is fragmentary and larger justifications are missing.

The F-statements—mostly positive, as contrasted with the mostly negative E-statements—are more substantive than the preceding ones. They partly follow the previous pattern and take their validity from SCK, particularly from the hierarchy of the objects of cognition (HO). The argument would be that since there is a hierarchy of the objects of cognition, there is also a hierarchy of human pursuits; consequently, the highest objects of knowledge correspond to the highest human pursuits. In the *Apology*, when Socrates criticizes the politicians for ignoring the most important things (21d4), he refers to those things as *kalon kagathon*, which clearly put the moral questions at the top of the hierarchy.

But in the F-statements, we find a more substantive streak—namely, the concept of the soul as a moral constituent of the human person. Socrates talked about "the element which" (in the original, he uses a pronoun, not a noun) that is concerned with justice and injustice. This element, as we learn elsewhere, is the soul. The expression that the soul "is concerned with" (*peri ho*) may mean both that the soul is an instrument to achieve justice and that it is the goal of justice. This translates itself into the statement that the highest human pursuit is to make the soul the best (*aristê*), and this best state of the soul Socrates calls virtue (*aretê*).

In making this claim, Socrates went quite far beyond the HO criterion. Until now, it was legitimate to talk about the soul as an instrument through which we attain knowledge, find consistencies and inconsistencies, formulate some meta-propositions about cognition, etc. Now it has turned out that the soul is also the center of a moral existence. This rapid transition from the intellectual to the moral is somewhat surprising. To make this transition, Socrates must have assumed that the person who argues well and whose intellectual skill is more potent has a better chance of living a good life than a person whose arguments are faulty.

This assumption could not have come up if Socrates had not had a strong and compelling sense of the sharp conceptual contrast between *adikein* and its oppositive, between injustice and justice (as between other basic moral concepts for which justice was often a shorthand), the contrast founded on EID, which made *adikein* purely evil, and its opposite completely free from evil. The chasm between the two was so commanding and had such striking clarity that the mind reacted not only to the formal aspect of the definition but also to the substance it conveyed. In the soul that recognized the absolute contrast between evil and good, the power of the moral *logoi* that refers to injustice and justice is expected to drive the human person away from the former and move him toward the latter.

The introduction of the soul as a moral force is thus far the only major substantive contribution to SBT. On the whole, however, SBT is more concerned with concepts and their relations, most of them grounded in SCK and EID, than about substantive propositions. Many problems that Socrates encountered in his elenctic examinations stem from the fact that some of his interlocutors treated his propositions as substantive: for instance, Polus vehemently objected to the thesis that *adikein* is worse than *adikeisthai*, the thesis that for Socrates must have been conceptually self-evident. This polemic will be analyzed in due course, but for now, it is enough to say that Polus considered the thesis to be a profoundly wrong description of human nature, whereas Socrates' rebuttal consisted in making Polus accept the power of the *logoi* that denoted the *eidos* of the concepts. In other words, Socrates' victory was more conceptual than substantive.

That Socrates was moving mostly on the conceptual level can be confirmed by another example. At a certain moment during his conversation with Polus, he made a point that a person who is noble and good (*kalon kai agathon*) is happy, whereas the person who is unjust and wicked is wretched (470e8–9). But can a person be happy when subjected to poverty, sickness, or suffering of the worst kind? For Socrates, apparently, it is possible. The argument would be as follows: (i) a just (noble and good) person is happy; (ii) the necessary condition of being just is not to commit the greatest evil (*adikein*); (iii) if a just person is a victim of lesser evils such as illness, poverty or torture, these lesser evils do not subtract any of the person's justice, nor of his happiness; (iv) therefore, a just person suffering from illness, poverty, and torture is happy. This conclusion—which neither Socrates, nor his interlocutors ever draw—is a consequence of the previous propositions, particularly about *adikeisthai* being a lesser evil and not a result of a reflection on happiness.

The G-statements sound familiar as they remind us of another criterion of knowledge—namely, HEX (the hierarchy of expertise). From Socrates' perspective, these should be as self-evident as the E-statements, and, indeed, he often used them in his arguments as unquestionably true statements, also during his defense speech in court. In fact, the first conversation he quoted to the jurors is about an analogy between the specialist (*epistaten*) who would make two horses "excellent in the kind of excellence proper to them" (*kalō te kagathō*) and the specialist who would be able to do the same with the two young men (*Apology* 20a5–b3).

On the other hand, one can argue that the G-statements are redundant in SBT as they can be derived from E and F. What makes the moral definition valid is its correct grasping of the *eidos*, not the political decision of this or that political group. Similarly, to achieve *aretē*, the soul should follow the true *logoi*, not the prevailing opinions. And yet, Socrates sets forth a lot of the G-statements, and it is not difficult to see why. By explicitly and repeatedly emphasizing the hierarchy of expertise in moral matters, he categorically distanced himself from the democratic habit of conforming to the views of the majority and treating such views as closer to the truth. This habit must have been so embedded in the Democratic Man's mind that Socrates does not hesitate to make the rejection of it one of the criteria of knowledge.

This explains why for Socrates, the problem was less sociological and more epistemological. The popular views, precisely because they were popular, created and endorsed by *hoi polloi*, must have been so pervasive that they deleteriously interfered with the process of any serious intellectual inquiry. The intellectual perception of the conceptual *eidē*, such as the absolute separation of justice from injustice, requires a clear mind, freed from the popular entanglements and *hoi polloi*'s constantly changing fads. Given that Socrates so often criticized *hoi polloi*, he must have considered their influence an ever-present and ultimately irremovable hindrance to knowledge that had to be constantly opposed. We could see it both in the reaction to the E-statements (the claim that *adikeisthai* is worse than *adikein*) and in the reaction to the F statements (resistance to Socrates' view that virtue supersedes wealth and fame in excellence).

All this leads to another problem. We know that the G-statements postulated the epistemological hierarchy, and since for Socrates justice (virtue) was also a kind of knowledge, the epistemological hierarchy transformed itself into a moral one, with the moral experts being at the top. But this opens the question of whether these two hierarchies should not embrace another one—political. With *hoi polloi* being blamed for interfering with knowledge and for preventing it from taking its proper place, it was, in a way, natural to think of some other political order where the multitude would have their power substantially reduced, and its destructive influence would diminish. This problem occupied a lot of Socrates' attention, but the conclusions are somewhat indeterminate.

6.3 Socrates' basic theses (SBT)

As reconstructed above, SBT consists of three pillars, each derived from and justified by the criteria of knowledge: the first is the rejection of *adikein*; the second is the positive concept of the human pursuit toward the best state of the soul; and the third is the directive that the first and second must develop independently of and in opposition to the mind of the Democratic Man and *hoi polloi*.

Before examining the possible relations among the three parts of what might constitute Socrates' theory, let us recall what was said before in the context of the *elenchus*. The elenctic arguments proceeded either vertically or horizontally—that is, one concept or statement relating to it would lead to another one of the higher (more general) order or it could be logically linked with the concept or statement relating to it of the same order. The first arrangement, as I said above, was more interesting because it led upward, possibly to a more general and unifying concept.

If we were to imagine what kind of theory Socrates would like to have at his disposal, had he had knowledge in the full sense of the word, we have two examples that illustrate both the horizontal and vertical structures. The first one—the grand theory from the *Meno*—was already mentioned and commented upon. On the basis of the scant information and the context (solving a geometrical problem), we can suppose it was a horizontal model, with one sub-theory leading to another and indirectly to all other sub-theories. One could start from geometry and reconstruct the theory of the cosmos or start with the theory of cosmos and reconstruct the theory of the soul.

The other model is mentioned in the *Phaedo* in the passage in which Socrates described his philosophical development. In the beginning, his interest was in the philosophy of nature, and then he became fascinated with Anaxagoras' concept of the Mind, which he interpreted in a specific way. Later he discarded it, disenchanted with how Anaxagoras used it. Initially, however, Socrates not only admired Anaxagoras' philosophy but turned it into another grand theory.

In Anaxagoras' *Nous*, Socrates discovered the reflection of his own moral intuitions extended to the entire reality. "I was delighted"—he said about Anaxagoras—"that I had found an instructor in the cause of things after my own mind" (97d5–7). Indeed, Anaxagoras' *Nous* behaved like Socrates himself—"the ordering Mind ordered everything and placed each thing severally as it was best that it should be; so that if anyone wanted to discover the cause of anything how it came into being or perished or existed, he simply needed to discover what kind of existence was best for it" (97c5–9, Bluck trans.).

This theory was vertical. There was one supreme concept, the Good, which applied to every part of reality and to its entirety—every being having its "best," and "the common good for all" (98b3–4). Therefore, in his life, the man was to strive for "the best and the highest good" (*to kaliston kai to beltiston*), some things being "better," some "worse," but both "are objects of the same knowledge" (97d4–5). The Good must have had its *eidos*, and the Mind grasping it arranged the entire reality accordingly. The concept of the Good was a combination of physical and moral, referring both to the celestial bodies and to the individual human life.

Occasionally, Socrates used horizontal arguments. For instance, in the F group, we have two such statements: "Living well is the same as living honorably or justly" and "The good are not unjust." In both, we have the logical linkage among related concepts—good, honorable, and just in the first, and good and just in the second.

Another example comes from the *Meno'* passage—already quoted above—where Socrates refutes the interlocutor's thesis that the virtues of men are different than those of women (73a1–c4), and that the man's virtue is to manage the state well while the woman's is to manage the household well. Socrates' argument is the following: good management is a *sōphrōn* and just management—that is, management with *sōphrosynē* and justice, thus the good implies *sōphrosynē* and justice; hence both the man and woman, if they are good at something, have the same virtues—*sōphrosynē* and justice. *Sōphrosynē* and justice appear as two virtues, and they are implied whenever one uses the qualification good/well.

But in Socrates' philosophy, the horizontal arrangement usually leads to the vertical one. If *sōphrosynē* and justice are related, then they must have a common *eidos* that unites them on a higher, more abstract level. The horizontal argument must, at a certain point, give rise to the question of this higher unity, whether in the form of the highest principle or concept, as in Socrates' reading of Anaxagoras' notion of the Mind, or in the form of a more concrete unity, for instance, the unity of the five virtues of which each might seem both independent of and logically related to others, but all being subsumed under the same concept of virtue, they must, according to EID, stem from one and the same *eidos*.

When we look at SBT, we might wonder about the possible arrangement of the three elements. It would seem that, logically, the basis should be the E-statements—the simplest and the most compelling, firmly grounded in EID—about the categorical rejection of the greatest evil. Having identified and separated himself from this evil, Socrates could proceed to the theory of the good. The next step would, therefore, be the F statements about the soul and virtue as the highest goals of human life, going beyond the formal criteria of knowledge and making strong positive claims. Consequently, the last step would be the G group about the epistemological and political obstacles that impede the achievement of E and F.

Such an arrangement seems logically preferable, but its consequence would be that the groundwork of SBT was the statement about the absolute inadmissibility of evil, which, in practice, would have implied that the core of Socrates' message is the avoidance of evil. But however essential this point is for Socrates, and despite the fact that the ban on *adikein* is for him irrefutable and non-negotiable, this is not the first and the main point that he made during his conversations. His mission was not primarily about telling people they should stop harming their neighbors. What he considered to be his first and most important message to deliver we find in the *Apology* passage quoted in the F group, and the passage clearly states that Socrates' primary message was positive—pertaining to virtue and the soul.

But let us note that in this passage, he articulated the strong substantive claim of moral anthropology—undoubtedly crucial for Socrates' philosophy—as an isolated statement, not a part of a more extensive theory. He did not provide any argument to support it, nor did he try to derive a justification from the formal aspects of knowledge such as *elenchus*, CK, or EID. He expressed it in the form of declaration—which is quite understandable in view of the context—rather than as a proposition logically linked to and supported by other propositions.

Perhaps the closest we can approach and read Socrates' intention is the first part of the *Crito*, where Socrates spells out three *logoi* that allow him to act rightly (46b1). The first stipulated that it is always necessary to act in keeping with "nothing ... but the *logos* that on reflection seems best..." (46b5–6). The second was the "*logos* about opinions (*doxōn*)" according to which the opinions of some people were more valuable than those of others (46c7–d2). The third *logos* stated that "[one must not] when wronged, inflict wrong in return, as the majority believe since one must never do wrong" (49b10–11).[26]

If we assume that Socrates enumerated these *logoi* in the order of importance and logical priority, we can reconstruct SBT in the following way. The first logos lays down a formal condition: before a person decides to act, he should first reflect upon the best course of action and come up with a good argument that justifies it. The word "best" (*beltistos*) does not mean "obvious," "self-evident" or "most effective," but has a moral sense: one should follow the logos which leads us as close to the good as possible.

We can see that the formal logos has a substantive aspect to it: human nature is such that it can—"upon reflection"—recognize the good, and this recognition may lead one to act accordingly. This is not an explicit statement about the soul in which the cognitive and moral functions coalesce but certainly points in this direction. At any rate, the first logos starts with the formal condition related to CK and then introduces the concept of the good as a regulative idea for human conduct. It seems, therefore, that in this version of SBT, we have a glimpse of what in the *Phaedo* Socrates expected to find in Anaxagoras' concept of the cosmic Mind, which emulated the human mind striving for "the best and the highest good."

The second logos comes naturally, as it were, indicating the epistemological and moral hierarchy, but also political obstacles that are in the way of achieving the aim of the first logos. And as low as in the third place, we have the ban on *adikein*, this time apparently as a consequence of the first logos (the priority of the good) and of the second logos (the defense of *adikein* being presented as the *doxa* of the multitude).

26   There is also the fourth logos which Socrates added ad hoc to explain his relation to the state. The fourth logos and the reason why it is not part of SBT will be analyzed in Chapter 3.

This pattern of SBT seems most plausible and congruent with Socrates' line of argumentation in his conversations. It is clear where the loopholes of this theory reside. There were at least three problems that required Socrates' attention.

The first problem is about unity: if Socrates or any person who strives to be *kalos kagathos* seeks the good or rather the best, then it seems legitimate to ask whether there are many "best" objectives and "best" *logoi*, or whether these objectives and *logoi*, because they are good, have some overarching *eidos* that covers all concrete instances. The broadest (maximalist) version of the second option—one overarching *eidos*—would be similar to what Socrates hoped to find in Anaxagoras but did not. We know that the latter's theoretical ambitions were lower. What kind of unity did Socrates expect to find, and how would this best logos affect human conduct?

The second problem relates to *adikein*, or, in general, to evil. The absolute ban on *adikein* was primarily conceptual, which left the more material problems unanswered, particularly those about human nature. Socrates' antagonists—Polus, Callicles, and Thrasymachus—considered *adikein*, i.e., some people harming other people or breaking the existing rules, deeply embedded in human nature and impossible to curtail. To use a somewhat mundane expression, we can say that there was a tug of war between Socrates, who defended the power of *logoi* against the unruly tendencies of human nature, and those who made those tendencies the defining factor of human conduct.

The third problem is political. On a more basic level, there is a question of the interaction between Socrates with his extremely demanding and abstract philosophy and the polis, which he severely and consistently criticized for falling short of the standards derivable from this philosophy. This interaction was far from obvious and certainly did not limit itself to the use of abstract arguments on his part and the interlocutors accepting or rejecting those arguments. Then there is a real political dimension. To what extent was Socrates ready to translate his notions of knowledge and virtue into the language of politics and make them the guidelines for a good political order? This, again, is far from simple. In Socrates' conversations, politics was usually present in the background, and although he was reticent in making explicit political commitments, he never dismissed or overlooked the political consequences of his philosophy.

These three sets of problems will be taken up in the chapters that follow.

Chapter II – Virtue and the Socratic Man

1. Background

Socrates' theory of virtuous conduct had to be a mirror reflection of his concept of knowledge. The concept presupposes a certain version of moral anthropology. The person this anthropology describes—let us call him the Socratic Man—is following the *logoi*, and since the *logoi* form a system, his behavior is systemic too. A clear statement to this effect comes from the *Crito*: "not only now but at all times I am the kind of man who listens to nothing within me but the *logos* that on reflection seems best to me I cannot, now that this fate has come upon me, discard the *logoi* I used; they seem to me much the same" (46b3–7 Grube trans.).[1] A similar statement we find in the *Apology* 33a.

---

1   These allegations that Socrates' ethics is essentially and excessively intellectualist can already be found in Aristotle (*Eudemian Ethics* 1216b2–10, 1229a12–16, 1230a7–10, 1246b32–36; *Nicomachean Ethics* 1116b3–5, 1144b14–30, 1145b21–34, 1147b14–17; *Great Ethics* 1182a15–23, 1183b8–11, 1187a5–13 1190b27–29, 1198a10–13, 1200b25–29). From the outset of modernity, Socratic ethical intellectualism raised serious doubts. Grote asserted: "Both Sokrates and Plato (in many of his dialogues) commit the error of which the above is one particular manifestation—that of dwelling exclusively on the intellectual conditions of human conduct, and omitting to give proper attention to the emotional and volitional, as essentially cooperating or preponderating in the complex meaning of ethical attributes" (1865:399–400). Of modern scholars, Segvic defended the opposite view. For her, "far from disregarding the volitional, desiderative, and emotional, Socrates attempts to build them into his account of virtue as knowledge" (2006:172). A different question was to what extent Socratic intellectualism grew out of and to what extent it dissented from Greek tradition. One could argue that the link between knowledge and virtue was not uniquely Socratic. Even Aristotle, while criticising Socrates for equating virtue with *epistēmē*, admitted that it was a different kind

The systemic conduct of the Socratic Man has three features that mirror those of knowledge. The first is unity: he is always the same man, whether in war or in peace, in a friendly conversation or in the face of death, who is never internally divided or labile. Second, as the quotation shows, it means consistency in words and deeds: he follows the *logoi*, regardless of circumstances, so imminent danger or other extraordinary situations could not subvert the validity of what is established as true and just. Third, he has a sense of hierarchy, always striving for the best—that is, the goodness (*aretē*) of his soul, which he discovers through the intellectual inquiries and examination of his life.

Socrates conceived of such a man not only as a result of pure reasoning but also in a critical reaction to various claims of his interlocutors. Those claims pointed to different models of moral anthropology that must have been characteristic of the democratic society in Athens. Here are some of them.

(1) *Logoi* are powerless and cannot motivate human behavior; they conceal weakness and practical helplessness, or they are never used in earnest but serve to cover the lower and more natural intentions (*Gorgias* 468e6–9; 471e1).

(2) Human beings are determined by the social conventions in which they live; different conventions—democratic, oligarchic, etc.—generate different rules and different moral requirements (*Republic* 338e1–339a4).

(3) Human beings naturally strive to have more than others and therefore

of *gnosis* (EE 1246b32–36). On Aristotle's indebtedness to Socrates see Cleary (1991). Several modern authors emphasize Socrates' roots in Greek tradition. Dodds said that ethical intellectualism "had long been an ingrained habit of thought" (1951:17). A similar opinion we find in Field: "To know what is good, ... nothing more is needed to make us do it ... this is not a peculiarity of Plato or of Socrates, but is simply a natural development of the assumptions of Greek thought and Greek language" (1967:105). O'Brien disagrees with such an intellectual approach to Greek tradition but takes his examples mostly from the tragedies (1967:22–55). In philosophy, however, Socrates was not alone—though most radical—in stressing a strong connection between knowing the truth and behaving accordingly. Among his predecessors Heraclitus is an obvious example (B45; B115).

tend to break the rules that have been meant to restrain such inclinations; one, therefore, should not wonder nor be critical that human beings easily succumb to *pleonexia* (*Republic* 349b11–d2) and *acolasia* (*Gorgias* 491e9, 492c4–5).

(4) Every human being lives in a world of subjectivity that is constantly changing in its interaction with the outside world, which is also in constant change; all this makes human existence fragmentary, which means that each individual is a collection of many existences (*Theaetetus* 166b–d).

Socrates rejects these claims, and in rejecting them, he formulates his own propositions, which he ably defended. But the concept of the Socratic Man also had its internal problems or could be challenged from the outside. In fact, the three characteristics of the Socratic Man might be accused for being derived from an erroneous view of human nature. Referring to the last paragraphs of the previous chapter, we can say that these problems are the direct consequences of larger problems: the alleged unity is too abstract, too rational, and too complacent concerning the disorderly part of our nature.

2. The unity of virtues

The unity of the Socratic Man resulted from and was guaranteed by his virtues. But do the virtues constitute unity? Socrates' philosophy, and particularly EID would suggest a positive answer.[2] After all, the definition

2 For this reason, I disagree with Santas' view that the theory of the unity of virtues poses two insuperable difficulties for Socrates' thought: (i) it presupposes that man possesses either all virtues or none (which is contrary to experience and human nature), and hence no man is virtuous, (ii) it assumes that virtues cannot be separated from one another even at the conceptual level, because the definition of each one comprises the definition of all of them and vice versa (Santas 1980:199–201). I think that Cooper is right when he observes that "engaging in this pursuit does at least raise the question of the unity of virtue in a sharply focused way: if one is attempting to formulate an ideal of human perfection, as a basis for doing everything possible to lead the best human life, it will certainly seem very attractive to suppose, at least as a de-

required one *eidos* as its object. In that sense, one can say that the unity of virtue was self-evident in the light of EID. But on closer inspection, this alleged self-evidence turned out problematic.

EID, which ascribed to the concept of virtue one *eidos*, implied unity in the sense in which parts of gold, differing in size, are the same gold. But there might be a different unity—namely in the sense in which nose, mouth, eyes, etc., are parts of a face (*Protagoras* 329d4–8). The Greeks spoke of several virtues—wisdom, justice, piety, *sōphrosynē*,[3] and courage. If they were different from one another, each had its own *eidos*. How do five *eidē* make one *eidos*, and if they do, what would this *eidos* be? If each of them has a distinct function or power (*dynamis*), one could say, for example, that in committing injustice, a man acted in accordance with *sōphrosynē* (*Protagoras* 333b8–c3). Could we call such a man virtuous?

feasible initial position, that there is some unified condition to be defined and sought" (Cooper 1999:78).

3   The abstract noun, derived from the adjective *sōphrōn*, combined two ambiguous words: *sōs* (healthy, sound) and *phrēn* (mind). The former denoted health in more than just the literal sense. Although pinpointing the exact meaning of the latter is difficult, the expression survived the ancient Greeks thanks to its the Latin equivalent "*mens sana*." A "healthy mind" meant a good awareness of what the human being is, which, according to the Greeks, included meeting a high moral standard. On the other hand, *sōphrosynē* meant discipline and self-restraint, especially with regard to sensory perception and the sphere of desires. Third, it implied the harmony and integration of man through a skilful combination and hierarchy of all the aspects of human nature. Finally, *sōphrosynē* denoted self-control, or the state of internal integration in which the most important part of man controlled all the rest, and man himself was the master of his own decisions, successfully resisting the forces of nature and social pressure (*Republic* 430d6–431b7). It is thus easy to understand the difficulty in translating the term into modern languages. All of its possible English counterparts, such as moderation, prudence, judiciousness, or self-control, suggest certain limitations being placed upon human nature, and sometimes even the reduction or elimination of certain of its aspects. The terms tend to be associated with something average, passive, devoid of risk, energy, and as a result, it smacks of a lack of fulfilment. In English, "prudence" has its pejorative derivative in "prude." For the Greeks, *sōphrosynē* communicated the fullness of humanity understood as a culmination of a demanding life. Someone described as *sōfrōn* was characterised by his lordliness and strength.

An affirmative answer to this question agrees with common sense. Why does it matter that there are people who have mastered *sōphrosynē* but are slightly deficient in piety or are pious but slightly deficient in courage? This is what we see every day in our lives, just as we see women who are on the whole beautiful but may have some slight physical defect, or philosophers who are wise, but have some problems with justice, just as there may be poems that are beautiful, but not absolutely beautiful, or a medicine that is good for health but has some unpleasant side effects. The imperfection of the qualities of people and their artifacts is a natural state of affairs, well-known to Socrates and taken into account in his concept of definition.

But this answer does not satisfy Socrates. The problem with virtue was not only linguistic—finding a definition that accurately captures the single *eidos* of all virtues. The problem was also practical. If the aim of the human person is to live a good life (*Republic* 352d8–354a9), then each virtue somehow encompasses the entire human existence and is directly or indirectly related to other virtues. Consequently, the absence of some virtues could contaminate the entire character. Justice, wisdom, piety, and *sōphrosynē* were perceived as related to the entire character, not to its part, so if in a person one of them were to be replaced by its opposite, justice by injustice, piety by impiety, etc., then to call such a person virtuous would not be easy. Such a person certainly could not be compared to a beautiful woman whose feet were slightly too big. Virtue is *kalon ti* in its entirety and did not contain any ugly or ignoble elements (*Protagoras* 349e7–9).

This is the reason why Socrates did not want to compare the unity of virtues to a unity of the face in which all parts were easily distinguishable and each might, even in a beautiful face, fall short of perfection, but be somehow an added value to the whole, showing intelligence, warmth, or a sense of humor. For virtue, this analogy does not hold.

The multiplicity of virtues would entail their separability (the explicit example was courage, of which more later), and hence the prospects of courage without justice, or justice without wisdom, or other combination of good and evil, which in turn, could cause the disintegration of the moral agent. In fact, one could then say that in one and the same person, there would be several moral agents: a respectable Dr. Jekyll and a cruel Mr. Hyde, or a pious and wise man and a coward fearing to stand up against injustice or defend his country.

Let us note that the thesis about the unity of virtues is not a part of Socrates' Basic Theses (SBT) but can be inferred from it, particularly from the EID-based absolute dichotomy between justice and injustice and from the proposition that virtue occupies the highest position of human pursuits.

SBT also implies that the best candidate for the *genus proximum* of virtue is knowledge. Since knowledge develops in a logically connected chain of *logoi*, and since SBT assumes the soul to be the supreme instrument of cognition, which at a later point turns into a vehicle and measure of moral excellence, it became clear that knowledge had to be a foundation of virtue (though, as I pointed out earlier on, this transition from the cognitive to the moral function of the soul lacks strong justification). Indeed, for Socrates, knowledge is the preferable *genus proximum* of virtue, although his language was sometimes evasive and terminologically inconsistent. In the *Republic I*, he calls justice a *technē* (332d2). But when discussing virtue in the *Meno*, he employs the term *epistēmē* several times. He also uses the concept of *phronesis*: "virtue, being beneficial, must be a kind of *phronesis*" (88d2–3). In the *Protagoras*, in turn, when considering the virtue of courage, he first uses the verb *epistamai* (350a2–3), from which the noun *epistēmē* is derived, only to later describe it as *sophia* (350c4–5).

The unity of the virtues is one of those Socratic conundrums that has inspired a lot of interpretative ingenuity.[4] Let us start with the definitions

---

4   There are several ways of making sense of the Socratic concept of the unity of virtues. Grote maintained that the concept was indefensible: "the position laid down by Protagoras, that men are often courageous but unjust—just, but not wise—is no-way refuted by Plato" (Grote II 1865:86). Vlastos, in his important article *The Unity of the Virtues in the Protagoras* (1981a), identified three formulae of the unity of virtues based on Plato's opinions contained in the *Protagoras*: (i) identity (piety, wisdom, *sōphrosynē*, justice, and courage are synonymous); (ii) similarity (these five virtues are similar to one another); (iii) mutual conditioning (possessing one implies possessing all). The first two formulae give rise to serious logical problems, but Vlastos did not reject them (as he had earlier done); instead, he modified them in the light of the third formula. The problems are obvious. If we take the formula of identity, by recognizing the five virtues as synonymous, we can use them interchangeably. When we substitute piety with courage, the phrase "piety refers to the *eidos*, through which things are pious" will change into the nonsensical "courage refers to the *eidos*, through which things are pious." The problem disappears

of certain particular virtues—justice, piety, *sōphrosynē*, and courage. Such definitions are quite numerous, but they clearly fall into three categories, and Socrates' attitude toward them varies.

2.1 Popular definitions

In the first group are popular definitions of the virtues, usually uttered by Socrates' interlocutors, with or without Socrates' guidance:

(a1) justice is the advantage of the stronger (*Republic* 338c3–4);

(a2) justice is helping one's friends and harming one's enemies (*Republic* 332d3–5);

(b1) piety is having the man who commits injustice prosecuted (*Euthyphro* 5d7–e2);

(b2) piety is what pleases the gods (*Euthyphro* 5e8–7a1);

(c1) *sōphrosynē* is quietness (*Charmides* 159b4–5);

(c2) *sōphrosynē* is modesty (*Charmides* 160e4);

(d1) courage is holding one's post and repelling the attacks of one's enemy (*Laches* 190e4–6).

if we do not predicate about the concept (universal), but about the *concreta* described by the term. This is the case with (iii). Thus, we can say about a particular person that since we attribute piety to him, he must also be courageous. The modification of formulae (i) and (ii) exploits Vlastos' observation that Plato does not use ordinary predication but "Pauline predication." When St. Paul writes that "love is patient, love is kind," he does not describe the concept of love, but the people who possess the virtue of love. For the criticism of the "Pauline predication" argument, see Wakefield 1991. Most scholars have tended to favor the identity option. Irwin writes that "all the virtues are really a single virtue, knowledge of good and evil" (1991:86). Penner (1992:167) claims that the unity comes from the fact that the names of particular virtues refer to the thing, namely "the motive-forces or states of the soul." According to Cooper: "virtues are one, and virtue itself is one, in that they and it are a single, comprehensive knowledge of all the considerations that ever present themselves for decision and action" (1999:89). Devereux (2009) points to "striking inconsistencies": Socrates defended the identity view in the *Protagoras*, but in the *Laches*, he supported the conditionality view. My point is that both views are present, that EID compels Socrates to opt for the identity view ("parts of gold") but he fails to refute the conditionality view ("parts of face").

The definitions may be called popular because they appeared as an immediate reaction to the question and, as an almost automatic response, illustrated widely accepted moral presuppositions or individual predilections. The mistakes the interlocutors made fall into several categories: (i) they selected certain particular practices and generalized them into norms, usually because they thought those practices typical; (ii) sometimes these practices justified their own conduct; (iii) they came up with their definitions in disregard of the instructions that Socrates gave them in connection with the concept to be defined.

Most of the above definitions fall under the three categories. All take one concrete type of behavior and raise its description to the status of the *definiens*, whether it is *sōphrosynē* defined by quietness ("doing everything orderly and quietly—walking in the streets, talking and doing everything of this kind" 159b2–4) or by modesty ("makes men ashamed or bashful"); or whether it is courage defined by behavior in battle; or piety defined by pleasing the gods; or justice defined by extending conflicts between the weak and the strong to the entirety of human relations.

The most general of these definitions is (a1), but it is not general enough. Shortly before presenting this definition, its author, Thrasymachus, reprimanded Socrates for using abstract qualifications in defining justice, such as "useful" or "beneficial" or "dutiful" or "advantageous," only to use one of them himself a few moments later. He failed, however, to explain the concept of advantage, and a lot of what he said looked like a hasty generalization of selective empirical evidence, a sample of which is presented at 343b–344c. All this amounts to the claim that "a person of great power outdoes everyone else" and "a just man always gets less than an unjust man."

But generalizations were conceptually confused and confusing. When Thrasymachus said that "justice is what is advantageous to the stronger, while injustice is to one's own profit and advantage" (344c6–7, Grube, Reeve trans.), it is clear that in the first part of the sentence he repeated his own concept of justice while in the second, he used what we might call a popular concept of injustice (generally accepted in a society). The sentence suggests that its two parts convey the same meaning: justice as Thrasymachus defined it is injustice in the popular sense. But there are complications. No doubt an unjust man "that outdoes" others is unjust in the popular sense, but what about "a just man who always gets less"? Obviously, he is just in the popular sense, but he is also just in the Thrasymachian sense: by getting less, he succumbs to the justice, as Thrasymachus defined it. So, if we translate the quoted sentence into Thrasymachian language, we have: "some just men always get less than other just men." The statement might be true but is not particularly original.

This is not the end of the confusion. Even if it were empirically true that "a person of great power outdoes everyone else" and "a just man always gets less than an unjust man" with the adjectives used in the popular sense, it does not follow that justice is, in its essence, the advantage of the stronger. The problem is that Thrasymachus needs the concept of justice in both senses, the popular one justifying the Thrasymachian, and in the case of the just man, the denotations of the two senses partly overlap. His argument, therefore, takes a rather nonsensical form: because the just men always get less than the just men, justice is the advantage of the stronger.

In (b1), Euthyphro, who formulated the definition, previously admitted his intention of charging his father in court because of the latter's wrong and allegedly impious action against a slave. Let us only repeat that Euthyphro produced his statement almost immediately after Socrates specified EID's first thesis—namely, that this definition must denote the essence of the concept. By coming up with the definition that blatantly contradicts it, Euthyphro thus either failed to understand or disregarded Socrates' point.

Let us look at Euthyphro's entire argument. He says that (i) piety "is to do what I am doing now," that is, persecuting his father; (ii) then he turned it into a general statement that piety is "to prosecute the wrongdoer, be it about murder or temple robbery or anything else, whether the wrongdoer is your father, or your mother, or anyone else"; (iii) but then, as he and Socrates well know, the Athenian custom prohibited a son from prosecuting his father, and deemed such an act impious; (iv) but Euthyphro argues that this custom is invalidated by a widespread devotion to Zeus, who treated his father with shocking cruelty.

Euthyphro's remarks about piety are the opposite of what Socrates advocated in the first proposition. Piety and impiety are mixed because they are so profoundly unclear: the action that is pious for Euthyphro is glaringly impious for the Athenians. The introduction of the gods did not help. People were devoted to Zeus, which might pass for piety, but then praising

Zeus for having put his father in bonds contradicts a basic intuition about a pious attitude. Socrates, at least, found it ungodly and "hard to accept" (6a9–10).

The chaos that pervaded Euthyphro's thinking about piety has one basic cause: the definition is subservient to an individual desire or preference. He started with the concrete action which expressed his individual intention: the pious is, he said, "what I am doing now." He immediately translates this individual action into an ad hoc general proposition—piety is "to prosecute the wrongdoer." A further justification of this proposition was again a concrete action, this time, Zeus putting his father, Cronus, in bonds and Cronus castrating his own father, Uranus.[5]

Unlike (b1), (d1) does not result from transforming a personal decision into a general principle. Instead, in the relevant passage, we have a military commander speaking about courage and, predictably, reducing courage to what he knows from his military experience. Since, in the traditional narratives, at least since Homer, courage manifested itself in battle and other military endeavors, it seems natural that the army commander when asked about its meaning, would present a narrow and rather conventional view and, as *pars pro toto*, unreflectively extrapolate its meaning to all forms of courage.

In (b2), we have all the three categories of error. Euthyphro formulated this definition not only after EID's first thesis but also after the second and third, which stipulates that the definition of piety must provide "the paradigm" for pious actions. His previous examples—referring to (b1)—about the gods imprisoning and castrating their fathers, were rather drastic and certainly did not allow for providing the moral standards. Apparently,

---

5   Nehamas was right when he argued—against a well-established tradition—that Euthyphro's (and other interlocutors') error was not in indicating a concrete act as an answer to the question that required a universal. Euthyphro's definition was not that piety is Euthyphro's prosecuting his father who was a wrong-doer, but that piety is to prosecute the wrong-doer. The problem is, however, that the definition clearly served to justify his action and emotions. After all, one can always infer the justification for one's action from some ad hoc general statement. In formulating this definition, Euthyphro never bothered to search for anything that went beyond the type of behavior with which he identified himself (1999a). In contrast, Socrates expected one and only one *eidos* that could cover all pious actions (Benson 1992a).

Euthyphro did not see any problem with such a picture of the gods; what is even worse, neither did he have any problems with claiming that pleasing such gods was pious. Again, this was the antithesis of what Socrates required: he wanted the definition to denote what was essential and, therefore, absolute in the concept, whereas Euthyphro's proposed *definiens*—pleasing to the gods—negated these qualities.

No better are the definitions of *sōphrosynē*. Before Charmides formulated them, Socrates was telling him how important the good health of the entire human person is, body and soul, how "everything in the body and in man altogether was sprung from the soul.... Wherefore that part was to be treated first and foremost..." (156e6–157a2). And the way to treat the soul is through the right *logoi*, and "by such *logoi sōphrosynē* is engendered in the souls" (157a5–6, Sprague trans.). Charmides either failed to understand Socrates' remarks or chose to ignore them, but the two definitions were obviously not compatible: they are narrow and, most importantly, do not say anything about the role of the soul as that part from which everything else might emerge.

With (d1), the situation is partly similar and partly different. Socrates made some remarks that should make it clear that virtue is a quality of the soul. In his conversation with Nicias, he distinguished between the means that the teacher/expert uses and the object of his expertise: in the case of eyesight, the means was the medicine and the object the eyes; in the case of horsemanship, the means was the bridle, and the object the horse (185b1–d7), etc. As the conversation was centered around the virtue of young people, the object that the teacher of virtue pursued was the soul and its goodness (185d10–e2). The Laches definition was certainly not about the soul but, at best, about some means to make the soul courageous or, more precisely, about the outward image of courageous behavior. Laches committed the same errors as Charmides.

On the other hand, one might defend Laches and blame Socrates for having misled him. Since the conversation often touched upon military matters, it was natural for Laches, a famous general, to relate courage to the behavior in war and on the battlefield, especially since Socrates pushed him in this direction, himself associating courage with "fighting in armor" (190d4). Socrates, let us add, admitted misdirecting Laches on this point (190e7–8, 191c7–e2).

Most of those definitions—let us repeat—generalize the concrete into the essence, by which they contradict EID. Because of the gravity of this error, the definitions are relatively easy to refute. But—and it is worth emphasizing—Socrates did not have it easy but used this opportunity to make important points, crucial for his philosophy. In the *Euthyphro*, the erroneous definitions (b1) and (b2) have serious theological and conceptual implications that Socrates refused to accept. When in (b1) Euthyphro invoked the examples of the cruel and vindictive gods, Socrates distanced himself from such a view. He does not develop his point, but his remark signaled that his interpretation of the gods was markedly different and this suggests that this interpretation—as I will argue in later in the book—has a lot to do with his concept of knowledge.

The same problem comes to the fore in his reaction to (b2). Socrates managed, in a seemingly long and tedious argument, to reiterate the basic message of EID about the *eidos* being independent of human attitudes, but this time with an addition that the *eidos* is also independent of divine intentions or predilections. This changed both the status of the *eidos* and the view of the gods. The *eidos* acquires the position superior to the gods, which, however, does not depreciate their status but makes them truly perfect beings who love what was essentially and unconditionally good.

The discussion of (a1) resulted in establishing an important proposition about the *technē* as such and the *technē* of justice in particular. Thrasymachus' conclusion that the strong act to their own advantage is challenged by Socrates when the latter introduces the concept of *technē*. For Thrasymachus, justice as he understood it was a sort of natural reaction and a political fact rather than a craft. Socrates' argument was that it is in the very essence of *technē* that it is not self-regarding, but other-regarding. To explain the crafts associated with "both public and private kinds of rule" (345e1–2), he employed an analogy to medicine and sailing. The end of all the proper *technai* is to take care of others: the doctor takes care of the health of the patients, and the captain takes care of the ship and the sailors. The ruler of a city-state is likewise concerned with the good of its citizens. Accordingly, the proper end of the craft of ruling never includes the ruler. This not only refutes Thrasymachus' argument by pointing out that his empirical evidence refers not to the *technē* of ruling but to other crafts, for instance to money-making, but was also a major step to his own view of what the rule of justice should be like.

Likewise, Socrates' polemics with (a2) formulated by Polemarchus in *Republic I* contain an important message—namely, harming people contradicts the essence of justice. This is a direct consequence of the SBT principle that one should never *adikein*. In his conversation with Polemarchus, Socrates does not state explicitly but nevertheless implies that justice is not about conflict, but about peace and unity and that it stabilizes and not antagonizes people against each other. He will develop this point explicitly in his conversation with Thrasymachus that follows (251a et seq.).

2.2 Parts-of-face definitions

There is a second group of definitions, also rejected, but clearly of a higher quality than the previous ones:

(e) justice is giving everyone what is appropriate (*Republic* 332c2);
(f) piety is caring for the gods (*Euthyphro* 12e5–8);
(g) *sōphrosynē* is doing one's own (*Charmides* 161b6);
(h) courage is wise endurance (*Laches* 192d10).

All these definitions can be defended and, more importantly, they are related to one another. If we revisit the question posed in the *Protagoras*—whether the virtues are more like parts of a face or pieces of gold—the former metaphor would best capture the intuition. In this approach, the virtues can easily be interpreted as being complementary to one another, and in that sense, they illustrate a horizontal unity: justice refers to the relations between people, *sōphrosynē* to internal discipline, and piety to the attitude toward the gods. Courage consisted in acting boldly, yet within the constraints set by *phronesis*; which, in turn, endowed the individuals possessed of the other features with resourcefulness and dynamism.

The virtues in question need not always manifest themselves simultaneously, but, on the other hand, their coexistence appears to be an anticipated outcome. It is hard to imagine someone who is just in his dealings with others and who is not internally disciplined; just as the appropriate attitude toward the gods should entail the same attitude toward people. But, as Protagoras noted, courage is the most independent of all virtues inasmuch as it designates bravery in action rather than moral relations with the gods, other persons, and oneself. This might imply—and probably many would intuitively agree—that courage could coexist with injustice, impiety, or the lack of *sōphrosynē*.

Socrates occasionally seems to consider the parts-of-face concept and spoke of the virtue as if it were composite and consisted of various parts, each being a specific virtue. For instance, the definition (f) appeared as a reply to Socrates' question about piety as a part of justice (12e1–2), with a presupposition that other virtues are other parts. In the *Laches*, he spoke explicitly of various parts of virtues (198a7–8). This, of course, does not mean that this was the concept he would defend. On the contrary, everything suggests he found the notion of the composite virtue hard to accept.

The definitions that fall under this category fare quite well not only on their own merit but also because Socrates' elenctic arguments against them are conspicuously weak, far weaker than those against the definitions of the first group. Let us first take (e), which states that justice is *to prosēkon hekastō apodidonai*, "giving to each what is appropriate to him" (332c2). The definition is also as enthralling as, arguably, the first version of the famous definition of justice, *suum cuique tribuere*, which remains with us to this day.

It may be true that Polemarchus did not see this definition clearly—he absorbed it from his father Cephalus, or rather from Socrates synthesizing the former's loose remarks into the statement that justice is truth-telling and paying debts (331c), but also from Simonides whose exact words are unknown to us and from whom Polemarchus did not provide a quotation. But whatever his intentions were, the reasons why the definition seems quite promising are precisely those that Socrates not only ignored but further distorted.

The word *to prosēkon* has various shades of meaning—from social to moral: belonging, appropriate, pertinent, befitting, seemly—and to grasp its essence would have undoubtedly required an elenctic examination. It is quite obvious, however, that the word does not compel us to think in terms of binary divisions. Appropriateness implies gradation and not a sharp opposition. And the sharp opposition was exactly what Socrates pushed Polemarchus into, elaborating on the division between friends and enemies that Polemarchus found (or thought he found) in Simonides.[6] Giving each

6   Polemarchus attributed to Simonides the statement that we should do friends good and no evil (332a8–9). Only later does Socrates introduced the problem

person what is fitting, appropriate, due, etc., blurs such a division as the distribution of *to prosēkon* must result in a more complex picture. The image of a just society where a criterion of distribution of material and non-material goods stipulates that every person receives—in whatever form—what befits him or what is due to him should have seemed, at least *prima facie*, worth considering.[7]

Socrates is not interested in it, probably because this view makes the picture of both human nature and political order somewhat opaque. He seems to want an unmistakably self-identical *eidos* that primarily reflects the nature of virtue as human excellence, and only indirectly, perhaps, the principle of the polis. By taking the theme of friends and enemies and making it, somewhat arbitrarily, the center of Polemarchus' definition, Socrates opens the problem that will structure the remaining part of Book I— namely, how the popular views of justice have absorbed the notion of injustice and sanctioned coercion, conflict, power, violence, etc., and how they, for this reason, condone evil conduct and undermine human virtue. The concept of *to prosēkon* is not very adept in steering the narrative in this direction.

Also promising is the definition (f). After several elenctic trials, the final version is that piety is to take care of the gods, by analogy to the slaves taking care of their masters and that the goods it means to provide are "many fine things." The definition adequately emphasizes the asymmetric relation between humans and gods, and the humans' dependence on the gods. This theological view is acceptable unless challenged by another theological view, which Socrates apparently did not intend to do in his criticism.

---

of enemies and asked Polemarchus whether we also should do them good as well, to which the latter replies that it is befitting to do the enemies evil (332b5–6). Whether this last point was really Simonides' opinion we do not know.

7   Let us also note Polemarchus' other interesting point. He suggested that in the time of peace justice manifests itself as a guarantee of the security of deposits. Socrates ridiculed the idea as being useful, but only with regard to *ta achresta*, the "things that are not used" (333e2). Polemarchus' intuition that the basis of a just order in peacetime was a financial system based on trust was original. Still, it completely missed the thrust of Socrates' thought and discommoded the philosophical narrative of the dialogue.

His attack on the definition was unfair since he expected Euthyphro to specify "many fine things," which was beyond Euthyphro's competence (despite his alleged reputation as a person well-versed in divine matters). Socrates' argument was based on the concept of "caring" (*therapeia*), which he thought to be a *technē* and, as such, was expected to bring benefits, "many fine things," to those to whom it was directed. What "many fine things" man could offer the gods through his *therapeia* was indeed difficult to envisage, considering the radical asymmetry between men and gods. One can, of course, argue against Socrates that if the relation between the humans and the gods is analogical to the relation between the servants and the masters, then the latter relation may be interpreted not in terms of the benefits that the servants bring about but in terms of the duties they should exercise toward their superiors. And if so, the humans' caring for the gods may also be a kind of religious duty.

This counterargument has an additional force. Socrates' critique of the definition made a certain assumption about the gods, namely, they were—so to speak—Euthyphro's gods, or in more general terms, the traditional Greek gods with their vices and weaknesses. One might surmise that such gods required and expected many fine things and, therefore, the question of what those things are might be legitimate. But Socrates had already expressed his profound distance from this view of the gods and rejected any idea of pleasing the gods as a criterion of piety. This rejection substantially weakened his critique of Euthyphro's definition: to those who, like Socrates, dismissed the idea of pleasing the gods, the question of "many fine things" that the gods could possibly receive was rendered less pertinent.

We have reasons to believe that when Socrates mentioned service (*hypēresia*) to the gods in the *Euthyphro* (14d6), he was speaking seriously. We know he thought about himself as being a servant (*homodoulos*) of Apollo and consecrated (*hieros*) to him (*Phaedo* 85b4–5), which, undoubtedly, he regarded as a form of piety and which had nothing to do with pleasing the gods. About his service (*latreia*) to the god he also talked during his trial (*Apology* 23c1). And this service—testing people's claims to wisdom in Athens—resulted, as he emphasized in the same passage, in his poverty and in neglecting public matters and family life. This type of service and of following the religious duty at the expense of other non-religious duties could, perhaps, exemplify the definition (f) modified in the light of Socrates' theology.

Even more unfair treatment we encounter in the case of (g) definition—*sōphrosynē* as 'doing one's own' (*Charmides* 161b6). The phrase recurred throughout Plato's works: in the *Republic*, justice was defined as such (433a7–8), and in the *Timaeus* we read about an old proverb that "to do one's own and to know oneself belongs (*prosēkein*) only to a man who is *sōphrōn*" (72a5–6). It seems that the definition did not sound extravagant, and, contrary to Socrates, its author neither spoke in riddles nor was simple-minded or silly (162b1). One might easily make a case that the definition describes a person fully developed, being in control of himself, and having the moral stature that the Greeks also indicated by the word *enkrateia*. Socrates' main counter-argument consisted in equating "doing one's own" with "doing everything for oneself": it was absurd, said Socrates, that one should "weave and wash his own cloak, make his own shoes and oil flask and scraper, and perform everything else by this same principle of keeping his hands off of other people's things and making and doing his own" (161e10–162a2, Sprague trans.). It is indeed difficult to understand why Socrates employed such an inferior argument, misrepresenting the import of the proposed definition.

This definition harmonizes with another one, proposed by Critias, that *sōphrosynē* is self-knowledge (164c–165b). Critias invoked old Greek maxims such as "know yourself" or "nothing in excess," cherished by Socrates, and they directly applied to the moral intuition encapsulated in the concept of *sōphrosynē*. "Knowing oneself" here means focusing on one's own moral education, and knowing the truth about the human soul and its proper aspirations. Socrates said as much when directly referring to the Delphic maxim in *Alcibiades I*: "If we know ourselves, then we might be able to know how to cultivate ourselves" (129a8–9, Hutchinson trans.). Similar passages include Xenophon's recollection of the conversation with Euthydemus, in which Socrates offers his interpretation of the Delphic maxim: "And what do you suppose a man must know to know himself, his own name merely? Or must he consider what sort of a creature he is for human use and get to know his own powers" (*Memorabilia* IV, 2.25).

The definition (h) of courage seems quite close, and, again, Socrates does not give it the justice it deserved. Courage is endurance (*karteria*) of the soul accompanied by *phronesis* (192c7, d10). The first part came from Laches, the last qualification—accompanied by *phronesis*—was supplied by

Socrates, but one can assume that it was not incongruent with Laches' intention. It is to Socrates' credit that he improved the definition, although later, it turned out that he was unable to refute this new version: strictly speaking, the definition remained unscathed. The only thing he managed to do was to elicit from Laches the statement that courage can be imprudent, which clashed with the definition, but since Socrates himself thought this statement false, the argument failed its purpose.

The difference between the arguments employed to refute the first group and the second group of definitions is striking. To abolish the popular definitions, Socrates makes use of the crucial theses of his philosophy. To overthrow the parts-of-face definitions, he employs the arguments of less importance, sometimes inferior and misdirected. This might indicate that either he had no better arguments to refute the definitions or was not particularly keen on refuting them. Every attempt to refute them showed, at best, some of the internal problems they generated but certainly did not lead the mind astray to the presuppositions or conclusions that, as in the case of the first group, contradict Socrates' criteria of knowledge (SCK), his basic theses (SBT), or EID.

2.3 Parts-of-gold definitions

The third group of definitions seems closest to the concept of the unity of virtues in analogy to the parts of gold. All of them have the same *genus proximum*, which is knowledge/*technē*. The listed definitions can be reconstructed as follows:

(i) justice is a *technē* whose purpose is to produce "what is the best" in the soul (*Gorgias* 464b3–c5);

(j) piety is "a knowledge of how to sacrifice and pray" (*Euthyphro* 14c5);

(k) *sōphrosynē* is the knowledge of good and evil (*Charmides* 174b9);

(l) courage is "wisdom about what counts and what does not count among *ta deina*, [and] is the opposite of ignorance (*amathia*) in these matters" (*Protagoras* 360d4–5); courage is "the knowledge of all that is good and evil at all times" (*Laches* 199c6–7).

All listed definitions say more or less the same, although (j) seems slightly different. The fact that the definition of piety stands out is easy to explain. Whereas the remaining three virtues could be defined essentially as the qualities of the soul, the concept of piety should extend outside the soul and relate to the gods. The quoted definition has obvious drawbacks. First, although it was formulated by Socrates, the suggestion came from his interlocutor, Euthyphro, a man of dubious credibility. Second, the definition seems narrow, primarily because it refers to Euthyphro's gods, and in this theology, as Socrates rightly said in his critique, sacrificing and praying was a "trading skill between gods and men" (14e5–6). This critique would be, however, less convincing if Euthyphro's gods were replaced by Socrates' god(s). Then sacrifice and prayer, usual religious practices, would lose their trading character and become closer to the care of the soul. It must be admitted, however, that, despite his piety, we do not see Socrates praying.

The exception is the testimony in the *Phaedo* (which could but did not have to be Plato's invention), where Socrates prayed to the gods before drinking the final cup. "At least"—he said—"one may pray to the gods, and so one should, that the removal from this world to the next will be a happy one; for this, I offer my prayer; and so may it be" (117c1–3, Gallop trans.). As the happy resettlement to the afterlife depended on the quality of the soul, and it was Socrates', not Euthyphro's gods that were to assess its value, Socrates' prayer could represent what he himself might regard as a more genuine version of piety.

The most Socratic seems to be (i), though it appeared in a comprehensive argument about *technē*, and not as a final definitional product of the elenctic analysis. In the passage in question, Socrates called justice a *technē* and did not use the word "virtue." But in the *Republic I*, he referred to justice as both a *technē* (332d2–3) and a virtue (335c4–5). The definition from the *Gorgias*, however, though having a good grounding in Socrates' philosophy, is involved in different problems. On the one hand, it is so general that it may denote virtue as such, but not necessarily justice.

On the other hand, (i) seems too specific: Socrates mentioned it paired with the craft of law-making (*nomothetikē*), both taking care of the soul and aiming at excellence (and both being parts of another more general *technē—politikē*), and juxtaposed them to gymnastics and medicine, both taking care of the body and also aiming at excellence. The analogies suggest that justice cures the sick soul, just like medicine cures the sick body, rather than keeps the healthy soul in a good state in analogy to what gymnastic does to the healthy body. In other words, justice rescues the soul from the disease but does not necessarily lead it to excellence—that is, to "what is best"—as the initial statement stipulated. Justice would thus be one of the conditions of a good life, yet not its crowning achievement.

Definition (l) is also unmistakably Socratic. Although it has two versions, they express more or less the same idea. The first version speaks of the person who aims at the good and noble, and whenever he fears, his fear comes from the knowledge that his actions will be wrong. *Ta deina* are thus evil things. The knowledge of what counts and what does not count as *ta deina* is, therefore, the knowledge of good and evil. Nothing that Socrates said anywhere can contradict this statement.

Definition (k) is likewise Socratic. One can imagine that if *sōphrosynē* stands for self-control, then the knowledge of good and evil will be responsible for all that makes this self-control possible: internal harmony, awareness of one's limitation, self-restraint and all conditions of a good life. In the small passage in which the definition appears, Socrates makes a point that this knowledge does not replace other *technai*—medicine, navigation, house-building, etc.—but that on its merit all the things that the *technai* produce we will be "well and beneficially done" (174c9–d1).

The four definitions—let us repeat—say practically the same thing. The two main words that stand for *genus proximum*—*epistēmē* and *technē*—partly overlap and partly complement each other. The definition of piety looks different, but the difference disappears once we replace the traditional Greek gods by "the gods wise and good" about whom Socrates spoke in the *Phaedo* (63b6–7) or by the god whom he called "truly wise" in the *Apology* (23a5). If the god's principal qualities are wisdom and goodness (and wisdom is goodness), then devotion to the god(s) is tantamount to one's devotion to wisdom.

The definition "virtue is the knowledge of good and evil" is obviously too general and, in that sense, not sufficiently eye-opening within the framework of Socrates' philosophy. On the other hand, this obviousness was unavoidable, given that the parts-of-gold format blending four virtues into one *eidos* had to produce precisely such an effect. No wonder Socrates is not quite satisfied with this definition, apparently expecting that he could come up with a version that would be sufficiently general and, at the same time, give an account of the specificities. But because he had difficulty indicating the differences between the virtues, he was compelled to stress—

in rather vague terms—their similarity rather than dissimilarity. In the *Protagoras*, he equates—or at least links—the virtues of justice and piety intimately: "justice is the same as piety, or very similar, and, most emphatically, that justice is the same kind of thing as piety, and piety as justice" (331b4–6). Since piety and justice were "similar," of "the same kind" or "almost the same" (333b6), and so were justice and *sōphrosynē* (*Gorgias* 507e6–508a4), these three virtues are therefore very close, similar, of the same kind, almost the same, or simply the same. One might suppose that the remaining virtues could be qualified in like manner.

Socrates may have been dissatisfied with these definitions, but despite their imperfections, he did not refute them, nor even seriously attempted to do it, which is quite remarkable when compared to his reactions to the definitions from the second and, particularly, first group.

Closest—but not close enough—to some sort of refutation might be Socrates' response to (j). He disposes of it through nitpicking (I might say unfairly) rather than through an argument. To the question what gifts we offer the gods, Euthyphro answered: *timē, gera,* and *charis* (15a9–10). These three words mean more or less the same thing—gifts or signs of honor, gratitude, and respect—and this answer is perfectly sensible and rather uncontroversial given his religious context. But Socrates picked on the last of these words, *charis*—prompted by his interlocutors' interjection "as I have said"—and related it to the word *kecharismena* that Euthyphro used before (14b2, b6). This word—the nominalized *participium perfectum* of *charizō* (to gratify) in the plural—understood as "things pleasing" immediately brought the conversation back to the earlier definition of piety as "pleasing the gods" (included in the first group above), which contradicted EID and was bound to fail.

Euthyphro agreed, but his admission did not make Socrates' argument any better or fairer. If he had not mentioned the word *charis*, the definition may have survived. It is true that Euthyphro did not consider any gods other than those he imagined, and in their case, *charis* could indeed bring to mind "things pleasing," but Socrates should have known better: respecting and honoring the wise and good gods did not clash with EID.

The definition (i) was not even discussed as it appeared in Socrates' own exposition. It would be hard to imagine how and for what reason Socrates could ever contemplate undermining it. All concepts there—the best, *technē*, and the soul—are impeccably Socratic and are at the heart of Socrates' philosophy.

Definition (k) also remained intact. Socrates did not say that *sōphrosynē* was not the knowledge of good and evil. What he said was that if *sōphrosynē* was the knowledge about various kinds of knowledge, as his interlocutor previously suggested, then the knowledge of good and evil could not be *sōphrosynē*. But Socrates has already demonstrated that the definition "knowledge about knowledge" failed. This way of dismissing the definition "knowledge about good and evil" is, therefore, unsubstantial. The justified conclusion would be that the person who defines *sōphrosynē* as "knowledge about various kinds of knowledge" cannot define it as "knowledge of good and evil." It does not mean, however, that the latter version is refuted.

Definition (l) also fared quite well. In the *Protagoras*, Socrates did not even try to refute it but concluded his remarks by pointing out the contradiction in his entire argument about defining virtue. He said he had started with the claim that virtue could not be taught and ended with the definition that virtue was knowledge, and knowledge was something that obviously could be taught. The alleged contradiction is only apparent. We already know that Socrates proposed such stringent criteria of knowledge that they seemed to be beyond the reach of any human person, but this did not induce him to weaken those criteria and adapt them to human possibilities.

His claim from the first part of the *Protagoras* that virtue cannot be taught (319a–320c) consisted of two arguments: (a) in politics, there are no specialists, and everyone is entitled to voice his opinion; (b) fathers are usually unable to inculcate virtue to their sons. As regards (a), this was precisely the main reason why Socrates criticized democratic politics (to be discussed in the next chapter). As regards (b), this was an empirical observation that had no bearing on Socrates' *logoi*, including SBT.

Definition (l) from the *Laches* also survives. The only reservation Socrates raised was that it clashes with the initial assumption about courage as a part of virtue, whereas the definition of courage as the knowledge of good and evil refers "not to a part but the whole of virtue" (199e4–5). The initial assumption was thus that the unity of virtues resembles that of the parts of the face, but the final definition rejects this model of unity and assumes the parts-of-gold model. The tone of dissatisfaction that one can detect in Socrates' reaction is due to the consequences of the latter model that already were indicated above: within this model, it is difficult to grasp the specificity of courage.

2.4 The eidos *incarnate*

The inquiries into the unity of virtue(s), though ostensibly aimed only to synthesize the definitions of moral concepts, were, on a deeper level, the inquiries into the unity of the Socratic Man. If the five virtues sufficiently and closely merged into one, then this oneness had to reflect itself in his character and conduct. But, as I said above, Socrates' final position on the unity of virtues remains ambiguous. The parts-of-face definitions seemed most promising, and, at the outset, Socrates considered them inferior and, as could be expected, took no interest in them; moreover, the arguments he used were of a dubious quality. On the other hand, although he accepted the parts-of-gold model and its *genus proximum* seemed pretty well established, Socrates was apparently not satisfied and found the final outcome rather disappointing.

His preference for the parts-of-gold concept over the parts-of-face concept results—as was said above—from EID and its predominant role. Gold is gold, just as virtue is virtue. But Socrates could not simply stop at this statement: the five virtues could have one *eidos*, and yet they could be distinguished from one another. How does one combine their respective distinctness with their identity? Any distinction between different parts of gold or parts of virtue seem either secondary—a small piece of gold does not make it less gold than a large piece—and then we cannot account for their differences or those differences related to the purity of substance. For some pieces of gold are purer than others just as some virtues are more virtuous than others, but then the identity of these seems doubtful and, in fact, should be excluded in the light of the Socratic concept of the definitions—in the end, none of the virtues can be said to be less pure a virtue than the others.

This closeness or even identity of the five virtues makes the unity of the Socratic Man less intelligible: he seems to dissolve into an obscure figure of moral perfection to which the distinctions inherent in the five-fold classification of virtues no longer apply. Once they are identical, or similar, or of the same kind, they lose their descriptive power, and then the Socratic Man is likely to turn into a morally perfect being but too nebulous to be described in more concrete terms. (How then can one 'follow' him or 'aspire toward'?) And yet, it is this model that Socrates makes every effort to examine, and let us add he never considered it elusive or unrealistic.[8]

To imagine how the blending of virtues could be carried out and what type of knowledge would correspond to this merger is not a simple task. But for Socrates—contrary to what might have seemed apparent—the perfectly virtuous man was not a figure from the world of the divine, and the problems with the definitions of virtues and their unity did not diminish this man's power and attraction. The awareness of ignorance, so important in Socrates' view of knowledge, does not play any role here. He might have doubts about the propositions concerning the unity of virtues, but the unity itself—both as regards the virtues and the human character—is unquestionable.

In the *Crito* we find some information about the human type who is undoubtedly very close to moral perfection. Socrates calls him "the one," "he who knows" and "the trainer" (47b10–11) and "the expert on matters of justice and injustice, the one (*ho heis*), the Truth" (48a7–8). In these qualifications, the word "the one" is of particular interest. It has two meanings. In the first sense, numerical, it means, simply, one person in contrast with more than one. This meaning is implied by the juxtaposition of one and *hoi polloi*, and it is the few, not the many, who are more reliable as regards the truth. The other meaning is non-numerical, that is, it excludes "many" altogether. The perfectly virtuous man represents the truth itself, and it is the only truth there is. Even if there had been more perfectly virtuous men, they would have represented the same truth. In other words, they would have been "the one." The *Meno* states it explicitly: "All people are good in the same way since they all come to be good by attaining the same things" (73c3–4, Day trans.).

8   The merging of the five virtues into one was a tempting perspective also for Plato who, as it seems, took over this model of moral perfection and made use of it in the *Republic*. He wrote about the creators of the just polis that they look "toward the natures of justice, beauty, *sōphrosynē*, and the like, on the one hand, and toward those they're trying to put into human beings, on the other. And in this way, they'd mix and blend the various ways of life in the city until they produced a human image (*to andreikelon*) based on what Homer too called the divine form and image" (501b1–7, Grube, Reeve trans.).

It is not clear whether Socrates was really searching for this type of moral excellence that cleansed a person of all concrete attributes—social role, sex, age, predispositions—or whether EID pushed him in this direction. One cannot fail to notice that he never talked of this ultimate moral authority as a divine or quasi-divine figure, the way he talked about the soothsayers, poets, or those who acquired true opinions that led them to great successes. A possible explanation is that the concept of such a moral master was a consequence of Socrates' concept of *technē*. If justice is a *technē*, then by definition it has to have its highest expert and an incarnation of excellence. Whether such a person really exists does not matter, as the hierarchy of expertise (HEX) points in this direction. In this sense, he was neither a prodigy of nature nor a divinely inspired creature.

The non-numerical view of oneness definitely favors the parts-of-gold concept rather than the part-of-face, although the former looks somewhat outlandish, whereas the latter seems more realistic and causes fewer problems. Should Socrates choose the latter, the Socratic Man would be a person in whom wisdom, justice, piety, *sōphrosynē*, and courage, though distinct from one another, are all harmoniously correlated; wisdom, perhaps, might have the superior function of overseeing the other four, and each of those four are responsible for different moral skills. If the harmonious correlation of the parts of the face accounts for its beauty, then, by analogy, an appropriate arrangement of various moral skills in the Socratic Man would account for his virtue.

Perhaps the only passage in Plato where one might look for some evidence that Socrates contemplated this view is in the *Republic I* (349e) where he makes a distinction between a musical man and a non-musical man. Assuming that the term "musical" in this context retained a basic connection with the literal meaning, the musical quality in a human character meant a harmony of the elements that constituted it. We could then imagine that these constituent elements were virtues, and in the process of education, these virtues were inculcated but also balanced and coordinated so that they formed harmony. A well-developed human character would be a complex horizontal structure rather than a unified monolith of a vertical structure. This picture was certainly closer to educational practice: the teaching of various virtues—different skills responsible for different aspects of human existence—and then harmonizing them into one complex, but integrated personality, made more sense than teaching one virtue covering the entire moral conduct.

But on closer inspection, the passage about the musical man does not support the parts-of-face unity. Talking about the musical man in the *Republic I*, Socrates compared him to a lyre that was finely tuned by the proper tightening and loosening of the strings, and the question he asked was whether in such fine-tuning a *pleonexia* was possible, that is, whether the quality of the tuning could depend on the ever-increasing of tightening and loosening of the strings. The analogy to this possibility would be wealth which one could increase infinitely and where having more of it (*pleonexia*) would be superior to having less. But since in tuning the lyre, this cannot be the case, the musical men—Socrates argued—do not compete with each other in trying to acquire more and more of the harmony, in contrast to the entrepreneurs who compete in having bigger and bigger profits.

It seems that this picture of the musical man favors the parts-of-gold rather than the parts-of face view of virtue. According to this latter view, one could, at least theoretically, imagine various arrangements or various harmonies of the five virtues, just as there are many variants of a beautiful face, each with peculiar proportions, shapes, or colors of its parts.

However, such a line of thought was foreign to Socrates. Let us take *pleonexia*. The musical man is free from it, but not because he managed to tame *pleonexia* through the proper coordination of five virtues, but because the very notion of the musical harmony excludes it both in a human character and in a musical instrument. The just men could not compete in their musical character, just as the musicians could not compete in the fine-tuning of their instruments for the simple reason that such a competition was objectively impossible due to the nature of harmony. In other words, the just men and those who tuned the instruments could be subsumed under the category of "the one" in the non-numerical sense rather than as an opposition to "the many."

The parts-of-face metaphor does not impose such stringent conditions. Perhaps, the word "competition" would not be adequate, but considering that the parts-of-face unity allows various arrangements, at least a choice was possible among different types of well-integrated moral agents. Such moral agents would probably not give in to *pleonexia*, not because this was objectively impossible, but because they were able to resist it through proper moral training, habituation, and adequate coordination of virtues.

Did SBT provide grounds for choosing the parts-of-gold rather than the parts-of-face option, or was this option only a consequence of EID? Finding such grounds is not easy, but one might think of some plausible ones. SBT contained very categorical statements and directives such as "one must never in any way do wrong willingly" (*Crito* 49a4), or "one should never do wrong in return, nor mistreat any man no matter how one has been mistreated by him" (49c10–11), or "injustice is the greatest of evils for the man who does injustice, and an even greater evil than the greatest, if that is possible, is doing injustice and not paying justice" (*Gorgias* 509b1–3). The moral precepts—it will be recalled—were derived from analytical statements whose obviousness was equal to the power of the imperatives, exhortations, and prohibitions ("never in any way").

Are such unusually strong moral precept, one may ask, more compatible with the parts-of-face or the parts-of-gold unity of a moral character? Perhaps—although it cannot be proved by referring to the text—Socrates considered the former unity insufficient. The direct transition from the analytical propositions to the imperatives and directives, without any mediation or additional provisions, was possible only when the moral agent had an unusually high degree of integration, without any internal conflicts, divergences, or tensions. And only a comparably high degree of integration could explain this unshakable obedience to the practical precepts such as "never do wrong in return," which seemed to go against the deep propensities of human nature. It does not mean that a moral agent modeled according to the parts-of-face metaphor could not achieve a similarly high degree of integration, but the process of making a moral decision is certainly more complicated, probably based on long-term practice and habituation as expounded by Aristotle's ethics, without this unhesitant directness that characterized the Socratic Man.[9]

---

9   Some authors emphasize the psychological—not only conceptual—aspect of Socrates' pursuit of the unity of virtue. I generally agree with Penner, who says that virtue is "a psychological state" (1992:165), except that we know next to nothing about this state in the case of the virtue *tout court*. One can intuitively agree with Socrates that each of the virtues—courage, justice, etc.—has its *dynamis* (*Protagoras* 349b5) and can imagine the psychological state of a brave man—Socrates said something about it in the *Protagoras* and the *Laches*, but it is not so easy to describe the psychological state of somebody with the virtue

To the question of whether Socrates justifies the unity of the Socratic Man convincingly, the answer would be, "yes and no." No doubt, the Socratic Man is unified and integrated. It seems, however, that Socrates was searching, but does not succeed in finding a deeper form of unity where the human character and the *eidos* of virtue coalesced. He is unsuccessful not only because of the definitional problems he had with the final version of the concept of virtue. There is not really much to be said about the person who would represent such a perfect example of moral excellence except that he is the *eidos* incarnate. The question is whether SBT and the theory of knowledge allowed Socrates to turn toward the horizontal parts-of-face notion of unity, which certainly promised a more inspiring philosophical perspective. The fact that he never really showed any interest in pursuing this road would suggest that he must have found it alien to his philosophical intentions.

3. The hedonistic argument

The hedonistic argument—identifying pleasant and good—is strange in the context of Socrates' philosophy, particularly in the context of the unity-of-virtue theory with the Socratic Man resembling the *eidos* incarnate. When one compares both arguments on a very general level, one will immediately discover the contrast between them. The unity-of-virtue argument starts and ends with the abstract concept of virtue and the highest possible moral ideal in which all differences are purified and blended into one, as remote from concreteness as one can imagine. The hedonistic argument starts with the lowest, most common and very concrete part of the experience, namely, pleasure. The aim of this argument is probably to arrive at the point from with the other argument started—namely, the abstract concept of unity and the highest possible moral idea.

unified. Socrates does not give us any specific information about it. Clark (2015) argues that Socrates conducted his search for the unity of virtue on two levels—conceptual and psychological; the first focused on the *eidos* and *ousia* of the concept, the other on its *dynamis* affecting the state of the soul. But again, not much can be said about the state of the soul of the *eidos* incarnate.

The main question that one has to ask is whether the hedonistic argument succeeds in reconstructing the Socratic Man from the hedonist perspective—that is, whether the commonest aspect of human experience, such as pleasure, not intellectual and not self-reflective in the least, provides the material from which the Socrates Man can be conceived. If this were the case, the Socratic Man would not be only the *eidos* incarnate but also a person more entrenched in human experience.

What prompted Socrates to link pleasant and good was the problem of courage. One of the five virtues seemed different from the other four in that it often seemed to defy human rationality and could hardly be subsumed under the category of knowledge. Courage apparently had its source in other parts of human nature, unrelated to intellectual skills and logical propositions, which proved that human nature also includes non-rational faculties, equally important as the rational ones because of its producing its own form of virtue.

It was Protagoras who came up with a more specific version of it (349d–351b). Against Socrates' allegedly too-restrictive intellectualism, Protagoras formulated his own view, which can be summarized as follows. Man, he says, consists of body and soul. Naturally good bodies and souls, when supported by education ("good food"), attain considerable physical strength and become more courageous. But, Protagoras argues, apart from these natural or acquired components, other elements constitute human nature. Originating from various sources, Protagoras called them "power" (as regards the body) and "self-confidence" (as regards the soul). This self-confidence is larger than courage and comes from "passionate emotion (*thumou*) and madness (*manias*)" (351b1). While courage is a virtue and as such, results from "the proper nurture of the soul," it also has an element of self-confidence.

Protagoras never claimed the person strong in body and self-confident in the soul is superior to the strong and courageous man, nor did he hint at any relationships between the two. He might not even be speaking in earnest but, rather, formulating a polemical hypothesis. But what he said provided an alternative to the Socratic view of human nature. It was, perhaps, seen as a more attractive and complex picture comprised of more elements.

Socrates' response to Protagoras' allegation was an argument—

called "utilitarian" or "hedonistic"—that has long perplexed commentators and contributed to many misunderstandings.[10] After presenting it, Socrates revisits the problem of courage while continuing to defend its definition as knowledge. The excerpt of interest consists of four distinct parts.

3.1 The hedonistic argument: Parts one and two

The hedonistic argument emerged when Socrates induced Protagoras to associate good with pleasure and evil with distress and suffering, or, to be precise, a good life with a pleasant life and a bad life with a life full of distress and suffering (351b3–c2):

(i) if a person lives well, his life must be free from suffering;

---

10 The argument was a source of controversy from the very outset. Many scholars have doubted whether Socrates and Plato actually presented it as their own reasoning. After all, they repeatedly speak out against the overriding role of pleasure, which they thought should rather remain under the disciplining control of reason. There are two main interpretive directions of the hedonistic argument. The first recognises that Socrates actually advances a theory equating good with pleasure. Grote makes a most emphatic statement: "Throughout all the Platonic compositions, there is nowhere to be found any train of argument more direct, more serious, and more elaborate than that by which Sokrates here proves the identity of good with pleasure, of pain with evil" (Grote II 1865:87). Likewise, Ritter thinks that in the *Protagoras*, "the words *pleasure* and *pleasure giving* included everything which in any way furthered human existence" (1933:59). Adams, in turn, asserted that this theory corresponds to the views held by the "historical Socrates" (Adam, Adam 2001:xxix). Irwin argues that Socrates promotes "epistemological hedonism" to justify happiness as the supreme good (Irwin 1991:102–14; 1995:81–83). The other interpretation of the hedonistic argument focuses on its adversarial nature, here presented from Protagoras' point of view or that of "the masses," whose hedonism reveals the possible assumptions of Protagoras' concept. This view has been supported by Taylor (1948:259–61); Sullivan 1961; Russell (2007:244), Denyer (2008:186–87). No doubt Socrates attributed this view to the masses, and yet he used it for his own purposes. My point is that he tried—unsuccessfully—to prove that hedonism, if properly interpreted, could lead to the same results as his philosophy of virtue.

(ii) to live a good life is to live a pleasant life, to live a bad life is to live a life full of distress;

(iii) therefore, to live pleasantly is good, and to live a life full of distress is bad.

In the next step, Socrates introduced the thesis, which he attributed to Protagoras and the masses (351c3), according to which some pleasures are bad, whereas some painful things are good. The paradox is that Socrates positions himself on the opposite side, questioning the distinction between good and bad pleasures. What makes it paradoxical is that the distinction should have been acceptable to him; after all, he elsewhere states explicitly that good things are not the same as pleasant ones (*Gorgias* 497d5–6). But this time, his position is different:

(iv) "a pleasant thing [is] good just insofar as it is pleasant, that is, if it results in nothing other than pleasure" (351c4–5); likewise, painful things are bad unless they have other consequences.

The explanation of this paradox is simple: Socrates set out to prove that it was impossible to separate good and bad pleasures on strictly hedonistic grounds, that is, by starting with pleasure as a given category and not going beyond it. Pleasure in itself is good (351e3–4), just as suffering in itself is bad; the provision "unless they have other consequences" ("if they result in nothing other than...") settled the matter in the sense that one may distinguish between good and bad pleasures by pointing to their consequences, but that is a completely different question. One cannot discern anything bad in pleasure itself, just as one could not discern anything good in suffering. In order to make further value judgments—distinguishing bad pleasures from good pleasures, etc.—one has to go beyond the strictly hedonistic perspective and analyze the context, which is no longer confined to the very sensations of suffering or pleasure.

The words "good" and "bad" do not have a moral sense because so long as we remain within the world defined solely by pleasure and suffering, no moral qualification is possible. We can only say that pleasure is good while suffering is bad because human nature accepts pleasure and rejects suffering.

Within this world, *pleasant* and *good* are synonymous, and so are *painful* and *bad*.[11]

In the first part of the argument, we do not have the explicit statement essential to descriptive hedonism that seeking pleasure and avoiding pain defines human nature, but we can legitimately infer this conclusion from (i) – (iv). Since Socrates talks of pleasure in itself and pain in itself, the former being always good and the latter always bad, he apparently presumed that on these assumptions, man naturally seeks pleasure and avoids pain. Those are the primary data of human experience and the basic signals of orientation. If there had been some other defining factors of human nature, equally basic, then (iv) would not be tenable: separating pure pleasure from other defining factors would make no sense and would give a false image of human nature.

In the second part of his argument, Socrates put forward a proposition that seems to contradict the first part—namely, that knowledge (*epistēmē*, *phronesis* 352c5–7) is the ruling authority in human nature. To this Protagoras agreed, calling *sophia* and *epistēmē* "the highest of all human things" (352d1–3). Socrates arrives at this proposition by confronting his interlocutor with an alternative: either man is ruled by knowledge, while all the other elements of human nature—emotional, volitional, instinctive, and others—should be subordinated to its authority, or man is ruled by various factors unrelated to knowledge but which hold sway over it, such as "… temperament [*thymos*], sometimes pleasure, sometimes pain, at other times love, often fear" (352b7–8). Faced with this choice, Protagoras was compelled to embrace the first option.

The proposition that attributed to knowledge an authority over pleasure, pain, anger, love, fear, etc., can indeed contradict the first part of the argument, except that we do not know how knowledge is defined. It is likely

11 Cf. Taylor's comment: "Socrates' assessment of pleasure and unpleasantness has lacked moral implications; a pleasant life is something good in the sense of something worth having from the point of view of the person who has it, an unpleasant life is something bad in the sense of something undesirable from that point of view" (1976:165). This interpretation clearly differs from another one suggested by Vlastos: "what Socrates most likely meant to assert is …: (a) that pleasure is *a good* (not the only one), and (b) that whatever is best will *in fact* be the most pleasant" (1956:xli).

that Socrates and Protagoras had something else in mind, considering how much their views differed. So, although they agreed, the meaning of the accepted proposition is still unclear, and the subsequent part of the argument will clarify it.

3.2 The hedonistic argument: Part three

Part three of the argument starts with an attempt to reinforce the hedonist position: the reason is the ruling faculty, to be sure, but it may be defeated by succumbing to desires. In extreme cases, knowledge may be "utterly dragged around by all these other things as if it were a slave" (352c1). Such a dramatic description of the fall of reason must have sounded convincing to the Greeks, just as it sounds convincing today. After all, yielding to intense passions has been a recurrent theme in literature at least since the times of Homer. "The spirit is willing, but the flesh is weak," as Christ would say several centuries later (Mt 26:41; Mk 14:38). But Socrates did not agree with this view and, characteristically, attributed it to *hoi polloi* (353a7).

His argument to refute it follows up on the previously discussed theme:
(i) pleasant things in themselves are good, and unpleasant things in themselves are bad "unless they have other consequences."
     Premise (i), although true, does not reflect actual human experience because in real life the human being always bears the consequences of his choices:
(ii) sometimes, the human being chooses short-term pleasure, whose outcomes turn out to be bad because it eventually results in suffering; conversely, sometimes, he chooses short-term suffering, whose outcome turns out to be good because it eventually brings pleasure.

Point (ii) implies that:

(iii) choosing a good thing or pleasure rather than a bad thing or suffering consists in making decisions that lead to the advantage of pleasure over suffering;
(iv) hence, if someone chooses a short-term pleasure over a more lasting one, when viewed from the long-term perspective, he does not necessarily yield to desire but may be making a mistake in judging the proportions between pleasure and suffering;

(v) in other words, choosing a pleasure with bad consequences is due to ignorance;

(vi) if the man were able to anticipate the consequences of his choices and make appropriate calculations, he would not choose something that resulted in greater distress and less pleasure;

(vii) therefore, to live a pleasant life, we need a kind of knowledge called "the art of measurement" (*technē metrētikē*–356e4), which allows for such calculations to be made.

The above reconstruction indicates that Socrates' intention was to show that although hedonism reduces human aspirations exclusively to pleasure and suffering, it could also be combined with a kind of knowledge:[12] the hedonists could fairly easily assume the superiority of knowledge over desires because the only way to organize pleasure and distress was to check their balance and calculate one's conduct with a view to deriving more of the former and less of the latter. From this, Socrates inferred two additional propositions expressing roughly the same idea: (a) the hedonists must also acknowledge that man never chooses evil deliberately but only in ignorance; (b) *akrasia,* impotence of will, is impossible: yielding to one's desires always results from the misperception of what will produce pleasure.

The question is, of course, what exactly is this form of cognition that Socrates called the art of measurement and whether it is similar to or convergent with his own concept of knowledge. Undoubtedly, the art of measurement is based on the hedonist assumption that Socrates later attributes to his interlocutor explicitly: "If you are content with that and aren't able to call anything good or bad except what results in [pleasure and pain]..." (355a3–4). But this assumption need not be Socrates'. His philosophical language is richer than that, and nowhere do we find any inclination to reduce it to the two concepts of pleasure and pain. If this were indeed his intention, the art of measurement would be identical with or close to his concept of knowledge.

12 Hence, the controversial interpretation proposed by Irwin (cf. footnote 10 above), who argues that utilitarianism was a Socratic doctrine (not that of "the masses"), and that pleasure is the end product, and therefore the goal of virtue understood as *technē* (Irwin 1991:103–09). Vlastos (1996c) and Roochnik (1992), among others, take issue with Irwin's reading of the passage.

We can imagine what the art of measurement could mean, as Socrates provides some explanation. "If you weigh pleasant things against painful, if the painful are outweighed by the pleasant, no matter which are nearer and which are more distant, you have to do whatever brings the pleasant about, and if the pleasant are outweighed by the painful, you have to avoid doing it" (356b5–8). Rephrasing it in Socrates' somewhat metaphorical language, we could say that the art of measurement starts with the experience of pleasure or pain and is a never-ending laborious comparison of these experiences as regards their intensity and possible consequences for the future. The objective is to come up with such a strategy that will guarantee the maximum of lasting pleasures and the minimum of short-lived sufferings.

Given that the art of measurement is an art of weighing, it obviously requires a modification of the picture of human nature by supplementing the initial assumption about pain and pleasure with an additional concept of an intellectual faculty that would make such weighing possible. This need not be a highly developed faculty but certainly one capable of making a rational long-term evaluation of pleasures. This art of weighing is obviously not the same as Socratic knowledge for the simple reason that it does not meet important SCK requirements: while it might have some theoretical justification, it does not constitute a system of *logoi* subject to elenctic testing. Besides, pleasure and pain are certainly not high in the SCK hierarchy of objects of cognition.

The art of weighing does not resemble Socrates' usual inquiries. It does not start with the general concepts or definitions but with the assessment of pleasures and pains as primary data, and a theoretical reflection—of a rather simple kind—comes afterward. If this is a way to a good life, then certainly Socrates himself did not take it. We do not see him comparing pleasures and pains, nor do we hear him encouraging others to do so.

But, for some reason, Socrates seems to hint that this art has a purpose, not unlike that of knowledge. After mentioning the misleading appearances that we might have of pleasure and pain, he maintains that the art of measurement could lead to "a salvation of our life" (356d3). And then he repeats it in a more elaborate form. "[The art of] measurement would have made these appearances powerless and given us peace of mind by showing us the truth and letting us get a firm grasp of it, and so would have saved our lives.

In the face of this, would they agree that it is the art of measurement that would save us, or some other?" (356d7–e4). To this the answer is of course 'no other but that of measurement.' This means that through the art of measurement, we can practically reach the same objective that the Socratic Man is trying to achieve—peace of mind, truth, and liberation from illusionary concerns.

Before we solve this apparent inconsistency, it would be instructive to consider Socrates' argument about happiness from the *Republic* I. Thinking in terms of happiness is certainly more congruent with his philosophy than thinking in terms of pleasure. At 352d8–354a9, Socrates introduces the concept of *ergon*, or a function proper to something or someone. The argument proceeds as follows:

(i) *ergon* is something that determines the constitutive function of an object, an animal, or a man (that which "it alone can do," and it "can do it better than anything else");

(ii) this *ergon* is correlated with a virtue (perfection) that this object, animal, or man can acquire;

(iii) the *ergon* of the soul is life (caring, managing, and deliberation);

(iv) the virtue of the soul is justice;

(v) thanks to the just soul, the man leads a good life (cares, manages, deliberates);

(vi) the man who leads a good life is *eudaimōn* and *makarios*, but the man who does not is *athlios*, that is, a miserable wretch;

(vii) the just man, or the man whose life is just, is *eudaimōn*, whereas the unjust man is *athlios*;

(viii) being happy is beneficial, whereas being miserable is not.

The difference between the hedonistic argument and the happiness argument is obvious. In the hedonistic argument, pleasure appears in the first premise as a basic datum of experience, from which—together with suffering and the art of weighing—the entirety human conduct can be derived. No matter how much later the meaning of pleasure develops and how the definition is extended, the basis of it is this sensuous experience to which every human being has direct access. In other words, human life, even if organized by the art of measurement, is inherently fragmentary. This art integrates the pieces of pleasure into more extensive and stable constituents, sometimes perhaps with much success, but the fragmentariness will not disappear for it inheres in the very experience of pleasure.

In the happiness argument, the notion of happiness appears in the conclusion, as the culmination of the entire reasoning. What is primary is the oneness grounded in the human *ergon*, particularly in the excellence of the soul. This unity provides the conditions of a good life, which in turn leads to the pursuit of virtue, that is, the excellence of the soul. Happiness arises as a consequence of a good life and is not a motive for a good life. The Socratic Man may have mastered the art of measurement to calculate the pleasures and sufferings with respect to a virtuous and happy life, but this art might be a by-product of the excellence of his soul, not a skill developed through the accumulation and sublimation of pleasures.

This solves the apparent inconsistency. Let us repeat. The Socratic Man, or at least someone who desires to become one, can use the art of measurement and look at his moral development through the perspective of the maximization of pleasure, but his primary concern and the main objective is the excellence of the soul. The happy life he has lived may be also a pleasant life, but not on account of the careful search for and selection of pleasures.

The hedonist man equipped with the art of measurement is unlikely to endow a human person with a sense of unity comparable to that of the Socratic Man. The fragmentariness and discontinuity of the hedonist person make it difficult to conceive of knowledge that would embrace and act in the interest of an entire human life. As Socrates (or Plato) argues elsewhere, such a person is not one being, but many, each of resulting from different and changing interactions with the outside world, depending on the circumstances, opportunities, and other unpredictable factors (*Theaetetus* 166b–d). Whatever successes in internal integration may await such a man, Socrates did not test this strategy, nor did he advocate it.

This implies that part three does not justify the proposition that *akrasia* is impossible and that knowledge cannot become a slave of passions. The proposition is defensible in the case of the Socratic Man but not necessarily in the case of the hedonist, whose only weapon is the art of measurement. The art of weighing pleasures, if it is to function correctly, presupposes a well-organized human character, but such a character is not a product of the art of weighing pleasures.

3.3 The hedonistic argument: Part four and the problem of courage

The fourth and final theme in this argument returns to the problem of courage with the intention to demonstrate that courage falls under the *genus proximum* of knowledge, and that, therefore, Protagoras was wrong in claiming that courageous conduct proves the essential role of non-rational aspects of human nature—passions, frenzy, etc. Such a role would have demolished the unity of virtue because it would indicate that a courageous man need not necessarily be just, pious, wise, or self-controlled.

3.3.1 Courage, confidence, and *technē*

The illustration of the problem comes from the *Laches*, where Socrates mentions a man who is not competent in diving but who, thanks to his perseverance (*karteria*), could descend to the bottom of a well (193c3–4). Socrates did not value such perseverance, nor did he think much of the diver and his ilk, considering their behavior irrational when compared to that of the divers who mastered their *technē* (193c8–9). The reckless diver reappears in the *Protagoras* (350a1), this time plunging "confidently" (*tharraleōs*). And again, this confidence was not something Socrates valued.

The criticism is, of course, controversial. After all, courage is usually thought of as an ability of daring more than other people, to go beyond the barrier of fear that, for many, is unbreachable. Consistent transgressing of these limits may indeed be a form of ignorance, as Socrates maintained, and can hardly be called a virtue. But, on the other hand, courage does not exhaust itself—as some might interpret Socrates' remarks about the competent diver—in following those acts of audacity that the diving *technē* (or any other *technē*) permits.

Socrates presents the full argumentation in the *Protagoras*. The key word in this argument is *deinon*, usually translated as "fearful" or "dreadful," and the entire passage deals with the man's attitude toward "the fearful things" (*ta deina*). Socrates also used the terms *phobos*, which simply means "fear" understood as being unwilling to pursue something, and *tharreō* meaning "to dare" or "to confront something with confidence" (as in the case of the recklessly daring diver).

The problem with *deinos* is that its meaning is broader, and the word denotes the things that cause not only fear but also awe and admiration. Perhaps the most famous usage of this word comes from the first stasimon in Sophocles' *Antigone* (334–75) where Chorus sings that there are many "wondrous creatures" (*ta deina*) in the world, but none is "more wonderous" (*deinoteron*) than man. In the Sophoclean sense, a *deinos* man was a person able to do things that other creatures feared to do, including evil deeds, but also to do the great things for which he would be admired and worshipped. And this is not what Socrates had in mind. In the argument, the meaning is negative: "the fearful things" are those that are detrimental to the doer.

Socrates' argument aims to refute the thesis, allegedly widely accepted (359c11), that cowards go for things they are confident about (*ta tharralea*) whereas courageous men go for *ta deina*. The argument runs as follows:

(i)   no one goes for *ta deina* (this follows from the previous parts of the hedonistic argument, which preclude that people knowingly seek what is unpleasant); hence, the cowards and the courageous alike go for the same things, those they are confident about;
(ii) Protagoras introduces the problem of war, which should contradict the above—the courageous go to war willingly while the cowards do not;
(iii) to Socrates' question whether going to war is noble (*kalon*) or disgraceful (*aischron*), Protagoras answers that it is noble; then Socrates continues—what is noble is good (*agathon*); what is noble and good is also pleasant;
(iv) if the cowards do not go for what is noble, good, and pleasant, then they are motivated by ignorance; the hedonist argument implied that no one could knowingly avoid what was pleasant, noble, and good;
(v)   the courageous, on the other hand, go for what is noble, good, and pleasant;
(vi) whatever the courageous fear and are confident about, their fear and confidence are not disgraceful;
(vii) their confidence, not being disgraceful, is therefore noble and good;
(viii) whatever the cowards and the overconfident (*thraseis*) fear and are overconfident about, their fear and overconfidence are disgraceful;
(ix) therefore, their confidence results from their ignorance and stupidity (*agnoia, amathia*);

(x) cowardice is thus ignorance about *ta deina;*[13]

(xi) courage is "wisdom about what counts and what does not count among *ta deina,* [and] is the opposite of ignorance (*amathia*) in these matters" (360d4–5).

The argument has two threads: the first starts in (i) and then continues in (ix), (x), and (xi), except that, for the sake of clarity, the word "confidence" in (ix) should be replaced by "overconfidence"; the second thread also starts in (i) and then takes its turn when Protagoras introduces the problem of war in (ii), and next Socrates develops it in (iii)–(viii).

Let us start with the first thread. In such a restricted form, the argument distinguishes three groups of people—the courageous ones who have the knowledge of what counts among *ta deina,* and their confidence in action is justified; the cowards, who are ignorant about *ta deina,* have little confidence and because of fear often refrain from acting; the daring and reckless ones who also have little knowledge about *ta deina* but because of this ignorance feel overconfident and do things that are not wise.

The argument bears a certain resemblance to the *Laches* 193c passage about the diver, the difference being that in the latter passage, we have the concept of *technē,* which in the *Protagoras* argument, Socrates does not use. The passage suggests, though does not state explicitly, that the divers with a *technē* are more courageous than those without a *technē,* the latter doing reckless and foolish things that many mistake for courage. The *Protagoras* passage does not mention *technē* but stays within the limits of the hedonistic argument and ultimately relates knowledge of *ta deina* to pleasure or avoiding distress.

There is one more thing that distinguishes the *Laches* passage—namely, the use of the concept of *deinos* in a different sense. The competent divers, those who have mastered the diving *technē,* Socrates calls *deinoi* (193c3–4). The word then has a positive meaning in this passage and describes adeptness. Let us refer to *deinos* from the *Protagoras* as *deinos*[P] and that from the *Laches* as *deinos.*[L]

If we combine the two passages, we have the following argument. The courageous man who is *deinos*[L] in this or that *technē* will only go for those

13 A similar formula appears at 345d6–e4. Cf. *Meno* 77b6–78b2.

things that the *technē* allows him to do, and by so doing will ultimately avoid *ta deina*[P]. The coward and the reckless man, on the other hand, who are not *deinoi*[L] in any *technē* dare to do—out of fear or out of overconfidence—much less or much more than the relevant *technai* allow.

Let us now compare this argument with what Sophocles says about *ta deina* in *Antigone* (334–75). For Socrates, *deinos*[L] means being adept in a *technē*, and the adeptness entails a discipline of the type that his theory of knowledge stipulates—the proper object, theoretical justification, etc. It is, therefore, obvious that the man who is *deinos*[L] will not indulge in overconfidence, or *hubris,* or recklessness because these qualities contradict the essence of *technē*/knowledge.

The courage of the *deinos*[L] man is not a power to break the limits and to confront *ta deina*[P], the fearful aims which, when imprudently chosen or devised, may bring suffering, destruction, or injustice. It is, on the contrary, a virtue that stabilizes and strengthens the character within limits imposed by knowledge. If we take the diving *technē* as an example of what other *technai* practice by adept people could achieve, we could surmise that for Socrates, the condition for the good functioning of the world would be such a self-controlled use of the *technai*, with courage as a power to prevent transgression and not to induce it. Transgression generates disorder, while courage, like other virtues, must generate ordering.

Perhaps, the closest approximation of this would be the view that Socrates ascribes to "the wise men," according to which the world is held together by communion, friendship, orderliness, *sōphrosynē*, and justice (*Gorgias* 507e5–508a3). Since the virtue of courage is defined as "wisdom about what counts and what does not count among *ta deina,*" we can suppose that Socrates, if he agrees with the wise men, could also make it responsible for holding the world together. Courage, after all, has been placed between two extremes—cowardice and overconfidence—both deviating from what was right and both adverse to orderliness.

Sophocles, in contrast to Socrates, talks about the world in the process of constant improvement and praises the *technai* as a means to conquer nature—ploughing the soil, hunting the game and taming the beasts, and primarily making human life more secure against external conditions and illness. For Sophocles, nature is not orderliness that the human *technai* should preserve or had to accommodate, but something unfinished and imperfect and, therefore, requiring the human craft and the "windy thought" to enact improvements in her.

So, unlike Socrates, Sophocles believes that the *deinon* characteristic of the human person consists precisely in an ability to break limitations through intelligence and inventiveness: "Clever beyond expectations the inventive craft that he has may drive him one time or another to good or evil." The *deinon* part was, therefore, responsible for human greatness as well as for human fail. The expression "one time or another" (*tote ... allote*) indicates that both stemmed from the same source in human nature, although both were in dire opposition to each other.

Translating it into the Socratic metaphor, we would say that in this view, the same man could be both a competent diver and a recklessly daring diver, which gives human behavior a high degree of unpredictability. At the very end of the stasimon, Sophocles seems to moderate this view by distinguishing between "a citizen of a proud city" (*hypsipolis*) who respects the laws, justice, and the oaths sworn to the gods and, on the other hand, "a stateless outcast" (*apolis*) that boldly defied what was right. But this moderating tone, which—to use Socrates' metaphor again—might be the basis of separating a competent diver from a reckless diver, did not quite follow from the preceding text.

Sophocles did not use—as Socrates does—the word *andreia* for courage but *tolma*, which denotes a bold and daring act, and it was *tolma* that pushed the stateless outcast to bad things. But when in the earlier parts of the stasimon, we read that the man is "all-inventive," that he "lacks nothing to confront whatever must come," and that his "resourceful *technai*" are "beyond expectations," it seems that all these things also require *tolma*. The skills to subdue and improve nature undoubtedly derived from a conquering spirit, and *tolma* must have been an expression of it.

The difference between Socrates' *andreia* and Sophocles' *tolma* is not only a controversy about whether a competent diver is or is not a daring diver. At the bottom of this, there are divergent views about the interpretation of *technē*: for Socrates, it is a tool for self-control and moral self-improvement to preserve the unity and consistency of the moral agent; for Sophocles, it is a tool—magnificent, but morally ambivalent and, therefore, risky—to expand human inventiveness and conquer nature. Ultimately, the divergence is also about the view of the world—whether it is finished and harmonious and under no circumstances should human activity generate disorder, or whether it is unfinished and imperfect, and only intervening human ingenuity can make it better.

And although Socrates did not commit himself openly and explicitly to the former view, it is clear what his preferences are and where the logic of his arguments directs him. The two examples of all-encompassing conceptions—the grand theory from the *Meno* and the *Nous* theory from the *Phaedo*—illustrate what might be his wished-for image of the world, especially since the latter theory came into being through the extrapolation of his moral views. Nothing in Socrates' statements suggests that he envisages a world in a state of conflict or imperfection that requires constant human intervention. One can, of course, imagine the Socratic Man living in a Sophoclean world, but this would engender many basic problems that must be immediately addressed to make the entire theory viable. Nowhere in Plato's dialogues does Socrates voice any concern that would indicate his awareness of such problems or of the theory that might generate them.

3.3.2 Fear of injustice and fear of disgrace

The analyzed part of the hedonistic argument made some use of the concept of pleasure, mainly in (i), but the reasoning is more about how to recognize things that one should fear. More important than pleasure is the knowledge of what we as human beings need to live a better life and, depending on that, how daring we should become to achieve this end.

But there is another thread in Socrates' argument, and it starts with Protagoras challenging Socrates' proposition that cowards and courageous people go for the same thing: avoiding *ta deina*. The ground for this proposition is the hedonistic argument regarding people desiring pleasure and rejecting pain, distress, etc. To undermine this view, Protagoras points to a case that obviously and, one would think, conclusively falsifies this proposition: the courageous people go to war willingly, whereas cowards avoid it.

To this, Socrates replied with a simple implication: (a) going to war is noble (*kalon*); (b) if something is noble, it is good; (c) if something is noble and good, it is pleasant. The conclusion should be: going to war is pleasant. The cowards who eschew going to war do not know that it is noble, good, and pleasant. Yet the courageous know this and, therefore, go to war willingly. From this statement, one could infer—though Socrates does not, at least not explicitly—that had the cowards been aware of the pleasures of going to war, they would be behaving exactly like the courageous people. The difference between the two groups boils down to a difference between ignorance and knowledge.

The argument does not look compelling. Why should going to war be pleasant? To call war pleasant is to contradict an elementary human impulse.[14] But since Socrates infers "pleasant" from "good," and later from "noble," we have to modify the question and ask: Why should going to war be *kalon*? Certainly, the proposition does not derive from any of Socratic ethical *logoi*, whether iron and adamantine or otherwise. On the contrary, one may have doubts whether the praise of war is compatible with some of Socrates' propositions. Let us recall that he criticized Polemarchus for including the notion of harming the enemies in the concept of justice. Justice, as Socrates argued, implies friendship and harmony, not conflicts and divisions, and certainly not a deliberate intention to destroy the enemy.

In Socrates' statements there is nothing concrete about the pleasures or beauty of going to war and of war itself. The word *kalon* appears as an answer to the question of whether going to war is *kalon* or *aischron*, noble or disgraceful. Faced with this alternative, the answer must be *kalon*. The answer, obviously, begs the question: Why is going to war not disgraceful? We do not get the answer, but the text clearly suggests that both Protagoras and Socrates consider it self-evident that going to war cannot be disgraceful. And since this sense of self-evidence did not come from Socrates' *logoi*, it must be a generally accepted moral view rooted in the Greek tradition, in warrior culture, in Homer, Hesiod, and other great writers.

Socrates himself must have believed going to war to be honorable.

---

14 The Greeks cherished their heroism and patriotism in their war against Persia, of which the best-known example is the epigram celebrating the Spartans who died at the battle of Thermopylae: "Go tell the Spartans, stranger, that here obedient to their laws we lie." The Greeks undoubtedly believed that their death was *kalon*. But the Peloponnesian War that the Greek poleis were waging against each other did not produce similar sentiments. Aristophanes is a particularly conspicuous witness of the new attitude to war. His comedies did not hide its unpleasant and distressful side of war and recorded deep anti-war emotions.

Otherwise, it would be difficult to explain why he who did not mince words in condemning politics, politicians, the Athenian *demos*, and democratic as well as oligarchic institutions, who distanced himself from politics, was himself a disciplined soldier, went to war, was commended for his actions, and never undermined the moral aspect of his military involvement.

The exclusive distinction between noble and disgraceful is, of course, debatable. To be exact, Socrates' argument should read: (a) refusing to go to war is disgraceful; (b) if something is disgraceful, it is also bad; (c) if something is disgraceful and bad, it is also distressful, unpleasant, humiliating, etc. Thus, the conclusion should not be that going to war is pleasant but that not going to war is distressful. The cowards are not aware of the degree of disgrace that falls on them on account of their cowardice and hence refuse to fight. To put it differently, they do not see how *deinon*[P] this disgrace is and that it should be avoided at all cost.

This version of the argument seems more plausible than the one which emphasizes pleasure. To argue that by refusing to fight, a man meets with contempt, loses his honor, and becomes an object of widespread condemnation, which ultimately will make his life miserable, is more plausible than to argue that by refusing to fight, the man is unaware of the pleasure that goes with going to war and fighting. The first version—let us add—does not compel us to accept the conclusion that, ultimately, courageous people and cowards can be alike. To know the burden of disgrace and to resist every temptation to compromise in this respect is definitely more difficult and less obvious to achieve than to know the attraction of pleasure (however broadly understood).

It is especially difficult to compromise for the reason, something the hedonistic argument does not mention. Going to war may be honorable, and refusing to go to war disgraceful, but the urge to resist the former and to do the latter is equally strong. In war, one can lose one's life, and this is a fearful perspective. Fear of death has always been a part of the human condition, not only as a necessity of finite existence but as a sudden termination of one's life in an accident, war, illness, or extreme trial. Socrates' adversary could persuasively argue that dying in a battle is *deinon*[P] and that those who willingly and joyously go to war are indeed courageous, but more in the sense of overconfidence and recklessness. They are more similar to the recklessly daring diver than to the *deinos*[L] diver. The mastering of military *technai*, swordsmanship, etc., does not guarantee survival and need not dispel the fear of death.

Socrates does not raise this point in the hedonistic argument, but addresses it elsewhere. Obviously, courage and fearlessness toward death are realities Socrates could infer directly from SBT. In the *Apology*, we find a clue in a passage where Socrates explains why he does not care about death or condemnation by the *demos*:

> "You are wrong, sir, if you think that a man who is any good at all should take into account the risk of life or death; he should look to this only in his actions, whether what he does is just or unjust, whether he is acting like a good or a bad man" (28b5–9).

Death is not terrible, says Socrates, and the death penalty does not imply infamy since passing away should not be man's primary concern. Above all, he should care about two things: whether his deeds are right or wrong and whether his entire life stands up to scrutiny as a life of a good man. In short, we have the following argument:

(i)   there is only one valid criterion, which is the principle of justice (virtue, the best state of the soul, etc.);
(ii) every act should be judged on its conformity with the principle of justice;
(iii) everything a man does should constitute part of the entire life of a good (just) man.

All three points follow from SBT, particularly from the categorical and absolute priority of justice, and do not really go beyond it. The only slight modification we find is in (iii), which emphasizes not only the individual acts as in (ii) but the entire moral character. The expression "a good man" (*aner agathos*) does not sound as demanding and abstract as "the one" or "the expert" in matters of justice and injustice. The man to whom the quoted passage refers and who did not fear death need not be the *eidos* incarnate.

While Socrates would have never considered himself the master of justice, he probably could justifiably call himself *aner agathos*: after all, he never committed injustice. He told his jurors with confidence: "Throughout my life, in any public activity I may have engaged in, I am the same man as I am in private life. I have never come to an agreement with anyone to act unjustly..." (33a1–3). What this statement, as well as the previous one (28b5–9), implies is that death, whether in war or in other circumstances, was not Socrates' primary concern, and his fearlessness results from his one-ness ("the same man"), but also his consistency—always following the principle of justice in private and public life. In other words, courage in the face of death is a rational choice based on the knowledge of justice.

But there is another reason for Socrates' fearlessness, which has little to do with SBT, but much more with old Greek ethics, traces of which we find in the fourth part of the hedonistic argument. But this time, courage proves itself in being able to risk life and face death. What matters for the Greek heroes is not the abstract principle of justice and its knowledge or ignorance, but social sanction.

The crucial passage that reveals to us this traditionalist side of Socrates comes from the *Apology* (28b9–29a1). To the question of whether he is not "ashamed" to have lived such a life that now he can be put to death, Socrates answers by indicating a similarity between his situation and those of "all the heroes who died at Troy," and particularly of Achilles, the hero who "was so contemptuous of danger compared with disgrace (*to aischron*)," who "despised (*oligorese*) death and danger and was much more afraid to live a coward," who would rather die than, quoting Homer, be "a laughing stock" (*katagelastos*) and "a burden upon the earth." Socrates added that when "a man has taken a position that he believes to be best or has been placed by his commander, there he must ... remain and face danger, without a thought for death or anything else, rather than disgrace (*tou aischrou*)." He invokes his own military service at Potidaea, Amphipolis, and Delium where he remained in his post "without a thought of death." Similarly, in the current situation, when he was on his philosophical mission, he could not desert his post through fear of death.

The passage differs from countless other passages in which Socrates evaluated actions and propositions in the light of justice, virtue, truth, etc. The language he uses here—"disgrace," "despise," "contemptuous of death," being "a laughing-stock"—does not lead us to philosophy or the unity-of-virtue theory but to Greek heroic tradition. One would think that Achilles—

famous for his bravery yet also impulsive, cruel, and not possessed of a particularly sharp intellect—might not be a particularly appropriate ethical model for Socrates. The Greek hero was neither a philosopher, nor an expert in the matters of justice and *sōphrosynē*, nor even was he aware of such aspirations. But the fact that Socrates made the comparison proves that regardless of how intransigent and uncompromising he is in adhering to SBT with all its abstractness, he also shows some attachment to a living Greek tradition.[15]

On the basis of this small passage, we can glean some basic information about what he might have found attractive. Most importantly, the tradition endorses a military model based on a hierarchy and a discipline based on the warrior ethos; hence Socrates makes a reference to his conduct in the Athenian wars and suggests an analogy between the battles he participated in and his current conflict with the Athenian society, both requiring submission to a hierarchy and discipline. As we know, thinking in terms of hierarchy is not alien to Socrates' philosophy, but this time the hierarchy is of a different kind.

In the SBT hierarchy, both extremes—high and low—are well-defined: the Socratic Man who cares for his soul should strive for virtue, knowledge, justice, etc., and he must never *adikein*. What motivates the Achillean-Socratic Man from the *Apology* passage are primarily the things he should fear—disgrace, cowardice, and being an object of contempt and ridicule. The other extreme is not clear and hardly touched upon. Usually, the opposite of disgrace is rendered by the adjective *kalos*, or by the noun *timē* (honor) and its derivatives, or *doxa* (reputation). But the top of this hierarchy does not interest Socrates much, and he uses the Achilles example primarily to make the point that for him, as for Achilles and the heroes of Troy, the fear of death is nothing when compared to the fear of disgrace.

15 Commenting on Hector's death in the *Iliad*, Redfield wrote: "Hector's fear of death is overcome by his greater fear of disgrace. ... The Homeric culture ... is a shame culture. The heroes do not distinguish personal morality from conformity; in a world where 'what people will say' is the most reliable guide to right and wrong, the two are practically identical ... *Aidōs* is a vulnerability to the expressed ideal norm of the society." The expression "what people will say" should not be treated literally. It is not people in the sense of *hoi polloi* that determine what is disgraceful and what is not but the well-established mores created by the ruling groups and creators of ancient culture.

There are at least two more passages supporting the view that the imperative to avoid disgrace and to behave honorably is, for Socrates, of the utmost importance. Both passages indirectly relate to his courageous attitude toward death. The first is the scene from the *Apology*, in which Socrates explains to the Athenians why he refused to use tricks meant to appease the judges, soften their hearts, and win him a more lenient punishment (34b7–35b8). Such acts of self-humiliation might be effective, but Socrates did not think them appropriate (*kalon*): they were unworthy of the reputation (*doxa*) of the city of Athens and would also tarnish his own reputation (*doxa*) and his name (*onoma*) and did not become him in his old age. Those who enact these pitiable scenes (*ta eleina*) and desperately try to save their lives, even if they previously managed to gain some amount of reputation (*dokountas*) or high esteem (*timais*), now bring shame (*aischynēn*) upon the city and make it a laughing-stock (*katagelaston*).

The other passage comes from the *Crito* (53c8–e4). This time it is not Socrates himself, but the Laws that make this statement, although we may assume that the Laws appealed to what Socrates must have considered persuasive. They imagine what might have happened if Socrates had accepted the offer of help in escaping from prison to save his life, and ironically comment on the possible circumstances of the escape. Socrates, they say, would behave in a most absurd (*gelaiōs*) and unseemly (*aschēmon*) way by sneaking away in some disguise, shamelessly (*glischrōs*) and greedily clinging (*epithymein*) to life. His behavior would draw opinions that toward him would express disgrace (*anaxia*), and he will be forced to accommodate the multitude, becoming their toady (*hyperchomenos*) and slave (*douleuōn*).

There seems to be a tension between the argument that one should not fear death but injustice and the argument that one should not fear death because such fear is disgraceful. For some reason, however, Socrates does not separate those two arguments. The *Apology* passage in which he compares himself to Achilles follows—without any transition—the passage in which he says that the man should take into account only whether he acts justly and is a good man, which I interpret as a consequence of SBT. Apparently, those two arguments Socrates found to overlap.

Several instances confirm this where Socrates directly links the word *aischros* (disgraceful) with bad/evil, or treats it as the opposite of good. It therefore seems that he did not see his more traditionalist bent in certain matters as diverging from his essential moral principles (SBT). One can, of course, find justifiable reasons that the tension between these two attitudes is real and that such categories as shame, unseemliness, reputation, high esteem, good name, and appropriateness are not easily translatable into the rather austere system of the *logoi* surrounding justice, virtue, knowledge, and soul.

On the other hand, one can argue that a person like Socrates, with a moral character well-integrated and determined to be consistent, must have developed—as a by-product, so to speak—a strong sense of nobility and, therefore, of propriety that also motivated his conduct. Someone who recognizes the primacy of the rational soul and is determined to follow the best *logoi* must also disparage all human proclivities associated with common pleasures and passions, as well as everything common and disorderly in human nature.

Both attitudes have a clearly aristocratic slant. Both presuppose the existence of a hierarchy with a small élite at the top. Both conceive the human being as potentially facing great expectations—so great, in fact, that few people are capable of meeting them and only on rare occasions. It is, therefore, understandable that the distinction between good and evil might overlap with the distinctions of superior/inferior and noble/disgraceful.

Both SBT and traditional ethics recognize the principle of consistency, though each in a different way. But whatever the differences, in both a single instance of violation of the principles impinge on man's entire conduct. Whoever loses his dignity through an act of cowardice jeopardizes all his accomplishments because disgrace contaminates everything. If Socrates had begged for mercy before the jury or employed rhetorical tricks by pandering to the emotions of the jurors, he would have lost the dignity he had earned with his good life. Likewise, if he had committed an unjust act, for example by escaping from prison, he would have undermined his basic principle of persevering in justice.

4. The argument from human nature

The third problem—beside those of unity and consistency—that Socrates' anthropology entails is the problem of evil. Since SBT established a hierarchy and urges the Socratic Man to strive for the best, it would be natural to ask about the status of the worst. Socrates' message is puzzling. On the one hand, *adikein* is "the greatest evil," and because the meaning of *adikein* covers many things, probably too many, one could imagine that the world is full of evil and that it is evil that makes the world what it is. On the other hand, the description of human nature, which follows from SBT, points in the opposite direction. People are endowed with the moral-intellectual faculty that governs their nature and strives for the best. Human nature favors the good, not evil. Evil is mostly negative—it results from error, ignorance, misunderstanding, wrong reasoning, faulty calculation, etc.

Polus, another of Socrates' interlocutors, made an extremely strong and controversial claim challenging the latter's view of human nature and argued that human nature is governed by a desire for power over other people, a desire so commanding that it tends to violate social constraints (466c9–470c3).[16] The person that best incarnates this radical hedonism is the tyrant. All of us—according to the view—would be potentially tyrannical, or at least, all of us would dream about fulfilling the desires that only the tyrants could fulfil. This dream about the unbridled pursuits of desires includes even the most brutal acts, such as those perpetrated by Archelaus, who—as Polus' story tells—murdered the members of his family to gain power and wealth.[17] In short, human beings would be either tyrants or tyrannophiles. But since these desires are so deeply entrenched in human nature, they are not properly evil. Polus, a tyrannophile and Archelaus' admirer, did not call them evil but thought they are a key to a happy life.

16　Polus was a teacher of rhetoric. Socrates in the *Gorgias* mentions that he has recently read the sophist's rhetorical treatise (462b11). In the *Phaedrus* he is credited with the invention of various terms related to rhetorical techniques (267b–c). In the *Gorgias*, he is presented as a young man with certain noteworthy achievements in rhetoric; but a rather unpleasant character all things considered. See Dodds 1990:11–12; Nails 2002:252.

17　I am using the name of Archelaus to denote the prototype of the archvillain as Polus described him. Whether the real Archelaus deserved this disqualifying description is a debatable point. Thucydides praised his achievements: Archelaus "built the strongholds that are in the country now. He also cut straight roads and made other improvements. In addition, he strengthened the cavalry, the hoplite force, and other armaments more than all the other eight kings who had gone before him" (2.100).

Socrates refuted Polus' view in a complicated reasoning, which consisted of several parts interspersed with asides and digressions, and which can be summarized as follows:

(I)   Socrates' first thesis: tyrants are admired for their ability to rule, which purportedly consists in their doing what they wish; in fact, they do not do what they wish, but what they misguidedly consider to be the best.
(II) Polus' first response: tyranny is part of human nature because everyone envies tyrants.
(III) Polus' second response: undoubtedly, the greatest misfortune is to be the victim of brutal treatment and made to suffer anguish and torture.
(IV) Polus' third response: the tyrant, Archelaus, and by default any other evil tyrant, is not unhappy and has no sense of guilt.
(V)   Socrates' second thesis (reply to Polus' first response): one should never *adikein* (inflict injustice).
(VI) Socrates' third thesis (reply to Polus' second response): *adikein* is worse than *adikeisthai* (suffer injustice).
(VII) Socrates' fourth thesis (response to Polus' third comment): not only are tyrants unhappy people, but they are also villains because what they harm in turn harms their souls.

The problem that the argument poses is whether the Socratic Man can defend himself against Polus' claim or whether the power of evil in human nature is so great that it makes SBT and its anthropology untenable.

4.1 Socrates' first thesis: The tyrant does not do what he wishes

Each step in Socrates' reasoning calls for further comment. Let us start with Socrates' first thesis, which is a direct reply to the following claim by Polus: the tyrants have "the greatest power in the cities" because "they kill whoever they want to, and expropriate and expel from the cities whoever they think fit" (466b8–c2). Socrates replied that the tyrants "do what they think best" or "fit" but denied that "they do what they want to" (467b2–9).

Socrates' argument that followed is something like a theory of human action. It consists of the following propositions:

(i) one should distinguish between acting and the goal of this acting or, in other words, between means and ends;

(ii) eating, walking, killing, expropriating, etc., are means to some ends;

(iii) the ends might be wisdom, health, wealth, etc.;

(iv) if the tyrant, by killing, expropriating, and banishing, achieves the result that is better for himself, then he did what he wanted; if the result is worse for himself, he did not do what he wanted (468c);

(v) killing, expropriating, and banishing cannot be the ends because they are sometimes beneficial and sometimes not, and the qualification depends on the ends they serve;

(vi) those that use such means for evil ends and do not do what they want have little power.

The backbone of the argument is a distinction between doing something and achieving something. When Socrates mentions the ends—"wisdom is a good, and health, and wealth and other such things" (467e6–7)—it is not clear what these "other such things" might refer to. It seems, however, that the items on this list meet at least two criteria. First, they are objective, not subjective, which means they cannot be reduced to personal feelings, pleasures, or sense perceptions. Second, they are final: once reached, they do not go beyond themselves; otherwise, they would also be means to other ends, not the ends themselves. This last criterion is controversial, if not outright dubious.[18] After all, health and wealth are gen-

---

18 This passage and related ones have attracted numerous comments. Most interpretations turn on the distinction between subjective (inauthentic, apparent, *de dicto*) and objective (authentic, real, *de re*) notions of the good (right) that, according to Socrates, people desire. For Gould, what we really want should be decided by our true self, and bad moral conduct results not so much from ignorance but from "the absence of a sure and personal spiritual driving-force" (1955:47–55). Dodds agrees that this was Plato's intention but adds that the distinction between the real self and the pseudo-self "too easily becomes an excuse for dictation," as Erich Fromm and Isaiah Berlin warned (1990:235–36). According to O'Brien, Socrates had in mind the objective sense, and a "desire for the truly good is something all men have all the time" (1967:217). According to Gulley, "Socrates recognises the legitimacy of speaking of the aim which appears to the individual to right as the 'right' aim"

erally and rightly perceived as means to other ends—such as happiness, power, or long and comfortable life, etc.

We can, however, save Socrates' assumptions by reformulating them in the following way. People naturally prefer what is real and lasting to what is ephemeral. This tendency might be related to an inborn desire to anchor one's life in something sufficiently stable to provide a strong and reliable sense of orientation. Without it, human existence is confused and desultory, and this is what no balanced person really wants. Considering that one's life is finite and exposed to unpredictable hazards, this assumption seems rational.

As a corollary to this, Socrates also assumed that the search for stability could be successful. Those who desire wealth sincerely believe it will be the safe fulfilment of their existence. Their hope might be wrong, as it would certainly be wrong in the case of those who try to find such fulfilment in acquiring political power. But it has been generally believed—and Socrates appears to have agreed—that we desire such an end for our striving that would no longer see beyond itself. We may not achieve this end in its entirety, and wisdom is a good example of this incompleteness, but even if incomplete, it will not point to anything else. It does not mean that such a life will be unproblematic; it might even have a dramatic ending, as it did in the case of Socrates. But whatever the problems, those who chose this goal would not replace it with another.

With these assumptions, Socrates' first thesis is far more plausible. Whoever wants to be a tyrant so as to be able to kill, banish, and expropriate

---

(1968:93). McTighe argued that Socrates committed a fallacy by equating the *de dicto* and *de re* notions of the desired good: "Socrates tacitly shifts to the *de re* reading and pretends that the *de dicto* is no longer valid—even though it was the very reading presupposed at the beginning of the argument. On the *de re* reading the apparent good is not necessarily desired—true—but only on that reading" (1992:207). Segvic maintains that when Socrates speaks of wanting or desiring, he "announces a certain ideal" of the cognitive-volitional unity of the soul striving for "the good proper to a human being" (2006:180). My interpretation goes in Sigvic's direction: I agree that knowledge, for Socrates, is not a passive intellectual act of assenting to the *logoi* but has a great power on entire human nature, but such words as "volitional" and "emotional" are misleading; they do not correspond to anything Socrates ever identified.

other people at will deludes himself by claiming that he really wants it. In fact, in the light of what has been said, the statement is absurd. Killing, banishing, and expropriating are means to something else, not ends in themselves. Those ends may be justified if the final result meets the two criteria, that is, if it produces some real good and if this good has a quasi-ultimate character. From this perspective, the tyrants' power looks illusory. Having so much at their disposal, they concentrate on the means that probably bring no satisfactory end. Their crimes reveal their inability and impotence rather than their power.

4.2 Polus' responses

Polus responded by adumbrating his own view of human nature, rather simple and, for him, of irresistible obviousness. Polus' first response was that what the tyrants do is a natural reaction and that all people in their heart of hearts wish to emulate the tyrants. Instead of perceiving man as a purpose-oriented being, Polus described him in terms of causes and motivations. From his perspective, the distinction between means and ends becomes secondary because what matters is the pervasive presence of hard-to-resist drives and desires. If a tyrant takes somebody else's wife, the reason for this action is not a plan for life, or happiness, or an intention to have offspring but an instantaneous and unstoppable yielding to desire. This yielding is both a means and an end: doing is achieving. On this view, Socrates' public protestations against Archelaus' crimes could not but be a hoax:

> "As if you wouldn't welcome being in a position to do what you see fit in the city, rather than not! As if you wouldn't be envious whenever you'd see anyone putting to death some person he saw fit, or confiscating his property or tying him up!" (468e6–9)

To that he added:

> "You're just unwilling to admit it. You really do think it's the way I say it is." (471e1)

Whence Polus took this view is not clear. Probably he repeated an opinion that was popular among those who envied the tyrants their power and had rather a simplistic image of what the tyrant's life was like. One may find a certain clue in the second response: the most unbearable state for every human being is to be subjected to pain, suffering, persecution, torture (472d9). Polus attempted to shock Socrates with a description of a man who wished to become a tyrant but who got caught and punished by suffering elaborate torture, after which his closest family members were punished in an equally cruel way (473b12–d2). He then asked Socrates whether he himself would rather prefer to be in the position of the victim or that of the tyrant who could do anything with impunity.

One can, of course, argue that even if being subjected to most cruel injustice is the worst that can happen to a human person, it does not follow that the best of what can happen is to inflict injustice on others. Apparently, Polus was of the opinion that those instincts and desires that are the principal causes of human behavior are so strong that the alternative—to inflict injustice (*adikein*) and to suffer injustice (*adikeisthai*)—must be a constant pattern through which one should perceive human existence. For a tyrannophile like Polus, such a view was somehow to be expected.

Equally expected was Polus' third response—namely, that the tyrant's behavior is beneficial to him and he does not regret putting people to death or exiling them. "Even a child" (470c4–5)—said Polus—would refute Socrates' claim that the tyrants were miserable people. Polus cited the example of Archelaus who in order to seize and maintain power, killed many of his relatives, and having committed those crimes—Polus added ironically—he apparently "remains unaware of how miserable he's become, and feels no remorse either" (471b6–7). For the truth is that "many people who behave unjustly are happy" (470d1–3). They are happy because they realize man's greatest dream, which is for them to do what they want with impunity and without any restriction.

Polus' responses might seem extreme, but they convey something that Socrates could not ignore. His own view of human action might be superior to that of Polus, but the latter touched upon a weak point in Socrates' philosophy: what to do with man's propensity for evil. Of course, Polus refrained from calling it evil, and there is a strong indication that he refused to accept the distinction between good and evil (468e–469a1). But for those who do not share his tyrannophilia, Archelaus is not *deinos* in the Sophoclean sense but an evil man.

The question, then, is about the origin of evil. Could it be that the propensity for evil has its roots in human nature, perhaps not in the extreme form suggested by Polus, but there all the same? What if human nature engenders desires and motivations so strong that the means to satisfy them would be identical to the ends, and these have nothing in common with the ends defined by Socrates? Once the propensity to do evil things is sufficiently powerful and sufficiently destructive, the claim that evil acts result from ignorance loses plausibility. Polus might have erred in his thoughtless tyrannophilia, but Archelaus committed his crimes with full awareness and not because he persistently failed to make a serious distinction between the means and ends.

Socrates responded to the above with what I call his second, third, and fourth theses. All of them refer in parts to Polus' responses, although it is easy to see that each of them is more closely related to a single response: the second thesis is primarily a reply to Polus' first response, the third thesis to his second response, and the fourth thesis to his third response.

4.3 Socrates' second thesis: The greatest evil is adikein

According to the second thesis, "*adikein* is actually the worst thing there is" (469b8–9). This is not a new proposition. We already know it belongs to SBT.

In a way, this statement appears to be a strange reaction to Polus' views. Socrates' position on injustice as the greatest evil was originally an analytical proposition, true *ex definitione*. This seemed a rather weak reply to someone who, like Polus, claimed that every human being is naturally conditioned to murder other human beings and grab their property. If Polus was right, at least partly right, then the analytical statement "injustice is bad" would be—without losing its definitional validity—miserably impotent against the powerful motivations of real people in real life. Injustice might indeed be bad, but what if in human nature there is a deeply imbedded propensity for evil?

But Socrates believed in the power of *logoi*, also regarding those who claimed to despise them. It is true that some of his interlocutors—Polus, Callicles, and Thrasymachus—defended what he considered unjust acts, but for Socrates, the crucial question was whether they were indeed willing to call it justice. Can anyone make a self-contradictory statement that to commit injustice is just, i.e., that *adikein* is *dikaion*? This was indeed the thrust of his second thesis: whatever extravagant or shocking definitions his interlocutors propose, it will ultimately turn out that those definitions will lead them to the conclusion that *adikein* is *dikaion*, and this they cannot accept.

There are three possibilities: one could either give those two words—*adikein* and *dikaion*—the meanings within the same moral philosophy, or take them from two different moral philosophies, or reject any moral philosophy.

The first possibility should be excluded. Regardless of whether someone defines justice as a power to kill and expropriate other people or as giving to everyone according to his needs, one cannot say that injustice is just or that justice is unjust. Certainly, this was not Polus' view. His was rather the third option. His praise of Archelaus suggests that the distinction justice/injustice is irrelevant. No matter how forcefully one condemned allegedly immoral conduct, everyone—even Socrates—had a tyrannical inclination. The justice Socrates defended was, therefore—in Polus' eyes—not a real thing but a kind of self-mystification. Polus implicitly advocated dispensing with moral concepts and satisfying oneself with a behavioristic language that described human conduct in a purely matter-of-fact way. For him, there was neither "must not" nor "ought." Whether he managed to be consistent with sticking to this kind of language will be answered in due course.

According to the second possibility, one could certainly make the statement "injustice is just" on the condition that the first word has its meaning taken from Socrates and the other from his adversaries, for instance, Thrasymachus and Callicles, and that only one of the meanings is genuine. According to the adversaries, this sentence would read "what Socrates wrongly called injustice is just" or "justice is what Socrates erroneously qualifies as unjust."

Thrasymachus and Callicles used a moral vocabulary that allowed them to say both "must not" and "ought." Initially, however, their intention was to reduce justice to fact or "ought" to "is," which would make it hardly distinguishable from Polus' view. Trasymachus' first definition—justice is what benefits the strong—made "ought" redundant. In tyranny, the strong is the tyrant; in oligarchy, the few, in democracy, are the many. In each system, justice expresses itself in the rules established by the strong, but these rules are a political fact, not a norm one should personally aspire to.

A similar reduction of "ought" to "is" we find in Callicles' first remarks: justice is *pleonexia*, meaning "to have more." As he says, "nature itself reveals that it's a just thing for the better man and the more capable man to have a greater share than the worse man and the less capable man" (483c8–d2, Zeyl trans.). Again, the concept of justice in this statement is descriptive rather than normative. Whoever is strong enough to have more has more justly.

But this initial non-normative use of the concept of justice is self-defeating. The core of Socrates' counter-argument is that one could never consistently stick to the rule that whatever is, is just. Tyrants can err and will not act to their own benefit, as he was telling Thrasymachus. And the possibility of error opens the question of what they ought to do, and what they ought to do may be different from they are doing.

His reply to Callicles started in a similar way, that is, by pointing out that strong and good need not be identical. This made Callicles reformulate his views according to which not every physical triumph was just and attributed justice to a special sort of people whom he compared to lions. But this was enough to raise the problem of what one ought to do to become a just man.

In the course of the conversations, it turned out that neither Thrasymachus nor Callicles could consistently follow the logic of their initial moral positions. Neither of them could say that what Socrates and others called injustice is just. On the contrary, they conceded to the Socratic view, and although they did not do it openly and never abandoned their views, it was enough to prove the power of the *logoi*. It was not a slip of the tongue on their part: the human mind simply cannot give its unconditional and unwavering assent to injustice as something good. Thrasymachus—at the beginning—absolved tyranny as a just system where the tyrant acting in his own interest justly imposes his own rules on the polis, but later admitted that tyranny is "the injustice of the most complete sort" (344a4). And the latter opinion was stated as his own view, not that of Socrates. Even Callicles, who tried to be consistent, did not quite succeed. He also used the concept of injustice in a Socratic sense rather than his own. "No man would put up with suffering what's unjust; only a slave would do so, one who is better dead than alive, who when he's treated unjustly and abused can't protect himself or anyone else he cares about" (483a8–b4, Zeyl trans.).

Both Callicles and Thrasymachus thus had to admit at a certain point in the long argument that *adikein* is bad, i.e., that hurting people and bringing suffering upon them is wrong. This did not make them embrace a conclusion about the absolute prohibition of injustice, but the admission they made, however unwitting or reluctant it was, gave Socrates enough evidence to expose not only their inconsistency, but the shaky foundations of their own views. The power of the *logoi* is real. Sooner or later, whether with full awareness or in agitation, whether a person's soul is in a good or not-so-good state, everyone will admit that hurting other people and making them suffer is wrong.

4.4 Socrates' third thesis: adikein *is worse than* adikeisthai

Socrates' third thesis stipulates that *adikein* is worse than *adikeisthai*. As has been already said, this is another of Socrates' self-evident propositions. It is morally worse, say, to rob than to be robbed, or to kill than to be killed.

In some respects, the problem induced by Polus may seem bizarre: the situations in which one is forced to choose between torturing and being tortured are rare and do not reflect fundamental moral dilemmas. Socrates was right when he said: "For my part, I wouldn't want either, but if it had to be one or the other, I would choose suffering [*adikeisthai*] over doing what's unjust [*adikein*]" (469c1–2). Yet for Polus, two reasons rendered them not unusual. First, his admiration for tyranny made him think in terms of incessant struggles to seize and sustain power: great opportunities opened up for the victors, whereas the losers died in agony (473b12–c1). Second, Polus concentrated on the human urge to satisfy one's desires. Hence, he imagined being a tyrant as the state of utmost pleasure, whereas being the tyrant's victim is a state of the greatest suffering, including exposure to torture and revenge on one's family.

Socrates made an attempt to convince Polus by proving that the statement "*adikein* is worse than *adikeisthai*" is true (474c4–475e6), and to do this, he had to lead him to accept the moral sense of "worse." At the beginning, Polus categorically denied that inflicting injustice is worse than suffering injustice. Here is a reconstruction of the argument:

(i)   according to Polus, *adikeisthai* is worse *adikein,* but *adikein* is *aischion* (more disgraceful, that is, more *aischron*);

128

(ii) according to Socrates, we call a thing *kalon* (as opposed to *aischron*) on account of its being beneficial, or pleasurable, or both, which means that things that are *kala* are beneficial, pleasurable, or both;

(iii) in relation to Socrates' statement, Polus associated *kalon* with pleasure and goodness, but *aischron* with pain and evil;

(iv) if—following (ii)—A is more *kalon* than B, then it is so in terms of being more beneficial, or pleasurable, or both;

(v) if—following (iii)—A is more *aischron* than B, then it is so in terms of pain, or evil, or both;

(vi) since, as Polus asserts, *adikein* is more *aischron* than *adikeisthai*, it may be so in terms of pain or evil, or both;

(vii) *adikein* is not more *aischron* in terms of pain;

(viii) in that case it must be more *aischron* in terms of evil;

(ix) *adikein* is thus worse than *adikeisthai*;

(x) no one will prefer *adikein* to *adikeisthai*.

The argument outlined above is considered controversial; however, its most important points can be defended successfully.

The crucial step that decided Polus' defeat is his decision in (iii) to include evil in the concept of *aischron*, which undermined the separation between *aischron* and evil stated in (i). Once he agreed that *aischron* may mean "bad," his admission that *adikein* is more *aischron* than *adikeisthai* was bound to lead, sooner or later, to the statement that inflicting injustice is also worse than suffering injustice.[19]

19 This is a standard assessment of the weakness of Polus' position. The first to have a different view on the weakness of the argument was Grote (1865 II:108–10). Vlastos offered a dissenting interpretation—starting with a similar observation—in his 1967 article "Was Polus Refuted?" (1996c). He pointed out that Socrates built the argument on the analogy that ultimately failed him. He defined *kalon* in beautiful objects as bringing pleasure and benefit to those who see them, and, by analogy, he should have—discussing the problem of *adikein* and *adikeisthai*—defined *kalon* as bringing pleasure and benefit to those who see such acts, and not—as he did—to those who experience those acts as perpetrators or as sufferers. Santas endorsed and even strengthened Vlastos' argument (1979:233–40), and so did Irwin (1979:157–58). But the refutations are not compelling, and their logic, although subtle, misses the

Why Polus made this step is not clear, especially since it renders his position rather confusing. Point (i) indicates that he distinguished between "bad" and *aischros* and, by the same token, between "good" and *kalos*. Saying that suffering injustice is worse than inflicting it, he implies that the concepts of good and evil are defined by pleasure and pain, respectively. But then, when in (iii) he unexpectedly introduces the concept of good and indirectly linked it with being beneficial, it appears that the distinction between *aischros* and evil, and consequently between *kalos* and good, no longer existed because both criteria that defined *kalos* and *aischros* contained, respectively, good and evil. To put it more generally, Polus—despite his tyrannophilia and occasional harsh rhetoric—hesitated to call *adikein* good and did not put up a fight to call it bad.

Socrates denied Polus an opportunity to explain what he meant by the adjective *aischros* when he said in (i) that inflicting injustice is *aischion* (more disgraceful) than suffering injustice. Socrates immediately took over and steered the course of the conversation. The most likely explanation is that for Polus, *aischros* meant "disgraceful." His argument might have been as follows: people do indeed—individually—have dreams of becoming tyrants and acquiring the power to fulfil the wildest desires, but the democratic society, such as Athens, strongly disapproved of brutal tyranny and considered it disgraceful.[20] Polus might have thought the social condemnation of tyranny was a sham or a conventional morality of the type Callicles criticized, but the indubitable fact was that in the light of the public opinion, *adikein* is disgraceful whereas *adikeisthai* is not. But even if this were his intention, he did not have an occasion to explain it.

Let us look more closely at the crucial parts of Socrates' argument. His first step was to refer to the word *kalon*—the opposite of *aischron*—first to bodies, colors and figures; then to music and sound; next to laws and practices; and finally to branches of learning (474d4–475a2). The word *kalon*

core of Socrates' position. Berman made a valid point: "Nowhere in the *Gorgias* does the pleasure or pain of contemplating something ever come up for discussion. Rather it is the *experience* of something—with respect to how it will affect one's life—that is under consideration throughout" (1991:276).

20 Tyranny was called "a thing more unrighteous and bloodthirsty than anything else on this earth" (Herodotus 5.92, transl. A. D. Godley); see also Thucydides 6.53.

he explained either as something that serves a purpose, satisfies a need, and bears a benefit (*kata tēn chreian*), or something that generates pleasure (*kata hēdonēn*). In short, *kalon* would mean "useful" (beneficial), or "pleasurable," or both. Consequently, one should define *aischron* as "painful" (distressful, hurtful, etc.) and "disadvantageous" (disparaging, useless, etc.).

This was not a controversial definition. The adjective *kalos* in the sense of serving a good purpose we encounter elsewhere, for instance in Xenophon's *Symposium* during Socrates' conversation with Critoboulos (5.4).[21] The adjective was also commonly used with respect to beautiful bodies or artifacts, but usually in connection with its pleasurable effect on those who perceived those bodies or artifacts. As Xenophon's Socrates says in the *Symposium*, a romantic dance between a beautiful girl and boy "offered [the spectators] most delightful sights and sounds" (2.2).

But the Greeks, and among them Socrates, broadened the meaning of *kalos* extending it to non-material categories—deeds, characters, moral qualities, but also laws and knowledge. It was this meaning that Socrates particularly stressed, both in Plato and in Xenophon. So, when in his conversations with Polus he referred *kaloi* to "laws and social practices," and then to "the branches of knowledge," alongside bodies, figures, sounds, and colors, there was nothing unusual about it.

Socrates' strategy was simple: he wanted to compare *adikein* and *adikeisthai* with respect to the two criteria of *kalos/aischros*—pleasure and usefulness and their opposites. It is obvious that whoever suffers injustice experiences pain and all kinds of agony. Whoever orders such injustice does not go through these experiences. In that sense, one is bound to say without the slightest doubt that *adikein* is not *aischion* (more *aischron*) than *adikeisthai* if the adjective is measured by the pain/pleasure criterion. But this statement is acceptable only from the tyrannophile perspective. It would be most awkward, to say the least, for Socrates to utter such a proposition as his own. His first thesis that the people like Archelaus do not really wish to do what they are doing does not allow one to interpret the absence of pain during committing injustice as a basis—even by association—for a positive moral judgment.

When in (iii) Polus changed Socrates' definition of *kalon* as pleasurable

---

21   It was Critoboulos who defined *kalos* in this way, but Socrates did not object.

and/or beneficial into *kalon* as pleasurable and/or good, one might wonder whether he replaced "beneficial" with "good" deliberately. What prompted him to do this remains unsaid. It seems that from the examples of things that are *kala*, the only ones that could be relevant in this case and that might have something to do with this move were the "laws and practices" and the "branches of learning." Colors, figures, sounds, and bodies are rather unlikely candidates.

If Polus had been consistent, he would not have so easily made the concession that secured Socrates' victory in the argument. His defense of tyranny—let us recall—derived from non-normative language that eliminates the distinction between "is" and "ought": people are what they are, and everybody wishes to have the greatest power to satisfy all desires even at the cost of breaking the existing constraints. But we have seen that Socrates already managed to open a breach in his non-normative discourse when in arguing for his first thesis, he made Polus agree that there are certain ends in human action such as "wisdom ... and health and wealth and other such things" (467e6–7), and that these ends are good. Human action is, therefore, ends-oriented and not determined by irresistible natural urges to satisfy desires.

Whether "wisdom" (*sophia*) mentioned in the above statement also covers "the branches of learning" (*ta mathēmata*) from 475a2, we cannot know for sure, but it is quite likely. If before Polus conceded that wisdom is a good, there is no reason why he should not make the same concession as regards the branches of learning. He says: "Indeed, you're defining beautifully (*kalōs*) now, Socrates, when you define *to kalon* by pleasure and good." The word "now" might suggest an indirect reference to the branches of learning from the preceding sentence, and the adverb *beautifully* may indicate a signal that Polus recognized something he already knew.

One may wonder whether among "other such things" from 467e6–7, beside wealth, health and knowledge, Polus could include "laws and practices," in which case the replacing of "beneficial" by "good" would also make some sense. This might clash with his praise of tyranny, but the tension is not as great as it might appear at first glance. Polus was, indeed, a tyrannophile, but he was not a tyrant and did not behave like one. One may wonder if he really dreamt about living the life of Archelaus. It is possible that his tyrannophilia was more a fad *pour épater* some of the Athenians than a manifestation of his natural impulses that he decided to let loose after rejecting the social norms. If this were the case, then calling "laws and practices" *kaloi* would have been quite proper and, in the case of Polus, might even have been sincere. Living under a tyrant but not being a tyrant is not a comfortable situation, and whoever thinks sufficiently clearly must appreciate the good sides of the existing laws.

This interpretation perhaps runs outside the text too far, but it is compatible with the general thrust of Socrates' argumentation. His third thesis, as the previous ones, relies on the power of the *logoi*, which must reveal itself sooner or later. The statements "knowledge is not beneficial and, therefore, knowledge is bad," or "to be ruled by laws is not beneficial and, therefore, it is bad" ultimately turned out to be unacceptable for Polus. And this impossibility accounted for his failure to defend the thesis, which seemed impossible to refute, considering his initial uncompromising position.

4.5 Socrates' fourth thesis: Injustice is a disease of the soul

The power of the *logoi* has its limits. This is at least what underlies Socrates' fourth thesis (475e–481a). The aim of the passage is to prove that injustice is the sickness of the soul in analogy to the sickness of the body. The analogy, as well as the image of the sick body and the sick soul, was not new to Socrates. We also find it in the *Crito* (47d–48a), where it serves a similar purpose, that is, to prove that as injustice makes the soul sick, justice makes it healthy, and as an expert in medicine can cure our body, an expert in justice can cure our soul.

The analogy has a rational justification. We might imagine a man who abandons himself to a life of pleasure and who believes that his cravings are really his own and that satisfying them is tantamount to acting in accordance with his bodily needs. The man binges on food and drink and pursues other pleasures with gusto. Such a way of life, pleasant as it may be, quickly damages his body and ruins his health. Similar reasoning can be applied to the human soul. Take a tyrant who satisfies all of his whims and commits terrible crimes in order to gain power, wealth, and women. He believes that what he obtains enables him to live his life to the fullest. His deeds destroy the moral order of his soul and infect it with an incurable disease, and to desire such a disease is not in keeping with human nature.

It seems that Socrates came up with the concept of the sick soul when he realized that his ethical intellectualism might be inadequate to interpret a certain type of behavior. The power of the *logoi* could be effective, if only partly, in the case of Polus, Thrasymachus and Callicles, but fail in the case of real tyrants. Ethical intellectualism that reduces wrongdoing to ignorance does not allow for the concept of evil. If what we do wrong results from ignorance, evil becomes a redundant category. The example of Archelaus is, therefore, too difficult to explain in terms of knowledge and ignorance, even if Socrates tries to prove that the tyrant did not in fact do what he wants.

By introducing the concept of the disease of the soul, Socrates not only made it possible to talk about evil that could be understood as a particularly sinister form of the disease of the soul, but gave it a more substantive status: evil exists and is real and should not be perceived as an absence of something, for instance as an absence of knowledge. But the concept complicates a relation between intellectual and non-intellectual parts of human nature. An argument, elenctic pursuits, self-reflection, and a search for knowledge are no longer the obvious answers to moral shortcomings. It will turn out that equally or even more important for moral improvement were flogging and other forms of corporal punishment. This, one should think, would be a rather unexpected turn of thought for someone who tirelessly advocated the paramount role of rational reflection.

Some passages in the *Gorgias* present a somewhat mechanistic picture of injustice and its consequences. When talking about curing oneself from injustice and from its analogies such as sickness or poverty, he used the verb "set free" or "rid" (*apallassō*): money-making ridding us of poverty, medicine ridding the sick body of sickness, justice ridding the unjust man of injustice, etc. This image associates the sickness with an alien element in a body or in a soul that has to be removed, and after the operation, the body and the soul regain their health.

This mechanistic image acquired additional force when Socrates stated that a way to rid the soul of injustice was punishment. Again, we have an analogy to the body. Just as a doctor cures the body by cutting out or burning the sick part, the soul is cured if it subjects itself to punishment: flogging, imprisonment, fine, or even death, depending on the gravity of the injustice committed. In both cases—the body and the soul— the operation is painful, but in both the effect of this painful operation is health.

This presents a rather simplistic picture: it is enough to subject oneself to punishment to free the sick soul from the disease of injustice. Getting rid of injustice is like extracting a sick tooth or amputating an incurably infected limb. There is a lot of pain and suffering that the unjust person must endure, and it is the judges who decide whether he should be sent to prison, or flogged, or executed (478a6). Do knowledge and intellectual reflection have a role to play in this process? Flogging and *elenchus* do not seem a suitable combination.

Socrates' answer is that the man with the sick soul should understand the nature of his moral error, and then he should agree or even desire to be punished (480d3) in order to cleanse his soul of the disease. But this, naturally, refers to cases where the disease is not serious. One may wonder what to do with the soul that is "rotten, unjust, and impious" (479b8c1). It is possible that such a disease is "chronic" and that it makes the soul "festering and incurable" (480b1–2). Although Socrates admitted a possibility of an incurable soul, the entire conversation is about the possibility of curing, not about those whose souls cannot be cured. When he mentioned those with the "rotten, unjust, and impious" souls, which suggested an irreparable moral infection, he still uses mechanistic language and talks of "getting rid of the greatest evil" (479c1–4), which certainly implies curability.

It is easy to see that to the incurably evil, the mechanistic notion of punishment becomes inadequate. Socrates said it explicitly in the final passages of the *Gorgias* when he described the greatest criminals who are punished not because the punishment would help them to get rid of the evil component of their nature, but as a warning and deterrent to other wrongdoers. "Those who commit the ultimate injustices and because of such injustices become incurable, the examples are made from them. And they no longer benefit themselves, since they are incurable, but others are benefited who see that for their faults they are undergoing the greatest, most painful and most frightening suffering for all time" (525c1–8, Irwin trans.).[22]

22 In the *Phaedo*, Plato radicalized Socrates' position. He said that after death the greatest wrongdoers would be entirely eliminated by being thrown into Tartarus never to emerge from it (113e1–6).

Conceptually, this interpretation should considerably limit the power of the *logoi* since in the incurable cases, epistemological categories do not apply, as if in those criminals the rational soul in the Socratic sense did not exist or was forever turned off.[23] Obviously, this form of punishment would be meted out to a rather small group of people, in point of fact, to those individuals who were not quite human because they lived their lives outside the human *ergon*.[24] As for the rest—that is, the entire human race—the *logoi* could, hypothetically at least, exert their power.

But the picture of such a restricted presence of evil in the world is not convincing. Having limited the incurable souls to the few perpetrators of the "ultimate injustices"—that is, to "psychopaths" as we would call them today—Socrates had to consider all other injustices, even the serious ones, as curable. But did he? He seemed to be deliberately ambiguous on this point.

How should we qualify the people with "rotten, unjust, and impious" souls, whom Socrates characterized as follows: "They go to all lengths to avoid paying justice and getting rid of the greatest evil, but equip themselves with money and friends and the most persuasive speaking they can manage" (479c1–4, Irwin trans.)? Are the souls of these people curable or incurable? The cure, according to Socrates, has the following pattern: (a) a wrongdoer understands he committed injustices; (b) he consciously seeks punishment; (c) he undergoes punishment; (d) he is cured. In Socrates' words, he "should

23 Let us note that the disease of the soul could be described using epistemological language: Plato did so in the *Timaeus* (86b1–4), when he wrote that it resulted from the disease of the body, that the disease was folly (*anoia*), and that there were two kinds of it—ignorance (*amathia*) and madness (*mania*). But the epistemological description does not convey the horrors of evil, what happens to the sick soul during life and after death, and finally the painful effort inherent in moral renewal. The metaphor of disease expresses all this content better. Elsewhere, Plato pointed out that apart from a disease resulting from ignorance (*agnoia*) there was another called wickedness (*ponēria*), a kind of evil that could not be explained in terms of ignorance (*Sophist* 228d6–11).

24 This was certainly Plato's view, who described the tyrant figure in *Republic* VIII and IX as both mad and deranged (573a4-c9); a dehumanized being who rejects all the human qualities and is transformed into a wolf (565d9–566a4); whose conduct is controlled by the "beastly and savage part" of his soul (571c3–d4).

denounce most of all himself ... and should not conceal the unjust action, but bring it into the open, to pay justice and become healthy" (480c1–4). In the case of the incurable souls, (a) never happens, so (b), (c), and (d) are impossible. The reason why (a) never happens is that the soul is so corrupted that it cannot produce any critical assessment of its own moral conduct and, as a result of this releases an uncontrolled stream of injustices to gratify whims and desires. The disease reveals itself not only in doing evil things that even a moderately developed rational soul would never permit or seriously consider, but in a persistent refusal to qualify these things as evil.

Now when we look at the above quotation, we can see that the people with "rotten, unjust, and impious" souls could be curable or incurable depending on whether they would be able to be convinced of the true character of their conduct. Equipping oneself with money, friends, and self-deception so as to avoid facing one's immorality is not a rare practice, certainly not restricted to psychopaths and "ultimate injustices." In fact, it is quite common. Whose soul is and is not curable, we can see this answered through actual recovery, not *a priori*. Socrates never claimed to be able to recognize incurability in the way the doctor diagnoses a fatal disease in his patient. Among the people referred to in the quotation, there might be, therefore, both curable and incurable souls. Consequently, incurability can extend further than a small group of the perpetrators of the "ultimate injustices." At least nothing that Socrates says ever precludes such a conclusion. Paradoxically, the ambiguity surrounding the scope of incurability proves that he approaches the disease-of-the-soul concept seriously.

The ambiguity intensifies in the final part of the conversation with Polus when Socrates states explicitly—in relation to (a)—that one could use rhetoric to denounce one's own or other people's wrongdoings (480b6–d6). But because for Socrates rhetoric was an inferior art unconnected with the pursuit of truth (464b–465e), such an act of denouncing did not stem from knowledge. Apparently, the power of propositions founded on SBT, even if self-evident, is not sufficient to convince a man that his soul is sick and that he should voluntarily succumb to a punishment. He needed a more compelling, if intellectually inferior, tool to shake his conscience. The paradox is that the same tool, rhetoric, he could use and probably did use prior but for the opposite purpose—namely, to defend "his own injustice

… [and that of] his parents or his friends or his children or his native state" (480b6–7).

We should, then, modify the curing process as sketched above and describe it in the following stages: (a) a wrongdoer understands he committed injustices, but the understanding or perhaps realization comes following rhetorical persuasion rather than argument; (b) he seeks punishment, but it is likely that the decision is emotional and not consciously taken; (c) he undergoes punishment; (d) he is cured. The role of the non-rational aspects in the new version of the curing process seems—by Socratic standards—disconcertingly high.

The most puzzling is (d), especially in relation to (a). What does "cured" or "healthy" mean? Did Socrates have in mind the Socratic Man with the perfect blending of the virtues or did he mean ordinary people with whom he frequently spoke, such as Euthyphro or Meno, whose souls were far from perfect but certainly healthy in a general sense? He certainly could not have meant that a person with "a rotten, unjust, and impious soul" could—moved by rhetoric to understand the evil character of his life—become the Socratic Man. He must have had a different human type in mind.

To be sure, the wrongdoer in (a) is not a psychopath, unresponsive to any distinction between good and evil and unmoved by *elenchus* or rhetorical persuasion. He is a criminal who committed grave injustices but who is not incurably corrupt. Morally, one could place him somewhere between the psychopaths doomed to undergo "the greatest, most painful and most frightening suffering for all time" and ordinary people such as Socrates' interlocutors. Polus, Callicles, et al. did not deserve flogging or any corporal punishment to improve morally, as did the wrongdoer from (a). They felt the power of the *logoi* and, even if they tried, could not reject the distinction between good and evil.

It would be difficult to justify, in Socratic terms, the claim that the curable criminal—awakened by rhetoric and subjected to punishment—would miraculously become morally superior to Socrates' interlocutors without having gone through the laborious process of acquiring knowledge and unifying the virtues. It would be more rational to suppose that the rhetorical persuasion and flogging would restore him to the level of ordinary people who, despite confusion and chaos in their minds, believe in the difference between good and evil and can, when involved in the elenctic inquiries, experience the power of the *logoi*. To their advantage, one might say that their grasp of this difference might be sharper and more serious than that of Socrates' interlocutors because of the sense of guilt for past injustices.

Unfortunately, this interpretation of "healthy" and "cured" has little textual evidence and does not give full justice to a weightier albeit somewhat murky meaning Socrates attributes to these words. On the other hand, the interpretation seems more congruent with his philosophy and makes the concessions to non-intellectualist conceptions of human nature less drastic. Otherwise, one would have to accept a rather fantastic hypothesis that in his picture of the curable criminal, Socrates anticipates Dostoyevsky's fictional characters who arise from complete wretchedness to achieve sainthood through suffering and spiritual revolution.

Chapter III – Politics

1. Socrates, the craft of politics, and the democratic man

Socrates' attempt to construe the unity of the human person in analogy to the unity of knowledge was only partly accomplished, as not all pieces of the system fit together. There were serious obstacles in the way: the complete unity of virtues turned human nature into a lifeless perfection; the utilitarian argument, which could bring the virtuous man closer to life, ultimately failed because it could not overcome its own assumption about the fragmentariness of human nature; and, finally, Socrates had to admit that his ethical intellectualism proved powerless in the cases of evil, i.e., when confronted with the incurable souls or the souls that refused to admit their moral diseases. Some of these weaknesses Socrates tried to elaborate by coupling certain aspects of traditional Greek ethics with his ethical intellectualism. Despite the problems, probably insoluble, the Socratic Man with his knowledge-based unity of virtues remains unchallenged, and Socrates never questions his model position.

Following the logic of Socrates' view of knowledge, one should expect that its systemic structure would extend beyond the individual life of the Socratic Man to cover the entire community, and that it would be possible to conceive of unity not only in the human soul but also in the polis. This consequence is so obvious that it would have been strange if Socrates had failed to see it. And fail he did not. In the *Gorgias*, in the passage already mentioned above, he presents the classification of the *technai* that take care of the human soul and the human body. In the first category, the supreme *technē* is *politikē*, which consists of two sub-*technai*—namely, law-making and justice, the former corresponding to gymnastic, the latter to medicine, both gymnastic and medicine being responsible for taking care of the body.

The passage provides, with great precision, a theoretical framework that could elucidate several crucial riddles in Socrates' philosophy, and in particular, the relation between the individual soul and the political order, or in more general terms between politics and ethics. One would expect Socrates to fill this general framework with concrete content and address specific questions—for example, how law-making influences the quality of the human soul, what law-making would be congruent with justice as an attribute of the soul, and many others. The most important of these is the question of politics as the supreme *technē*. But surprisingly, Socrates chose not to continue the subject and never returns to it with the seriousness it deserves.

The general picture that emerges from this passage is the following. Justice is a *technē* that liberates the human soul from ignorance and disease (injustice) and improves its moral state. The craft of law-making (*nomo-thetikē*) creates a system of laws that stabilize high moral standards and help to inculcate the virtues in the citizens' souls in analogy to gymnastics, which through the institutions of *gymnasia* develop physical education among the Athenians. The craft that unites and coordinates those two *technai* responsible for the soul is politics, and the good politician, equipped with the knowledge of law-making for the entire polis and educating the individual souls, establishes appropriate rules, mores, and institutions.[1]

This passage is surprising because it does not mention any of the formidable problems that these *technai*—justice, law-making, and politics—face and that could make the entire classification utterly unrealistic. The major problems are democratic politics and its product—namely, the democratic man. The basic charges are the following. Democratic politics does not respect the eidetic definitions but, on the contrary, because of its incessant struggle for power, adapts the abstract concepts to the logic of power, distorts them, and uses them as convenient political tools. The democratic man does not strive for unity and consistency, but, on the contrary,

---

1 Socrates did not give us any concrete information about this craft of *politikē*, but I assume that it largely depended on the new institutions and laws; otherwise, there would have been no need for *nomothetikē*. Another option would be not the laws but the "kingly knowledge" Plato mentioned in the *Statesman*: the ruler having this kind of knowledge could sit "beside each individual perpetually throughout his life and accurately prescribing what is appropriate to him" (295b1–2, Rowe trans.). In the latter case, any legal or institutional structure would not be necessary.

accommodates himself to democratic politics, and thereby becomes inconsistent, thoughtless, impulsive, and chaotic.

Perhaps the most significant insight into the epistemological shortcomings of the democratic man are Socrates' remarks about true opinion in the *Meno*, which are discussed in the chapter on knowledge. Socrates says that true opinions are not stable and had little power over one's moral conduct because they would "run away out of the human soul" (98a2) like a slave who escapes from his various masters or they move around like the statues made by Daedalus. "They are not worth much"—Socrates continues—"until one ties them down by giving an account of the reason why" (98a3–4, Grube trans.). And this tying them down by an account of the reason why (*aitias logismos*) is something that the people around him were unable to do.

While this description may refer to human nature as such, the political context clearly indicates that Socrates meant primarily the democratic man. The context was a short exchange with Anytus, Socrates' would-be accuser, a defender of Athenian democracy, and a declared enemy of the sophists.[2] The examples to which the interlocutors referred are the leaders of Athenian democracy, Themistocles, and others. So even if the problem of the volatility of true opinions is universal, the empirical basis from which Socrates drew his conclusion is the democratic man.

This has far-reaching consequences. When one cannot organize one's thoughts into a stable structure of ideas and regularly subject them to a process of elenctic verification, then one's opinions lack serious justification and are likely to be inconsistent, rendering one's decisions haphazard. And because the *aitias logismos* is said by Socrates to be hard to find in individual

2   Anytus, son of Anthemion, was a successful and wealthy tanner (*Meno* 90a1–b2). He had a son about whom Xenophon wrote that he was extremely gifted, but because of bad education he turned out a failure (*Apology* 30). Anytus was partly involved in the reign of the oligarchic tyranny in Athens, but later, as a result of a conflict with the oligarchs, he was exiled and became a defender of democracy. Numerous accounts exist of his fate after the trial of Socrates. Some say he was sentenced to death or stoned to death; or exiled in Heraclea, where the inhabitants were outraged at his complicity in Socrates' punishment, and banished him or stoned him to death. Others say the trial of Socrates neither weakened Anytus' influence nor discredited him (Nails 2002:37–38).

people, it is also hard to find in a society consisting of such people. This is a deeper reason why Socrates believed that the democratic society is not able to accumulate its experience, to distill its good elements and to transmit them to subsequent generations. Whatever good that happens in such a society is also haphazard—"the things that turn out right by some chance" as Socrates put it. The achievements of the leaders—as we remember—Socrates attributed to divine intervention rather than to their knowledge and competence. But precisely because those achievements are divinely inspired and not based on knowledge, they could not expect continuation. With every leader, in fact, with every decision, the danger of haphazardness re-emerges.

But the decisions that are haphazard are also peremptory, and there is no paradox in this combination. No matter in what manner the opinions are inconsistent, arbitrary, chaotic, volatile, once they are supported by the majority of like-minded people, they are considered—at least in the moment of their articulation—as ultimate and irrevocably true. Socrates, therefore, always sought to distance himself from "the masses" and from everything that bore the hallmark of general approval or alleged self-evidence. The views of the majority are not plain falsehoods but rather a collection of random and chaotic opinions. To his friend, who argued the opposite, Socrates replied:

> "Would that the majority could inflict the greatest evils, for they would then be capable of the greatest good, and that would be fine, but now they cannot do either. They cannot make a man either wise or foolish, but they inflict things haphazardly." (*Crito* 44d6–10, Grube trans.)

In the same dialogue, he made another comment on the masses' volatility: "those people who easily put men to death and would bring them to life again if they could, without thinking; I mean the majority of men" (*Crito* 48c4–6, Grube trans.).[3]

---

3   The last quotation is an allusion to the event that took place after Athens won the naval battle of the Arginusae Islands off the coast of Asia Minor in 406 BC.

Despite—or, perhaps, because of—this amorphousness of the demo-cratic men and their society, *hoi polloi*'s behavior does not allow for much dissent from the currently prevailing opinion. In the *Gorgias*, Socrates said that the majority expected everyone to change their natures and become like they are (513b3–5). Further in the same dialogue, he added that *hoi polloi* acknowledge only what agreed with their character and rejected all that contradicted it (513c1–2). To dissent from what was largely accepted at a particular time and to oppose the majority is not safe. Had Socrates behaved differently during the trial, he might have spared his life and even been acquitted (*Apology* 37a6–b2). Had the trial lasted not one day but two, the angry emotions of the jurors would have probably subsided, and the verdict may have been less severe. One of his closest friends, Crito, was certainly right when he advised him: "one must also pay attention to the opinion of the majority" (*Crito* 44d1–2).

When we look at the Athenian polis from this perspective, we discover that Socrates interpreted it differently than those philosophers who later tried to depict this Greek political structure, particularly differently from Aristotle. According to the latter's view, as expounded in his *Politics*, the polis was a community of communities. The state is defined as a commu-nity of agricultural communities (*kōmē*), and each *kōmē* consists of house-holds (*oikia*). This communal aspect is entirely absent from Socrates' description. We have, instead, a society of individuals, more or less alike, self-interested but also carried by collective waves of political emotions.

Risking an anachronism, one can say that Socrates' democracy in Athens is more like a modern society in which traditional practices and mores have relatively little effect. And since it is an egalitarian society—equality being, of course, the privilege of the citizens only—there are, as always in such a society, two basic mechanisms of its regulation: law and politics. The two are intertwined, and both heavily depend on the waves of collective passions that swayed the Athenian *demos*, the major actor in the democratic society. The craft of *nomothetikē*, which in the *Gorgias* Socrates makes a constituent part of politics, has therefore little chance of developing itself.

Socrates's conversations with the sophists or with those whom the sophists influenced enable us to identify a passion that animates the activity of the demos and the democratic men. This passion is power. The concept should be understood largely, not narrowly, as Polus meant it when he was expressing his admiration of brutal tyranny. Power means having a position of influence among other democratic citizens. The desire for such influence is understandable considering that equality—naturally, as it were—generates conflicts of power: first, because in the egalitarian society, more people feel entitled to aspire to the positions of influence, and second, because the precarious equilibrium of equality makes people seek their own security in getting an advantage over other people.[4] The sophists accurately identified the needs of the democratic men and offered them special training to make them more skillful in public and private affairs and to compete successfully with others.

This new democratic man strives to master the virtues of: "ruling," "doing/acting," "managing," and "directing" (*prattō, dioikeō*). More particularly, he wishes to "conduct the city's affairs and, in so doing, to help his friends, hurt his foes, and take good care not to get hurt himself" (*Meno* 71e3–5). These sorts of men should attempt to "run homes and cities finely, look after their parents, and know how to receive and send off both fellow citizens and guest-friends from abroad in the manner worthy of a good man" (*Meno* 91a3–6, Day trans.); as well as "how to realize one's maximum potential for success in political debate and actions" (*Protagoras* 318e6–319a2, Lombardo, Bell trans.). It is the art of "how to be as good as possible and how best to govern one's own house or the city" (*Gorgias* 520e3–4).

Among those instruments that could help to achieve success is the art of speaking and persuading. As Gorgias, a famous teacher of rhetoric, explains, the individual who practices rhetoric is thus "the craftsman of persuasion which yields conviction" (454e9–455a1). This person could achieve the "greatest and best" things that, contrary to what Socrates is teaching, are not goodness, beauty, or justice, but

> "the power to persuade by speech jurymen in the jury court, council-men in the Council Chamber, assembly-men in the Assembly, and in every other gathering, whatever political gathering there may be. And I tell you, with this power you will hold

4   Such a description of egalitarian society, we find in Hobbes' *Leviathan* (Part I, chapter 13).

the doctor as your slave, the trainer as your slave—and this money maker here will turn out to make money for someone else—not for himself, but for you with the power to speak and persuade the masses." (452e1–8, Irwin trans.)

The language used by the Athenian citizens became entangled in the democratic practices, and this had important consequences, and for the subsequent history of philosophy as well. What is peculiar about democracy, as observed by Socrates, is that it is both a highly intellectualist and anti-intellectualist system. It was obviously more intellectualist than other systems because, with the weakening of the traditional modes of conduct, the citizens had to express their opinions and defend them by using arguments. The institutions such as the assembly and the courts are the institutions where speech is paramount. The citizens, jurors, and leaders justify their claims more and more by appealing to general concepts so that they could convey their meaning to others and seek their understanding and support. Justice, freedom, piety, corruption, and law are the concepts through which the individuals rationalize their decisions and points of view. In an individualized egalitarian society, where the hierarchies grounded in social custom disappear, abstract concepts tend to play a far more significant role than in traditional societies.

Aristophanes, who satirized such a society as well as Socrates' role in it, noted the growing disdain for the traditional ways. As one of his characters, a young man, said to his father, "How agreeable is intimacy with novel and clever activities, and the power to scorn established customs!" (*The Clouds* 1399–1400). Aristophanes also noted that the main exponent of the new times was garrulousness (*lalia*) understood as incessant arguments, which, regardless of their purpose, undermined the traditional views and justified the modern ones (931). Whereas previously the main formative tool was the observance of custom, the new fashion of garrulousness offered young people an opportunity that was difficult to resist—they might ostentatiously disavow it. It also gave them an opportunity to do incredible and shocking things in the absolute belief that they were in the right. This is illustrated by the scene in which the aforementioned young man, resorting to quite bizarre argumentation, justified beating his father and threatened to beat his mother.

What Aristophanes wrote was, of course, a wild exaggeration, but he adequately captured the wave of intellectualism in a democratic society. But at the same time—and it was also Socrates' view—this was a fake intellectualism. Although Socrates' interlocutors used abstract concepts, they never inquired deeply into their meaning and usually related this meaning to their own subjective perspective and to the practical goal they aimed to achieve. A sample of this is to be found in what I call the popular definitions of virtues, discussed in the previous chapter. This is the reason why he says that the concepts, or rather their definitions, are moving like Daedalus' statues. And the more those concepts are used, the more their meanings become obscure, contextual, and inconsistent. They express the speakers' idiosyncrasies, not the well-argued conclusions. Their intention, as Socrates says in the *Gorgias*, is to flatter those whom the speakers want to influence and lure into their own political plans.

From Socrates' perspective, the democratic society did not present itself favorably. What superficially looked like intellectualism, a society of general conversation with a widespread practice of using abstract arguments, was in fact permeated by profound anti-intellectualism and a strong reluctance to reflection and self-reflection. It seemed that rational communication among people was no longer possible or necessary. If the meaning of the concepts depended—as Thrasymachus maintained—on which group holds the political power and interprets those concepts to its own advantage; if, as some sophists were teaching, one could learn to turn a weak *logos* into a strong *logos* to persuade other people; if, according to the art of anti-logic, two contradictory statements could be made about everything; then arguments no longer mattered and the choice of *logos* was entirely arbitrary. Ultimately, it was power that decided which *logos* prevailed and was accepted.

Socrates' philosophical activity, as Plato presented it, was to oppose this: to stabilize the concepts, to formulate correct definitions, to prepare the conditions for a discussion by agreeing on those definitions, to find logical connections between them, and finally to arrange one's life accordingly, etc. Socrates' just man is to be the opposite of the democratic man. If, as it is sometimes claimed, Socrates started a new era of philosophy, it would be legitimate to add that this new era of philosophy begins as a critical reaction to democracy, to its fake intellectualism covering a profound disregard for the meanings of general concepts, and to its political hijacking of intellectual reflection. Indulging in an alternative history of philosophy, one can say that without such a critical diagnosis of democracy and the democratic mind, there would have been no Socratic philosophy, and as a consequence no Platonic philosophy.

2. Avoidance of politics

It was obvious that having such a view of democracy, Socrates could not adjust himself to it: the differences between him and the democratic man were irreconcilable. The question is: what was a person aspiring to justice, such as Socrates, to do in a democratic system? And he did not give a clear answer to it. There are several variants of positioning Socrates politically.

The first way the philosopher could take—and also the best-known—was the avoidance of politics, all politics, including democratic. This would, of course, mean abandoning *politikē* as the crowning *technē* from the *Gorgias'* classification and abandoning *nomothetikē*. To be precise, what Socrates had in mind was a refusal to act via the state institutions, which he explains as follows:

> "Be sure, men of Athens, that if I had long ago attempted to take part in politics, I should have died long ago, and benefited neither you nor myself. Do not be angry with me for speaking the truth; no man will survive who genuinely opposes you or any other crowd and prevents the occurrence of many unjust and illegal happenings in the city. A man who really fights for justice must lead a private, not a public life if he is to survive for even a short time." (*Apology* 31d7–32a3, Grube trans.)

Socrates told the jurors he decided to quit politics on the strength of his experience of two events. One occurred under democracy, the other one under oligarchy (which resembled more a tyranny), but both highlight negative features of these political systems.

First was the hasty decision to call to account the military commanders who had failed to rescue the survivors of the naval battle at Arginusae. Despite the victory, the Athenian commanders were denounced, accused of failing to rescue shipwrecked survivors from the damaged ships, and of failing to bury the dead. Eventually, the popular mood became so turbulent and hostile that people demanded that the fleet commanders be jointly punished by confiscation of property and death. Socrates was a member of the Council who opposed the decision, considering it unlawful, to the outrage of other politicians who threatened him with arrest, punishment, and even death (32a9–c3). The emotions of the people were swinging from one extreme to the other. Finally, the commanders were executed, but soon the Athenian citizens regretted the decision and their anger turned against those who instigated the execution.

Then, under the Thirty Tyrants, he and several others were ordered to bring Leon of Salamis to the city to be executed. The rulers intended this ruse to serve to spread the responsibility for this killing as widely as possible. Socrates might have lost his life for refusing to participate if the tyrannic oligarchy had not collapsed (32c4–e1).

On the basis of these events, one could identify the dangerous features of the two regimes. About democracy, Socrates reiterated his well-known criticism: the rule of the *demos* invited uncontrolled (perhaps uncontrollable) and often violent and volatile emotions that could lead to hasty and unjustified decisions. In times of feverish agitation, resisting the majority was both strenuous and dangerous, and innocent people could easily be accused of treason. The tyrannic oligarchy was a system characterized by a brutal elimination of all opposition and implication of others in such criminal practices.

These events permit us to reconstruct the following line of argumentation that underlie Socrates' account of the first way:

(a) the rulers act in an arbitrary manner, which often means doing unjust things;
(b) the rulers not only act unjustly but also force the citizens to accept injustice;
(c) the philosopher cannot act unjustly, and hence he refuses to accept the rulers' conduct;
(d) the philosopher is not afraid of death and, therefore, cannot be intimidated;
(e) the philosopher involved in politics constitutes a permanent threat that can only be removed by killing him.

The argument is clear and convincing as far as it goes, but it does not quite prove what it set out to prove. Let us remember that in his speech, Socrates tried to explain why he refused to hold political positions while continuing to pursue philosophy as he understood it. If the argument was to come down to the fact that a philosopher involved in politics risked being put to death, it would not be a good one. First of all, death was not and could not be the first factor to be considered. Socrates himself, citing Achilles, dismissed it as an argument that could make him alter a morally correct decision. As we remember, Socrates cherished some attachment to traditional Greek ethics, and courage in the face of death was one of its vital constituents. The man, he said, "must I think remain and face danger, without a thought for death or anything else, rather than disgrace" (28d8–10). The threat to his life could not, therefore, induce Socrates to choose one tactic over another.

Besides, his chosen strategy of private conversations did not produce the expected results. Socrates ultimately lost his life as a result of political decisions, unsurprising in light of the above-mentioned dangers posed by democracy, including the *demos'* changeable moods. Let us not forget that the difference between a private life and a public life in such a democracy was much less pronounced than in other political systems. Given that the power rested with the people, all conversations with the citizens and all contact with or between them necessarily influenced their conduct in political bodies.

Privacy in Athens was, thus, rather limited, something that Socrates admitted indirectly when he mentioned "his first accusers" or the public opinion that provoked hostility against him, with all its legal consequences. It shows that regardless of how much Socrates tried to keep his activity private, it was generally perceived as public and he himself a public figure. Aristophanes must have correctly captured the perception of Socrates in Athens when he depicted him as a dangerous troublemaker. Socrates complained of it in his own trial defense, but this perception of his activity prevailed. In a democracy, the choice to remain uninvolved in the operation of the state bodies does not offer any real political security.[5]

5   Commentators point out that the distinction between the private and the public had a simple legal sense used in those times with regard to crafts, for

What is then the value of the prohibition against acting via state institutions? Perhaps the opening sentence from the above-quoted excerpt provides a certain intimation: "Be sure, men of Athens, that if I had long ago attempted to take part in politics, I should have died long ago and benefited neither you nor myself" (31d7–e1). It might be interpreted as follows. A conflict between the philosopher and the state is inevitable and puts the former in mortal danger. Pursuing an activity as a private person rather than as a public official had the advantage that the tragic end to the conflict was postponed. The fact that the divine mission is not associated with the political institutions prolonged Socrates' life, meaning that he had more time to pursue his mission.

The conclusion is sound but somewhat disappointing. The decision to live a philosophical life as long and as much as possible outside the state institution, which Socrates initially defended as an important moral act of defiance, is ultimately of little practical value, considering that it only postponed the inevitable. Socrates' "benefitting" himself and the Athenians by living longer could have been a plausible justification provided there was a clear positive end to which the elenctic activity was directed and its longevity affected. With no such clear end, prolonging Socrates' life, no matter how important psychologically, did not matter much within the moral framework of his philosophy.

There is another factor that might account for Socrates' alleged avoidance of politics. In the *Apology*, Socrates told the jurors that the *daimonion*[6]

example with respect to physicians (*Gorgias* 455b2, 514d3–5). The passage from the *Gorgias* is important and will be commented upon in due course. In legal terms the distinction was fairly clear. As Kraut put it, a private man (*idiōtēs*) in contrast to a public man (*dēmosieuōn*) "lacks an official connection with his city" (1984:115). This does not alter the fact that, in Socrates' case, the adoption of the status of *idiotai* led to the same consequences as being *dēmosieuon*.

6   In Plato's dialogues *daimonion* gained a distinct meaning. "This began when I was a child," said Socrates. "It is a voice, and whenever it speaks it turns me away from something I am about to do, but it never encourages me to do anything" (31d2–4). The *daimonion*'s main function was to oppose or dissuade. It spoke about the future—not predicting it, but warning Socrates against harm. This part of Socrates' conception, although well known, still requires

forbade him engaging in politics: "I have a divine or spiritual sign [...] [that] turns me away from something I am about to do. [...] This is what has prevented me from taking part in public affairs. [...] [I]f I had long ago attempted to take part in politics, I should have died long ago, and benefited neither you nor myself" (31c4–32a3, Grube trans.). He then outlined his unsettling experiences both under an oligarchy and democracy.

That instance of the *daimonion*'s intervention is perhaps the strangest of all those provided by Plato. First, Socrates recounted his traumatic experiences in politics in the very same dialogue. Perhaps the *daimonion* forbade politics quite late in the philosopher's life, after the fall of the Thirty Tyrants. But considering that the *daimonion*—as he, himself, admitted in the *Apology*—first spoke to him "when he was a child" (31d2), "on many occasions" and "even in small matters" (40a4–6), one may wonder why it remained silent for so long on such an important problem, only to decide to speak up at the end of the philosopher's life. Second, if Socrates' political

refinement. Socrates' words left ambiguous the *genus proximum* of his *daimonion*: it was variously "a voice" (*Apology* 31d3, *Phaedrus* 242c1–2), "a divine and spiritual sign" (*Apology* 31c8–d1), a "prophetic power" or "spiritual manifestation" (*Apology* 40a4), and a "sign" (*Apology* 40b1, c3; *Phaedrus* 242b9; *Euthydemus* 272e3–4). Sometimes, the word *daimonion* functioned as a modifier, for example, in the expression "something divine and spiritual" (*theion ti kai daimonion*), where it likely meant the same as *theion*. In conjunction with the word "sign," it could function as an adjective, for example, in the *Phaedrus* or in the *Euthydemus*, where the same expression was used. Possible translations included an adjective ("ordinary divine sign") or noun ("ordinary sign or *daimonion*"). Explicitly nominal uses are found in the *Apology* (40a4), when Socrates discussed the "prophetic monitor" or in the *Theaetetus* (151a4), when Socrates speaks about "the divine sign that visits me." Without consistent usage, it is impossible to identify the *genus proximum*. The *daimonion* could be a voice, or even a specific (mysterious, unknown) deity, who approached Socrates in order to speak to him. Other passages suggest that it was a voice or a sign sent to the philosopher by the god, *tou theou sēmeion* (*Apology* 40b1), perhaps indicating a transgression against "the divine [*to theion*]" (*Phaedrus* 242c3). If a voice, did it leave a literal statement, or only a sign to be interpreted by Socrates? In all likelihood, the *daimonion* was both, depending on the circumstances. Socrates seemed untroubled by the problematics of his *daimonion*, and so he was not terribly concerned to understand, describe, or define it well experiences were so unpleasant, his decision not to hold state office was completely rational—no supernatural intervention was needed. Each of the two instances of political turmoil, one democratic and one oligarchic, involved killing persons who were impulsively accused of harming the state. In both cases, Socrates refused to obey the rulers. These examples and probably others as well in politically turbulent Athens could legitimately provoke Socrates' aversion not just to a particular regime but to politics in general.

What could the *daimonion* have contributed to a matter that had already been so thoroughly contemplated by Socrates? Again, we can only speculate. Perhaps a strong aversion is one thing, whereas an explicit statement is quite another. If the *daimonion's* intervention really resulted in a kind of disavowal of politics, it did not so much predate the conclusion derived from his experience as it accorded it a superior rationale. After all, the god's voice was the only authority that could legitimize the renunciation of what was widely considered to be the essence of Athenian citizenship. Still, the greatest doubt remains unresolved—namely, the *daimonion's* longstanding silence on politics.

To sum up, Socrates' avoidance of politics is neither complete, nor entirely persuasive, nor definite. It would be more accurate to say that what passes for such an avoidance is expressed in his refusal to go along with the political practices he saw in democratic as well as oligarchic Athens. This negative reaction is quite understandable considering Socrates' views on knowledge and virtue and his criticism of the democratic man. But the reaction does not exhaust his notion of politics and how he saw his role in it.

3. True politics

The (partial) avoidance was not the only way Socrates dealt with politics to be faithful to his philosophy. There was also the second way, far more positive, when Socrates talked about "true politics" and "a truly political craft," presumably fulfilling the standards of his philosophy and moving closer to the craft of *politikē* from the classification of the *technai*. "True politics" was, of course, contrasted with actual politics as it was conducted in Athens. The basic information about it we find in the *Gorgias*, mainly in his conversation with Callicles. Socrates put forward three theses that shed some light on how he interpreted true politics. In the text they overlap and are often intertwined, but it is not difficult to distill them and present each in the form of a clear proposition.

3.1 True politics and political order

The first proposition: since man should strive to live a good life, not just to stay alive, a good politician caring for the city should also make every effort to make "the citizens possibly the best" (513e6, 515c1). And Socrates numbered among the few who followed this principle. He said: "I don't aim at gratification with each of the speeches I make, but aim at the best, not the pleasantest" (*Gorgias* 521d8–e1). This led him to a somewhat puzzling statement. In the *Gorgias*, when criticizing the Athenian politicians, he said: "I think I am one of a few Athenians—not to say the only one—who undertake the truly political craft and engage in political matters (*prattein ta politika*)—the only one among people now" (521d6–8, Irwin trans., slightly modified).[7]

---

7   This statement is not easy to reconcile with other statements. For a philosopher who made coherence and consistency his priority it appears somewhat puzzling. Not only did he contradict his previous statements—chiefly in the *Apology*—but he also undermined one of his best-known principles, namely, keeping one's distance from politics. Part of the solution of this problem is what was already indicated, namely, a difficulty to identify with certainty what counted and what did not count as politics. Some scholars tend to mitigate this contradiction, but they do not always do so convincingly. Dodds writes that Socrates engaged in the art of politics as a private man (1990:369). Similarly, Brickhouse and Smith: "one can live as a 'private man,' and yet be a genuine political craftsman" (1994:139). However, the cited passage does not refer to private matters, and the comparison with Miltiades, Pericles, and other statesmen suggests something more than private activity. Irwin argues that in 521d6–8, Socrates does not say at all that he is a politician, but that he "engages in" political art or that he "tries" to pursue it (1979:240–41); but, at the same time, Socrates says that he "acts politically" (*prattein ta politika*); in any case, the context is quite unequivocal, and the emphasis on "engaging" or "trying" does not change much. On this stronger interpretation, I agree with Kraut (1984:236, n76) and Vlastos (1991:240, n21). Stauffer reduces Socrates' political activity to education or rather to "a kind of "deeducation" or in a stripping away of the convictions that the young have already received from their primary education at the hands of the city" (2009:165). J. Clark Shaw goes a step or two further: "Socrates can expose whether someone con-

The statement is all the more puzzling given that earlier on, during his conversation with Polus, Socrates said, "I am not one of the politicians," (473e6) and as if to prove it he mentioned an incident when he was selected by lot to preside over the meeting of the council. Asked to put a question to vote, he "caused laughter" when it became clear he did not know how to do it. The passage suggests that Socrates did not think much of political procedures, particularly of the democratic ones, and that for him, apparently, practicing "true political craft" did not depend on the competent use of such procedures.

It would be reasonable to identify the true political craft with the concept of *politikē* as the crowning *technē*, which consists of justice and law-making. Once we make this identification, Socrates' statement about being a true politician loses a lot of its puzzling character. Whoever works for justice, as Socrates did by engaging others in elenctic pursuits about virtue and related moral concepts, conducts political work since justice was a vital part of politics. Socrates could then argue that his ignorance of the democratic procedures did not really matter because those procedures—insufficiently grounded in justice—do not contribute to *politikē*. Hence, he could rightly claim his superiority over the Athenian officeholders because they, assuredly more competent in the procedures, were ignorant in the matters of justice and virtue and, therefore, not reliable in their law-making job.

Of the few pieces of information that Socrates gave us about the true craft of politics, one is found in the passage contrasting the true politician (compared to a physician) and the pastry cook, which brings us back to the earlier classification of the *technai* and the concept of flattery. The pastry cook flatters the children by giving them what they like and find pleasant, just like a democratic politician offers or promises to offer the *demos* everything they like and find pleasant. But flattery is neither a harmless consequence of the majority rule nor a clever craft used by skillful politicians. It should be rather called a savvy and of the kind that is detrimental to the

tradicts what the expert would say," and then "using his own well-organized psychological attitudes" he could help to organize this person's psyche (2011:206). My own interpretation is a strong one. The true craft of politics was not a private occupation, and a lot of what Socrates pointed to is what he thought this craft to be.

human mind: it is *alogon* and therefore makes the mind unable to grasp the nature and the cause of things (465a2–5).

Flattery is thus both a form of obsequiousness and an instrument to exercise power. Therefore, Socrates called it a practice that required "a sagacious, brave soul, naturally clever at approaching people" (463a5–7, Irwin trans. slightly modified). The political flatterer could use it to influence the *demos*, for instance, by instigating the multitude against the true politician, just like a pastry cook can mobilize the children's emotions against the physician who orders them an unpleasant therapy. Socrates' interlocutor, Callicles, was perhaps an example of this combination: he both coaxed people and despised them. He must have been known for cajoling *hoi polloi* as Socrates attributed to him the love of the Athenian demos (513b4–5, c6). On the other hand, Callicles expressed contempt for *hoi polloi* and claimed that the few who are clever and strong should dominate the multitude of inferior and baser people (490a6–8).

But Socrates' view was that this stratagem could not work. The political system had a logic and dynamic of its own that tended to impose itself on all those who followed its practices. The democratic politician had to adapt his soul to democracy, not as a clever political trick, but by thoroughly immersing himself in democratic life. Socrates clearly indicated that the political system had the capacity to change people according to its nature. He said to Callicles:

> "If you think that some person or other will hand you a craft of the sort that will give you great power in this city while you are unlike the regime, whether for better or for worse, then in my opinion, Callicles, you're not well advised. You mustn't be their imitator but be naturally like them in your own person if you expect to produce any genuine result toward winning the friendship of the Athenian people [*demos*]." (513a7–b5, Irwin trans.)[8]

8   In his commentary, Dodds states that the *demos* becomes a tyrant (1990:350). This claim is correct though not in the sense of the identification of the two systems. In my understanding, Socrates says that the *demos* in democracy and the tyrant in tyranny not only refuse to tolerate anything that might jeopardize their power but also impose on everyone who operates within the system their own model of behaviors, standards, beliefs, ideas and objectives—democratic ones in a democracy, and tyrannical ones in a tyranny.

If true craft is the opposite of flattery, then it becomes fairly easy to identify its main characteristics. It will turn out that most of what can be said about this craft is already known and comes directly from the main constituents of Socrates' philosophy—namely, EID, SCK and SBT. "The best," according to EID, must correspond to the *eidos* and therefore be independent of subjective whims and inclinations and, by implication, also resistant to political power. It is this *eidos* that the true politician should have in mind and follow in political activity, not the prevailing views or imposed preferences; otherwise, he will lose his independence and, as Socrates warned Callicles, will assimilate himself to the political system in play and conform to its practices.

The true politician is thus independent of pressure groups and—as the concept of *technē* implies—acts in the interest and for the good of those he is responsible for. As it was said before, *technē* is other-regarding, not self-regarding (*Republic I* 345d5–e2). This gives the true politician a position of disinterestedness: he neither acts for his benefit nor for the benefit of this or that group. He is responsible—as Socrates made it clear—for the citizens, not for his *deme*, or the wealthy elite, or *hoi polloi,* or any other group.[9]

All this suggests that the concept of true politics invalidates the popular classification of political systems according to the size of the ruling group. There were three possibilities: one-man rule (monarchy, tyranny), the rule of the few (oligarchy, aristocracy), the rule of the many (democracy). The classification is, of course, not only quantitative but also qualitative. The few could be wealthy, or virtuous, or powerful, etc. The many could be the whole body of citizens or poor and uneducated, etc.

What the three types had in common was that in each case, the ruling group is a part of the polis and intended to extend its partiality to the entire political community, sometimes with good and other times with bad consequences. The constitutional debate in Herodotus exemplified these controversies (3.80–83). In other words, each represented a sort of collective egoism that resulted from the privileged position of one group, but in each, the ruling group could claim the special competence that justified their

9   In this context one should read Socrates' critique of the institution of compensation for holding a public office (515e5–7).

privileged position, and from this competence the entire polis would benefit. It was obvious, however, that each political system has its drawbacks resulting from the one-sidedness of the ruling group and its particular interests. The awareness of this inherent one-sidedness gave rise to the idea of the mixed regime, which, to put it somewhat crudely, was to combine various aspects of each system and incorporate them into one complex political structure.

The true politician could not be qualified for any of the three types because he was not a part of the polis, nor did he represent his own partial point of view. "The best" he was trying to achieve had the ultimate justification in EID and SBT, not in the beliefs of the citizens; the political *technē* is independent of the particularities of any political arrangement but has its own logic and requirements. The true politician stood outside and aloof of the polis, just like the physician did with respect to patients and the shepherd with respect to the flock. His political activity was, therefore, neither democratic, nor tyrannical, nor monarchical.

And yet the latter statement should be modified. One of the SCK criteria states that knowledge/*technē* presupposes a hierarchy of experts (HEX), which necessarily implies that the true political craft should establish a hierarchy in the polis. The hierarchical structure, by its very nature, makes the system closer—formally, at least—to oligarchy, as it puts the power in the hands of a small group of people or even to tyranny in the sense of having a single man at the helm of the polis.

We do not know much about this hierarchy. Socrates talked about the "citizens" without any indication that this group should be somehow structured or differentiated. Similarly, he spoke of the true craft of politics without specifying what sort of body would be responsible for it—a small group or a single person. We only know—in analogy to the craft of medicine and shepherding—of the two parts: many citizens and few (one?) true politicians.

3.2 True politics and knowledge

Socrates' remarks in the *Gorgias* contain the second proposition, a rather unsurprising one: a good politician must have knowledge and experience.[10]

10 Xenophon's Socrates also reflected—mostly in the *Memorabilia*—upon the question of knowledge and governance. While he did not say much about the

As usual, Socrates did not give us much in terms of details and particulars. The only general indication we have comes from an analogy between the architect and the politician, an analogy that was meant to explain the transition from their private occupation to public involvement. Socrates made the following point about the architects. First, they should be well educated in the craft by good and reputable teachers; afterward they should prove themselves skillful by building many fine private houses. Only then could they "proceed to public works" (514c4).

How does this apply to politics? The analogy makes the craft of politics both difficult and easy to attain. The first condition—having good teachers—is impossible to meet, considering Socrates' harsh judgement of the Athenian politicians. In his opinion, Pericles, Cimon, Miltiades, and Themistocles, despite their temporary successes, did not contribute to the moral quality of Athenian society (515d–516a). Socrates held them to be "the ones responsible for the evils" (519a6–7), as they made more serious the "swelling and festering" of the Athenian state's disease. Since the state as a whole was said to be a festering ulcer, Socrates must have noticed that it was a progressive condition stubbornly ignored by the leaders and that it would ultimately lead to the downfall of Athens (518e4).[11]

general theory of governance, his more mundane remarks were numerous, detailed, often concrete, though somewhat disorganized. Socrates, for example, claimed that good governance involved speaking, and all the greatest leaders were excellent speakers (3.3.11). He also associated skilful governance with the desire to attain fame (3.3.13) and with the ability to defeat one's enemies (3.3.6–7). Further, he mentioned justice and respect for human and divine laws (4.4.15–17). He stated, however, that there was no qualitative difference, only a quantitative one, between governing a state and managing a household, since both involve managing people (3.4.12). Xenophon's Socrates also emphasized the need to have a knowledge of the particulars, for example, when he proved to Glaucon that his intention to pursue a political career in politics was premature. He asked him about the sources of state income, the number of Athenian troops and the enemy troops, the number of necessary border posts, about grain supplies and several other things.

11   The passage presumably refers to the disastrous defeat Athens suffered in 404 BC. According to Dodds, Socrates' remarks suggest that a certain originally-implanted defect made the fall of Athens inevitable (1990:364). Irwin apparently agreed with this interpretation but criticized Socrates for holding such

Not only were the political leaders unable to set a political standard for others to follow, but the democratic system is essentially inimical to knowledge. Let us recall the *Meno*'s description of how the mind fails to accumulate and organize true opinions; the political achievements, if they happen, result from divine inspiration or chance. To put it in simplistic terms, teaching in democracy, as Socrates described it, is a rare commodity.

The second condition in the architect/politician analogy seems less challenging. The argument that before the architect constructs public buildings he must learn his craft by constructing private houses sounds rational. The architect responsible for designing a public structure should have a larger view of the context and be well aware of the function of the building, which in turn presupposes some kind of knowledge of the political system and the polis as such. Similarly, whoever wants to lead the polis should have acquired experience in leading smaller communities.

But this is not quite what Socrates had in mind. By distinguishing between the private and the public in the craft of house-building, he could imply that there is also a difference between a private activity within a family or a small circle of friends and a public activity that extends to the entire polis. This distinction should not surprise us once we remember that in the classification of the *technai*, he also distinguished between the craft of justice and the craft of law-making, corresponding, more or less, to the private and the public. The problem is, however, that Socrates was ambiguous on this point: he seems to treat private and the public governance as different, but when talking about them, he used the same language, which blurs this difference.

The distinction was clearer when Socrates criticized the Athenian politicians and their activities. The argument was simple: the politicians made bad laws, that is, they were incompetent in *nomothetikē*, which resulted in

a view: "Socrates does not trouble to show how Athenian moral sickness caused the defeat, or how moral health might have avoided it" (1979:239). It seems that the inevitability of the decay has its roots in democratic and imperialist politics. Socrates' true craft of politics—as it will become clear in the subsequent parts of the chapter—could not approve of Athenian imperialism. There is, therefore—contrary to Irwin's claim—some connection between, on the one hand, moral health and prudent foreign policy and, on the other, between moral sickness and hubristic imperialism.

the moral decay of the Athenian citizens. His example was Pericles' law that instituted compensation for holding a public office. Socrates asserted that the law had a morally devastating effect, and he spared no harsh words about the culprit: Pericles, he said, "made the Athenians idlers and cowards, chatterers and spongers, by starting them on drawing pay" (515e5–7).

The bad laws corrupted the citizens, but the question was how to improve them. The politician/architect analogy evidently indicates that the process should start from private activity, just as the architect responsible for public works starts with building private houses. Socrates made this point explicit when he talked about himself as a possible state-physician (514d3–7) and then about Callicles and his political plans. To these plans, Socrates reacted by advising Callicles to examine his record in this field so far and ask himself a question: "Has Callicles ever yet made any citizen better? Is there anyone who was previously base, unjust, intemperate, and who because of Callicles has become find and good?" (Irwin trans., 515a3–6). The implication was that so long as Callicles did not have any success in private activity, he should refrain from aspiring to political functions, just as Socrates—should he want to be a state physician—had first to prove his medical talent in private practice.

All this is, of course, perfectly congruent with Socrates' insistence on his elenctic method that required addressing individual people and inspiring individual souls. But considering that this method did not bring about any visible results and even granting that Socrates, by talking about justice, fulfilled his small share of the general craft of *politikē*, there is still a question of *nomothetikē*. Is there, under the circumstances, any place for it at all or should it be suspended until the *technē* of justice starts improving citizens? Since Pericles' law had such bad consequences, it would be reasonable to replace it by better regulation and expect an improvement of the civic spirit among the Athenians.

Unfortunately, Socrates remains silent on the craft of good law-making. It seems, however, that he did not suspend it and did not advise waiting until the *technē* of justice brings about improvement. A suggestion to that effect we find in Socrates' rather negative comment about the standard forms of the politicians' activity. He asserted that making one's polis richer, building ports, roads, and settlements did not constitute sufficient conditions for being a good politician. Certain politicians—he said—filled the city with "harbors and dockyards, walls, and tribute and that sort of rub-bish," acting "without *sōphrosynē* and justice" (519a1–4, Irwin trans.).

These last two terms could refer both to the polis as such as to personal qualities, and it may very well be that Socrates meant it to be ambiguous. Such concepts as justice and *sōphrosynē* were essential to his language, whether he talked about individual souls or other matters. As I said in the preceding remarks, this language blurred the distinction between the private and the public but, at the same time, implied the crucial role of personal virtues. In the above quotation, however, both concepts seem to refer pri-marily to the public rather than the private, and there is nothing unusual about it. We remember Socrates repeating with approval the opinions of the wise men that *sōphrosynē* and justice organize the entire cosmos. Since he could think of them—if only tentatively—as organizing the entire cos-mos, it is quite possible that he could also think of them as the organizing principles of the polis, with—presumably—the craft of *nomothetikē* being responsible for their implementation. Unfortunately, Socrates was rather laconic on this point.

3.3 The just polis

Socrates did not tell us what laws the true politician should launch to im-prove the citizens and establish the rule of justice and *sōphrosynē*, but he gave us an intimation of what a just polis would be like. And this is the third proposition: good politicians work in accord with the citizens to se-cure the internal harmony—*homonoia* and *philia*—of the polis. This is at least what one can infer from Socrates' conversation with Callicles and par-ticularly with Thrasymachus in the *Republic I*. The context of the latter con-versation was the question: which is stronger—injustice or justice (*Republic* 351a). Socrates asserted that justice is stronger than injustice and derived his argument mainly from the function (*ergon*) of injustice (351d7). Injus-tice—he said—generates hatred, and hatred leads to conflicts and divisions, which in turn makes any coordinated enterprise impossible: "injustice has the power, first, to make whatever it arises in—whether it is a city, a family, an army, or anything else—incapable of achieving anything as a unit, be-cause of the civil wars and differences it creates, and, second, it makes that unit an enemy to itself and to what is in every way its opposite, namely, justice" (351e9–352a3, Grube, Reeve trans.).

Injustice is thus—through its internal dynamics—self-destructive: it provokes "factions, hatreds and internecine conflicts" (351d4–5). Justice, as its opposite, should generate the opposite results—"unity of mind and friendship" (*homonoian kai philian*—351d5). Such an interpretation sheds a different light on the internal conflicts within the polis, especially when the citizens turned against their leaders. This attitude toward the leaders was particularly characteristic of the Athenian citizens, who could be extremely hostile to them, even the most famous ones whom they had formerly respected.

Socrates did not fail to mention this, for example, the case of Pericles whom at the end of his life the Athenians "convicted of theft, and nearly condemned to death, clearly because they supposed he was base" (*Gorgias* 516a1–3). Socrates rhetorically added:

> "Now tell me about Cimon. Didn't those Athenians he was caring for ostracize him so that they wouldn't hear his voice for ten years? And didn't they do the same to Themistocles, and punish him with exile as well? And Miltiades of Marathon—didn't they vote to throw him into the pit, but for the prytanis wouldn't they have thrown him in?" (516d6–e2)

The criticism is directed both against the *demos* and against the leaders, but the latter are clearly deemed more guilty. About those politicians, he said:

> "I notice that when the city lays hands on any of the political men for injustice, they are annoyed and scandalized, saying that it's a terrible thing being done to them; they've done much good to the city, and now they are being ruined unjustly by it—that's their argument. But the whole thing's false. For not a single leader of a city could ever be destroyed unjustly by the very city he leads." (519b3–c2, Irwin trans.)

Once it is assumed that the aim of the leaders is to create "unity of mind and friendship," a rejection of the leaders by the citizens is unmistakable proof of the failure on the part of the leaders. We can thus generalize and say that true politicians "improve citizens" and "aim at the best" by working for *homonoia* and *philia*, the qualities that resulted from and were the outward manifestations of justice. It was expected that the well-governed city, free from factions and internecine struggles, would create a relationship of mutual kindness amongst the citizens but also between the ruled and the rulers.

How committed was Socrates in defending the politics of friendship? Certain passages in Xenophon's *Symposium* and, above all, in his *Memorabilia*, associate friendship with political life: by promoting gentleness, mutual support, and harmony, friendship allows people to achieve political goals in service of their homeland (2.6.24–25; 24; 4.8.7). In Plato's dialogues, the prototypical idea of reciprocity between the leaders and those who are led was mentioned in the *Apology*. Socrates argued that he had not corrupted anyone, for if he had, the corrupted persons in his circle would have turned against him: "the wicked do some harm to those who are ever closest to them, whereas good people benefit them" (25c7–9, Grube trans.). While studying the Athenians in matters of wisdom, Socrates claimed he had treated them not like enemies but "like a father or an elder brother" (31b4–5).[12]

This picture of the polis integrated not only by mutual kindness but also by unity of mind is well in tune with his philosophy, but, surprisingly, Socrates did not develop it in the *Republic I* (nor elsewhere), limiting the argument to a few phrases while instead devoting considerably more space to the bad political consequences of injustice. A probable reason is that the state of unity in a polis is even more difficult to attain than that in an individual person through the perfect blending of the virtues. The latter presupposed the former, and the former did not seem realistic either.

The difficulty is yet more serious if we reflect on what kind of integration of the citizens and the leaders Socrates could have in mind. There are two versions if we bring back the distinction from the *Protagoras* between the parts of the face and the parts of gold. The parts-of-face metaphor is

12   Book VIII of *Nicomachean Ethics* is the *locus classicus*, wherein Aristotle considered the problem of friendship in the context of political systems. At 1155a20–25, Aristotle made a remark that is not quite dissimilar to Socrates' view, namely that friendship in the polis, if sufficiently strong, is self-regulatory and makes justice redundant.

clearly preferable politically if only because it may imply a more realistic strategy. Unity or friendship would then not mean the blending of political groups into a unified political body but harmony or a balance of various groups. Assuming that Socrates correctly diagnosed the excesses of democracy and its self-destructive tendencies, this could be a potential solution, perhaps only partial, to at least one of the problems that troubled and irritated Socrates: it would keep in check the indivisible power of the *demos*. The solution appeared later in Plato's *Laws* and then was elaborated by Aristotle in *Politics*.[13] The idea of a mixed system in which democracy is only one of the constituents, being checked and controlled by other constituents—oligarchic and monarchical—was to have a spectacular career in the centuries to come.

For Socrates, this would have been a rather diluted form of friendship, but at least it might indicate some more practical steps to remedy the ills of the Athenian system. Will this interpretation be reconcilable with Socrates' philosophy? Highly unlikely. For one thing, there is not a shred of evidence, not even an indirect suggestion, that a similar idea ever entered Socrates' mind. By relating "friendship" to *homonoia*, i.e. the unity of mind, Socrates excluded any such speculations and brought the concept considerably closer to the parts-of-gold metaphor.

In the same dialogue, the *Republic I*, Socrates' antagonist invoked a picture of a shepherd and a flock, with the intention of illustrating his point that ruling is always in the interest of the ruler: the shepherds tend the sheep for the good of their masters and themselves (434b3). But Socrates accepted this analogy and did not think it falsified his claim that "every form of rule in so far as it is rule considers what is best for nothing else than that which is governed and cared for by it, alike in political and private rule" (345d5–e2). If we develop this shepherding analogy and say that the political leader is a shepherd while the society is a flock, then we are certainly

---

13 One can find a glimpse of this idea even before Plato, for instance in Solon: "For I gave the common folk such privilege as is sufficient for them, neither adding nor taking away; and such as had power and were admired for their riches, I provided that they too should not suffer undue wrong. Nay, I stood with a strong shield thrown before the both sorts, and would have neither to prevail unrighteously over the other" (TLG-0263.5).

closer to the concept of the parts-of-gold homogeneity than to the parts-of-face system of a political balance.[14]

But the parts-of-gold option is somewhat extreme and, therefore, politically doubtful. It is one thing to say that the factions, hatreds, and uncontrolled powers of certain groups will destabilize the system and that the polis will not survive without public and private morality and without selfless leadership committed to the best interest of the people. It is another thing to claim that the solution to this should be a community comparable to a flock, built on *homonoia* and *philia*. Public morality, civility in political relations, a reduced influence of factions, and public-spirited leadership do not necessarily imply one-mindedness and political homogeneity.

And it was Socrates himself who made this option even more difficult by diagnosing certain types of collective behavior that ran counter to true politics and made the sanative measures more than problematic. The most notorious of these was the behavior of the *demos*, which was *sui generis*, that is, irreducible to the sum of the ways of behavior of the individuals that composed it. Socrates speaks of the *demos* as if it were a single entity with its constant features and typical reactions, for instance, its volatility that Socrates famously noted—the *demos* could "easily put men to death and would bring them to life again" (*Crito* 48c4–6).

In the second and third propositions that describe the true craft of politics, the problem of the *demos* does not exist, as if their behavior could be easily overcome and corrected by the true politician. This expectation would have been more plausible if Socrates had specified, if only by way of mere suggestion, some positive steps in law-making that would improve the state of the polis. But, as I pointed out above, if he was ever specific, it was only about the bad laws and their bad consequences. The disappearance of the *demos* and of the problems that the *demos* creates is therefore

---

14   To be fair, we should point out there are other pertinent craft analogies in the *Republic I*. One is the art of commanding the ship, and the other is medicine. The first one could well harmonize with the parts-of-face picture of the polis. The second does not directly address the problem in question, but it implies a complete separation of the ruler and the ruled. If the politician is a doctor, and the polis a patient, then not only is the ruler detached from the political community, but the polis is totally dependent on him. *Homonoia*, if not *philia*, seems an obvious consequence.

unwarranted. The harsher Socrates' comments are about *hoi polloi*, the less justified seems its omission from the description of the craft of true politics.

4. Good laws

It was stated previously that Plato's Socrates assumed the Athenian democratic society consists of individuals living in a world with loosened social bonds rather than Aristotle's community of communities. The fact that he identified the *demos* as a distinct collective entity only confirms this description: *hoi polloi* were the product of the individualistic and egalitarian tendencies in the Athenian democratic society; they had no stable identities inherited from the past or a firm common goal that could consistently organize their activities in politics. Their participation in politics was impelled by herdlike emotions, easy to manipulate but at times dangerous when the emotions were excessively intense. When, in the *Apology*, Socrates talked about the politicians, manufacturers and poets as three groups, he stressed their similarity—all, despite their ignorance, believed themselves to be wise—rather than their distinctness. Some, like the manufacturers, could very well be part of the *demos*, while others, the politicians and poets, were likely to adapt themselves to its dominant position. Politically, they made little difference. In any event, Socrates never says they do.

There is nothing surprising in this description. Since the basic problem of the polis and the individual man was that of knowledge and ignorance, all other identifications lost much of their importance, especially since the democratic society was full of *logoi*, usually expressed carelessly and arbitrarily, and it was precisely this fact that prompted Socrates to carry out his elenctic examinations. All those examinations—let us repeat—were individual, and the social background of the interlocutor, "citizen or foreigner" (*Apology* 23b5–6), an aristocrat like Charmides, or a son of a tanner like Anytus, did not count. The comments about the three groups in the *Apology* were therefore exceptional and primarily contributed to the understanding of the problem of knowledge, not to the description of the group identities in Athens.

For the same reason, Socrates, a critic of Athens' present and past, was not interested in the Athenian identity and its glorious tradition that the Athenians should activate and make their country great again. As someone who consistently argued for the power of *logoi*, Socrates could not have trust in the power of the tradition. He proffered his general image of society in response to such people as Anytus, who saw Athens as a harmonious unity sharing in a wonderful heritage of past achievements. Socrates mocked Anytus' image in the *Menexenus*, a humorous parody of the pompous rhetoric in praise of Athens. He sarcastically noted that he felt better, taller, stronger, better looking, and inspired awe in others when listening to the orators praising Athens, yet after a few days, this feeling faded, and his usual outlook on life returned (234c–235c). The rhetoric of praise cast a short-lived spell on people's souls, changing nothing significant either in man or in the state.[15]

But despite this low opinion about the alleged Athenian identity, he seemed to be aware of the differences between the *poleis* having distinct and rather unchangeable characteristics. In the *Crito*, the Laws noted Socrates' high opinion of two cities—Sparta and Crete—because of having what he thought to be good laws (*eunomeisthai*—52e6). The Laws used the same verb about two other city-states—Thebes and Megara (53b4–5)—that probably also met with Socrates' fairly positive assessment. The verb *eunoeomai* not only refers to a system of laws but also to its identity, that is, to all social practices, norms, and mores that are responsible for general orderliness permeating the life of the polis; therefore the Laws linked those city-states that were well-ordered (*eunomoumenas*) to the most orderly (*kosmiotatous*) men (53c3–4).

The opposite of the well-ordered city like Crete and Sparta was Thessaly, a polis known for *ataxia* and *akolasia*, that is, for "disorder and

15 Xenophon's Socrates held the opposite views. He distinguished between the *demos* that was a rabble consisting of "dunces and weaklings" (*Memorabilia* 3.7.5) and the elite—"true gentlemen [who] share public honors" (2.6.24). He also believed that reminding the Athenians of their famous ancestors and heroic past could persuade them that they could lead again: "As we want them to strive for pre-eminence in virtue, we must show that this belonged to them in old days, and that by striving for it they will surpass all other men" (3.5.8). Besides, "these men, like their fathers, are reported to have been far superior to all other men of their time" (3.5.11).

licentiousness" (53d3–4).[16] It was a polis where one could spend time "enjoying oneself" (54a4), "entertaining oneself," and "banqueting" (53e5). Socrates said elsewhere mockingly that in the past, the Thessalians had been famous for "their horsemanship and wealth" (*Meno* 70a5).

It is clear why Socrates could criticize Thessaly that in his description represented everything to which he objected. It is not, however, clear why he would praise Crete and Sparta, and possibly also Thebes and Megara. One could provide the following argument to justify his preference for the four city-states. Among his criteria of knowledge (SCK), he includes the hierarchy of experts in knowledge (HEX), which had its counterpart in SBT and which clearly disqualifies democracy but could—formally at least—give a provisional support to some form of oligarchy. According to this criterion, it was simply impossible to have a political system based on Socrates' concept of knowledge, which would not have a hierarchical structure with an elite at the top. And since all four city-states were closer to oligarchy than to democracy, this gave them an advantage over democratic Athens.

The problem is, however, that according to SBT, the hierarchy should be based on knowledge and the elite should consist of virtuous men. And nowhere do we find Socrates saying that the ruling elites in Sparta and Crete represented the high standards of knowledge or that the unity of the virtues in their souls was exceptionally high. None of the four city-states developed a sufficiently intellectual culture that could satisfy Socrates' attachment to philosophy and rational inquiry.[17] Why, then, did he praise them? We can only speculate.

16 The concept of *akolasia*—licentiousness, lack of discipline—is revisited in the *Gorgias* in Socrates' dialogue with Callicles. Callicles appeared there as an eloquent advocate of *akolasia*. He argued that desires and appetites, especially the most intense ones, should be pursued openly instead of being restrained (*mē kolazein*—491e9). Further, the notion of *acolasia* with its censorial function was invented by the weak who wished to subdue the strong, thereby disguising their own impotence (492a3–b1). He added that happiness and virtue were "wantonness, *akolasia*, and freedom" (492c4–5). Desires and appetites were a manifestation of life, whereas their absence led to inertia.

17 The praise of Sparta is more congruent with Xenophon's Socrates who did not emphasize knowledge to the degree Plato's Socrates did. The former, indeed,

When Socrates made derisive remarks about the Thessalians, it was not only their excessive interest in horsemanship and wealth that he mocked[18] but also their newly awakened intellectualism, or rather fake intellectualism. According to Socrates, it was Gorgias who spread this new fashion in Thessaly and taught its citizens "to give a bold and grand answer to any question you may be asked, as experts are likely to do," and as he himself was doing (*Meno* 70b5–c2). The Athenians—let us add—were also attracted by similar practices. In the *Protagoras*, we read about a meeting of sophists and the city elite, during which Hippias was answering all questions on astronomy and physics, Prodicus seemed "godlike in his universal knowledge," and Protagoras managed to collect a group of people, "enchant[ed] them with his voice like Orpheus and they follow[ed] the sound of his voice in a trance" (315a–316a).

Perhaps what made Sparta, Crete, Thebes, and Megara superior to Thessaly (and Athens) was precisely the absence of fake intellectualism, which prevented those city-states from unleashing the processes that Socrates found deplorable. But whence this resistance to the new trends? In the *Protagoras*, Socrates said that "philosophy, first of all, has its most ancient roots and is most widespread among the Greeks in Crete and Lacedaemon, and those regions have the highest concentration of *sophistai* in the world" (342a7–b1, Lombardo and Kell trans.). The word *sophistai* is most probably used not in the usual sense but rather refers to wise men, poets, musicians, that is, it is close to the meaning attributed to it by Protagoras himself (316c–e). Similarly, the word "philosophy" means "wisdom."

But whatever the shades of meaning, this statement is rather unusual, not quite serious, perhaps partly ironic.[19] Sparta was consistently hostile to

praised Sparta too and he gave explicit reasons. In Sparta, unlike in Athens—he said—the elders and the laws were respected (*Memorabilia* 3.5.15, 4.4.15).

18 The same opinion about Thessaly we find in the *Greater Hippias* (284a). The Thessalians apparently acquired a well-deserved reputation of excellent horsemanship, as their horses were considered "the best in Greece" (Herodotus 7.196). Also: Plato's *Laws* 625d.

19 Let us remember that admiration for Sparta became a sort of intellectual fashion in Athens. According to Aristophanes, "all men were crazy about the Spartans: they wore their hair long, went hungry, never bathed, acted like Socrates, brandished batons" (*Birds* 1281).

the modern *sophistai*, that is, to the sophists such as Protagoras or Hippias. The latter admitted it explicitly (*Greater Hippias* 283c–284c). As to the *sophistai* of old, that is, wise men, poets, and musicians, Sparta made no significant contribution to philosophy. Plato in the *Laws* (325d and seq.) criticized Sparta and Crete for concentrating mainly on warfare. Aristotle repeated this charge in the *Politics*: "The entire system of the laws is directed toward one part of virtue only, military valor, because this is serviceable for conquest" (1271b2–4).

But in his half-mocking remarks on Sparta and philosophy in the *Protagoras*, Socrates said something that could be taken seriously. He seemed to praise both Sparta and Crete for not exposing their citizens to the sophistic influence. "So that their young men won't unlearn what they are taught, [the Spartans] do not permit any of them to travel to other cities (the Cretans don't either)" (342c7–d2, Lombardo, Bell trans.). This seemingly anti-intellectual attitude might sound dissonant in the mouth of Socrates who himself debated the sophists, but there are good grounds to think that he meant what he said and that he indeed might have been favorable to preventing the young minds from being subjected to the sophistic teaching. We know, for example, that he did not admit to his company the young men whose minds leaned toward sophistry (*Theaetetus* 151b). Nothing he said ever indicated that he thought the sophistic training was intellectually edifying. On the contrary, what the sophists said dramatically clashed with Socrates' view of knowledge—logical consistency, justification of the propositions, a clearly defined object, etc.

In the *Phaedo*, we see Socrates developing this anti-sophistic argument to its conclusion. He stated that these exercises and games with contradictions because of the sophists' incompetence in the *technē* concerning *logoi* (90b6) results in misology, that is, a rejection of the *logoi* as unreliable, inconsistent, malleable, and unstable, rendering "all the things that are carried up and down, just like things fluctuating in the Euripus, and never remain at rest for any time" (90c4–5, Gallop trans.). Whether this was really Socrates' argument or instead Plato's, we cannot know, but it is consistent with Socrates' previous enunciations about the sophists' incompetence.

The unstable and inconsistent store of claims and propositions in the sophists' world where all things go up and down has an analogy in the democratic man's mind where true opinions move around like the statues made by Daedalus. Of course, one should not push this analogy too far. It is equally arbitrary to say that the sophists imposed their thinking on democracy as to say that the democratic system created the sophists. However, some interaction between the sophists and democracy did exist and was noticed a long time ago, but an elaboration of this interaction is not an easy task.

Socrates' positive attitude toward the oligarchic or quasi-oligarchic city-states was, as it seems, partly due to the fact that he thought them to have been free both from "all things going up and down" as well as from the opinions "moving around like Daedalus' statues." So what he praised was the stability of the laws and a corresponding stability of the minds that refrained from undermining those laws. Socrates must have assumed another criterion, not included in SCK and SBT, and primarily political: good laws are those that produce orderliness in people's conduct and in people's minds.

This raises, however, a problem of consistency. Since it is possible that the laws are stable, it must also be possible that people's opinions do not have to move around like Daedalus' statues even without *aitias logismos*, that is, without the discipline of the arguments and systemic thinking. It is also possible that there is a more or less unperturbed continuity of political tradition without centrifugal tendencies, mutually hostile factions, and disruptive, volatile emotions. Moreover, all this is possible even without grounding politics on a comprehensive and coherent system of *logoi* about virtue and the human *ergon*.

The fact that in the *Protagoras* Socrates talked about philosophy being most widespread in Sparta and Crete may be an indirect hint that he was aware of this inconsistency and tried to neutralize it by a half-serious remark. To admit openly that there may be a stable non-intellectual basis for good laws and the general orderliness of the polis would have undermined a lot of what Socrates said in his philosophy. To indulge in grandiose praise of Sparta and Crete as a bedrock of philosophy was perhaps a safe way to hide the problem behind a playful remark without really addressing it.

5. Parental state and tacit consent.

Another description of Socrates' position in the polis we find in the *Crito*. This dialogue has always caused considerable controversy. Socrates repeated his commitment to justice as a fundamental category that should organize all of human life and inform all decisions, but, unexpectedly, this assertion did not lead him—as it does in the *Apology*—to the conclusion about the inevitable philosopher-versus-state conflict. The dialogue argued that Socrates should submit himself to the state and that the act of submission was essentially just. The superiority of a collective entity over the philosopher has appeared for many as shockingly un-Socratic.[20]

The story in the dialogue is simple. Socrates' desperate friend Crito[21] visited him in prison early in the morning, two days before his planned

20 For this reason, the dialogue often has given rise – from the very beginning— to disputes about the credibility of its message. For Zeller, the *Crito* expresses "the same principle" as the *Apology* 1877:150–51). According to Grote, the *Crito* was deliberately written as a counterbalance to the *Apology*, in which Socrates treats the Athenians with condescension; in the *Crito*, Plato intentionally presents him as a patriot, a loyal citizen and an exemplary democrat (I 1865:300–05). Since that time a lot has been said about the relation between the *Apology* in which Socrates defies the city and the *Crito* in which he professes his obedience to the city: Martin (1970) argued that according to Socrates all should be obeyed (as stated in the *Crito*), but not all commands (as those described in the *Apology*) are laws. Wade (1971) claims that there is not a contradiction between the *Apology* and the *Crito* because both assume the hierarchy of excellence—the inferior should obey the superior. According to Young's interpretation (1974), Socrates' true position is expressed in the *Apology* whereas in the *Crito* he only persuades his interlocutor. McLaughlin (1976) takes issue with this interpretation and denies any contradiction between the *Crito* and the *Apology* as the principles each defends—obedience in the former and disobedience in the latter—relate to different cases. Woozley (1980) argues that the two dialogues can be reconciled and that obedience to the laws does not exclude civil disobedience if the protester stays "within the reach of the law" and even if his protest is somewhat "quixotic." Vlastos (1996a) maintains that "there is no inconsistency between Socrates' stand in the two dialogues, because the reasoning by which he justifies obedience in the *Crito* will itself show that a man with those reasons for obeying the law in the circumstances of the *Crito* would have as good reasons for disobeying it in the very different circumstances which he conjures up in the *Apology*."

21 Crito often appears in Plato's dialogues as a partner in conversation (*Crito*, *Euthydemus*, *Phaedo*); he is present at the trial of Socrates (*Apology* 33d, 38d). He also appears in Xenophon (*Symposium* 4.24; *Memorabilia* 1.2.48.2.9.9.1– 8). We know that he was the same age as Socrates, and came from the same

execution. Crito tried to persuade Socrates to save his life by escaping. The plan, it can be gleaned, had already been prepared; only the consent of the concerned party was needed. But Socrates categorically refused, offering his reasons. The *Crito*'s crucial part is the long statement made by the Laws of Athens (as anthropomorphized by Socrates), demonstrating to the philosopher that escaping from prison would be unworthy. The general impression of the Laws' speech is unequivocal: the state is to be recognized as something much more important than the individual, and, therefore, the individual has a duty to obey the state.

Each of the *Crito*'s elements deserves closer inspection: Crito's persuasion, Socrates's reply, and the Laws of Athens' speech.

5.1 Crito's offer and Socrates' reply

Three basic threads can be found Crito's attempts to persuade Socrates to escape. The first referenced Socrates' regrettable situation in prison while awaiting execution; escaping death seemed to everyone to be the obvious thing to do, especially on account of the children who needed their father

deme. According to the accounts in the *Phaedo*, the dying philosopher entrusted him with the task of sacrificing a rooster to Asclepius; he also closed the dead man's eyes and mouth. This closeness of the two men suggests that Crito should be the best illustration of the effectiveness of Socrates' philosophy. But what he says in the dialogue does not indicate he absorbed much of his friend's moral teaching. Perhaps it would be too denigrating to call him "one of the many" (Young 1974:6) or "unphilosophical" (Weiss 2001:43–49) or "a kind of Athenian Everyman" (Miller 1996:122). He may have been "well acquainted with philosophical arguments as used by Socrates" (Liebersohn 2015:105) or agreed to "several Socratic principles" (Harte 2005:240) but failed to internalize any of them. It should be noted that none of Socrates' close friends demonstrate any particular interaction between philosophy and life. Weiss incriminates Crito even more, quite unnecessarily and arbitrarily, by suggesting that since he mentions his friends in Thessaly (45c2–4) who offer to take care of Socrates after his escape, and since in the further part of the dialogue the Laws of Athens describe Thessaly as a place rife with "the greatest license and disorder" (53d3–4), it can be assumed that Crito engaged in shady business dealings (2001:53). Beversluis (2000:59–74) defends Crito as a morally noble figure; his book, let us add, is entirely devoted to the defence of a dozen or so of Socrates' interlocutors, which implies that most of them were wrongly treated by the readers and, above all, by Socrates himself.

to bring them up. The second thread is the social pressure exerted on Socrates' friends, who were expected to try to save him, even though their endeavors might prove to be costly and unlawful; failure to undertake such efforts would be interpreted as a betrayal of friendship and meanness. The third thread highlighted the negligence, bias, contingency, and injustice of the entire trial: Socrates, as the harmed party, should have no scruples about saving his life.

The arguments deployed here appear difficult to refute from the point of view of common sense and elementary human intuition. Following Crito's line of thought, it is reasonable to conclude that there was actually no good reason why Socrates should await his execution when an opportunity to escape presented itself. His duties toward his children, his friends' helpful hand, and the scandalous nature of the trial should suffice to take advantage of the opportunity.

However, Crito altogether ignored the question of justice. He referred to it twice (45a1, c5) but for rhetorical purposes rather than as an argument that would sanction the chosen course of action. He wanted the action to seem just if it could not actually be so. None of Crito's basic thoughts demonstrated an obvious association with justice as a general principle. Socrates' duty toward his children was presented as a psychological problem rather than a moral one; likewise, so is the problem of friendship treated. As to the trial, Crito never talked about it in terms of justice but described it as a social phenomenon.

By way of summary, we can say that Crito's arguments were based on what one might call a common morality. It manifested itself as a belief that in certain important life situations, the beneficial course of action becomes immediately so apparent that the abstract question of justice or virtue loses its relevance.

For this reason, Crito could not be considered a good citizen. He did not invoke his homeland, city-state, or the laws, but only *hoi polloi*. He appeared to have no clear or considered sense of community with Athens, even though he understood the mechanisms and social reactions of its people quite well. The paradox is that he did not realize the problems inherent in his attitude toward the state, just as the other citizens who thought similarly would not question an attitude he represented (44c2–4). Presumably, even overseeing Socrates' successful escape from prison would not undermine either his own self-esteem as a citizen or the attitude of other Athenians toward him.

In his reply, Socrates generally invoked justice as the primary category.[22] Before the Laws of Athens joined his conversation with Crito, Socrates formulated three *logoi* as a reminder of his basic moral teachings. These *logoi* are familiarly Socratic. They are already mentioned in Chapter I and, as I argue, corresponded to SBT.

The first is formal and stipulates that it is always necessary to act in keeping with "nothing ... but the *logos* that on reflection seems best..." (46b5–6). This *logos* invalidated Crito's first argument about the natural reflex to save one's own life, even if it was done for the sake of one's children. The second was the "*logos* about opinions" originally formulated by Crito, not by Socrates, according to which the beliefs of some people were more valuable than those of others (46c7–d2). This *logos* overturned Crito's second argument about *hoi polloi* and the importance of social pressure. The third *logos* stipulates that "[one must not] when wronged, inflict wrong in return, as the majority believe, since one must never do wrong" (49b10–11). This logos abolished Crito's argument from the miscarriage of justice: the status of a victim, Socrates argued, did not entitle the victim to do injustice, even to the wrongdoer.[23]

Each of the three *logoi* was itself sufficient for Socrates to reject Crito's offer. The escape plan lacked a satisfactory rationale in terms of justice (the first *logos*); it was supported by the majority or masses, which made it unreliable (the second *logos*); and there was a suspicion that accepting it would force Socrates to do something unjust (the third *logos*). The deployment of the three *logoi* together ultimately resolved the problem. Theoretically, the dialogue could have concluded approximately at line 49e2, where it was made clear that Socrates did not expect Crito to question his reasoning. Yet, for some reason, the philosopher decided that the previous arguments

---

22 As I wrote above, apart from the ethics of justice, there is also the theme of aristocratic morality based on the worthy/unworthy opposition.

23 I, therefore, cannot agree with Woozley who asserts that Socrates ignores or dismisses Crito's arguments (1980:309–10). For a rebuttal of Woozley's interpretation, see Barker 1977.

did not exhaust the case, and he encouraged his interlocutor to listen to the continuation of the argument (49e3) in the form of the speech of the Laws of Athens.

The arguments of the Laws may have added something to the justification of Socrates' decision not to escape from prison, but they were not necessary. The inadmissibility of the escape has already been proven. The arguments served to explain in what way the Laws interpreted the nature of Socrates' political obligation toward the state. Whether Socrates could have incorporated those arguments within his own philosophy remains to be seen.

5.2 The Laws of Athens speak

Let us reconstruct the main steps in the Laws' speech. As to the number of arguments to be found in the speech, usually four are listed. In my reconstruction that follows, these would be points B, E, F, and G.

A. Socrates' general proposition (the fourth *logos*): we fulfill an agreement on certain matters on the assumption that it is just.

B. The Laws' allegation if Socrates chose to run away: by escaping from jail, he would destroy the city, for failure to observe judicial decisions has precisely such devastating effects.

C. A possible reply to the allegation: the city harmed Socrates first, and thus—although not verbalized—the philosopher is not bound to accept the unjust verdict.

D. The reply of the Laws to C: the agreement between Socrates and Athens also includes accepting judicial decisions, including harmful ones.

E. The first justification of D: a comparison of the relation between Socrates and Athens to the relationship between the child and his parents.

F. The second justification: Socrates has made an agreement with Athens "through action" concerning the judicial verdicts and the management of state affairs (51e2–3); by escaping, Socrates would deny what he had implicitly agreed to.

G. Socrates could have persuaded the state as understood in E but did not.

H. Socrates could have persuaded the state as understood in F but did not.

I. The Laws' concluding remarks and Socrates' final words.

The speech is composed of four basic strands. The first is the fourth *logos* (A), which, strictly speaking, precedes the speech as an introduction. Nevertheless, it anticipated everything stated subsequently. The second strand refers to the conception of the state community as compared to the relation between parents and children (E). The third includes the concept of agreement between the state and its citizen (F), and the fourth one constitutes an argument from effects (I) and concludes the speech.

5.2.1 The fourth logos

To open the final part of the dialogue, Socrates formulated the fourth *logos*: "when one has come to an agreement that is just with someone, one should fulfil it" (49e6), or in a slightly different formulation, "we are sticking to a just agreement" (50a2–3). The Laws that immediately took over interpreted this *logos* as a reference to the relation between Socrates and his polis.

The fourth *logos* deserves closer attention, if only because it differs to a certain extent from the typical thrust of Socratic thinking. Socrates usually referred to justice or truth in keeping with the most fundamental premise of his philosophy that, among other things, is reflected in the first *logos*. Referring to an agreement or to consent (the verb *homologeō* and its derivatives mean both) introduced a new and unclear element, which led to the following problem. If the agreement concerned matters sanctioned by justice, then the very act of consenting to the agreement did not contribute anything new: for justice was a mandatory and self-justifying category. It was enough to refer to the first *logos* to recognize that certain things should be done, whereas other things, say, escaping from prison, were prohibited. One might ask whether any agreement was needed at all if the obligation to act in accordance with justice directly ensued from the rational recognition of what was good.

One could make sense of the Laws' strategy in the following way. They drew Socrates' attention to two kinds of his involvement in Athenian political life, its rules and institutions, as specified in points E and F of the above reconstruction. Those two kinds of involvement have something in common. Socrates was not aware of them before, or at least he never showed such awareness, and it is easy to see why not. His main and, one would think, only concern was justice, virtue, truth, etc., that is, the abstract moral concepts that were to organize his life and improve his soul. SBT did not say anything about these involvements. From this perspective, his participation in the Athenian polis was of secondary importance: the highest authority for him were the *logoi* that defined those abstract concepts, not the institutions of the city-state.

He could radically criticize Athens (which he did); he could distance himself from Athenian politics (which he said he did); he could also think of some better politics that would save the polis from its imminent predicament (which he also reflected upon). None of these ways allowed for the possibility that Socrates owed something to Athens and that these obligations were binding irrespective of his criticism of the Athenian system. The fact that he—until two days before his death—did not give a thought to or try to formulate a theoretical justification for his attachment to Athens revealed a big lacuna in his system. And that he had such an attachment, his military record and his rootedness in Athens demonstrated beyond any doubt.

So, the question that the Laws raised was legitimate and well-taken: what is the nature of Socrates' obligations to Athens, and how strong are they? The fourth logos suggests that these obligations are based on justice. The implication was, therefore, that there was not a contradiction between Socrates' attachment to justice as an abstract category and his duties to the polis. If this were true, then a lot of what was said before about Socrates' politics would have to be revised, including his avoidance of political involvement, his devastating critique of the Athenian polis coupled with the search for an alternative true way of conducting politics, and, finally, his claims about the superiority of the oligarchic systems in Sparta and Crete.[24]

24 Some commentators speculate whether obedience to the laws derived from the "agreement" mentioned in the *Crito* does not contradict the instances of disobedience mentioned in the *Apology*, such as, for example, Socrates' refusal to become involved in the execution of Leon of Salamis; or, whether there is no conflict between obedience to the law and obedience to morality. The *Crito*, however, deals with a different problem, namely, accepting injustice committed by the state against its citizen. On this I agree, among others, with McLaughlin 1976:190–92; Allen 1980:109–13. I, therefore, think that Socrates' alleged authoritarianism is a separate issue. The authors such as Bostock (2005) ask a legitimate question whether when according to the *Crito*, the citizen should obey only the decisions of the courts or all just laws in the

5.2.2 The state as parents

The "state as parents" was the first explanation of the relation between Socrates and Athens, point E in the above reconstruction. Two entities were posited: Socrates (*qua* citizen), and the Laws of Athens / *to koinon tēs poleōs* (50a8). This phrase could be translated as "political community," or "commonwealth," or even "homeland." Hence, the Laws themselves adopted the inclusive formula of, roughly, "the Laws and the political community" when talking to Socrates—variations include, "we, the Laws and the city" (50b1–2, 51d4–5, 52b2) and "your country and its laws" (51a2, 51a4–5).[25] The word "commonwealth" would seem the best to express those threads and associations, but I will stick to "the state," following the established practice.

Briefly in this vein, the argument marshalled by the Laws is:

E_1. The state brought Socrates into the world (thanks to the laws and institutions which allowed his parents to marry).

city, but this is not the core problem in the Laws' speech. Its implication is that Socrates would be as resistant to escape from prison if he had been incarcerated after the Leon incident, as he was resistant after his own trial. Obviously, he could have argued that during the rule of the Thirty Tyrants there were no Laws but pure injustice, but this would have forced him to engage in philosophical casuistry—alien to his attitude—about which regimes he could retaliate in kind and which he could not.

25 Grote goes further than all the other commentators, too far as I see it, in that he regards the entire speech of the Laws as a democratic manifesto, to which all the supporters of democracy in Athens would subscribe; it was even, according to him, a "commonplace" of democratic discourse, expressing the "most authentic spirit of constitutional democracy" (Grote I 1865:302–04). Against this claim, one might argue that the concept of democracy in Greece derived from the question of how numerous should be the ruling group— one man, a small elite or demos (the word denoting either the multitude of mostly the poor and uneducated or all citizens). This necessarily gave democracy an aspect of one-sidedness and partiality. In the Crito, we find the concept of the state unrelated to the threefold quantitative classification. This is the state in its entirety, a commonwealth with all its social and historical dimensions, irrespective of its political system or social structure. The phrase *to koinon tes poleos* had its continuation—as Burnet (1991:280) rightly pointed out—in the Roman concept of the state.

E_2. The state raised and educated Socrates thanks to its educational system.

E_3. By birth, upbringing, and education, Socrates became (a) a child and (b) a slave of the state.

E_4. One is not allowed to destroy the state because it would be (a) not only comparable to but (b) even more serious than destroying one's own parents.

E_5. The state is (a) not only comparable to but (b) far more important than one's parents.

What leaps to the eye is a disproportion between the premise (E_1 and E_2) and the conclusion (E_4 and E_5). After all, the fact that Socrates' parents got married according to the Athenian law and he himself was educated within the Athenian social environment does not justify such superiority of the state over the individual.[26] One might consider Socrates a child of

26 The obvious question is to what extent one can identify the Laws' speech about political obedience with Socrates' own position. Several interpretative options are possible: (i) obedience to the Laws is fully in line with Socrates' philosophy, since he consistently defended the law against abuse by one power or another throughout his life, and admired the stability of laws in Sparta and Crete (Adam 1980:xx–xxiii); (ii) obedience to the Laws is entirely consistent with Socrates' philosophy, since the law represents what is moral, and breaking the law is *adikein* and, therefore, destructive to the man's soul (Barker 1977); (iii) obedience to the state is fully compatible with Socrates' philosophy, although it is not absolute (Brickhouse and Smith 1994:141–55), or, in a different version, there is "no fundamental incompatibility between Socrates as we know him from the tradition and Athenian democratic culture" (Ober 2011:166–67); (iv) obedience to the state is entirely incompatible with Socrates' philosophy and hence the language of the Laws does not express his philosophy, but is rather intended for Crito (Miller 1996; Weiss 2001:98–112); (v) obedience to the state is totally incompatible with Socrates' philosophy, but in the *Crito*, the point is not to defend obedience to the state as a general principle but to address Socrates' particular situation (Vlastos 1996a; DeFilippo 1991); (vi) obedience to the state is inconsistent with Socrates' philosophy and the interpretation of the *Crito* as a defense of political authoritarianism is erroneous (McLaughlin 1976:192–97; Kraut 1984:161–71). My point—as I argue in the remaining part of the chapter—is that the Laws' arguments are not Socrates', but they touch upon certain problems that Socrates considered valid but could not justify within his own philosophy.

Athens, and this in a rather loose sense of the word, but calling him a slave seems unwarranted, to say the least.

> "Your country is to be honored more than your mother, your father, and all your ancestors, that it is more to be revered and more sacred, and that it counts for more among the gods and sensible men, that you must worship it, yield to it and placate its anger more than your father's. You must either persuade it or obey its orders, and endure in silence whatever it instructs you to endure, whether blows or bonds, and if it leads you into war to be wounded or killed, you must obey. To do so is right." (51b2–c1, Grube trans.)

This conclusion will be less puzzling once we note that in E_4 and E_5, we have two claims in each. The first—let us call it the argument from education—is an analogy between the two sets of educators: Socrates was born, raised, and educated—both by birth parents and by the polis. One might, of course, have doubts about the analogy: the biological birth that Socrates owed to his parents, and the figurative birth owed to Athens, were entirely different. The figurative birth seems to be what in today's language one might call social and cultural formation. The Laws said Athens gave birth to Socrates because the existing law permitted the marriage of his parents and, as a consequence of this, obliged them to educate him in the arts (*mousikē*) and physical culture (*gymnastikē*) (50d5–e4). Together *mousikē* and *gymnastikē* referred to the particular intellectual *cum* physical education that the Athenians proudly pioneered.

To translate into more mundane categories, this argument amounted to the following. A person's nature must realize itself in the course of one's life and in the process of education, through family life, and through life within the polis. Biological birthdays are accompanied by social ones— whoever is born enters not only the world inhabited by his mother and father but also by a larger community. Then his life is largely determined by both kinds of birth. Socrates could have thought that he would have been someone else if he had been born in Sparta or in Persia.

But the Laws also introduced another claim, even stronger; let us call it the argument from inequality—namely, that the state is more important and potent than the parents. Socrates hints at this fundamental inequality at 50e5, and next, referring to the opinion of the unspecified "gods and sensible men," asserts that the distance between a citizen and the state is far bigger than the distance between a child and his parents and so is a degree of inequality. This goes against many modern views: the Laws say that the parental quality of the state does not tend to diminish—as one would expect considering the more abstract character of the state institutions—but its authority becomes immensely higher, almost godlike.

The entire argumentation in E is sound as far as it goes, but one may wonder to what extent it is compatible with the Socratic philosophy and how it will change this philosophy once it is accepted. A simple answer would be that both claims are hard to reconcile with Socrates' system, but both contain important insights that Socrates could not easily dismiss.

As for the argument from education, Socrates might have accepted some kind of obligation toward the Athenian state for the reason already mentioned: without such a sense of obligation, he would not have had an unblemished military record in the Athenian army. He might have been grateful to his parents for being born in Athens with its *mousikē* and *gymnastikē*, and not in Thessaly with its license and horsemanship. Perhaps he could have even admitted that *mousikē* and *gymnastikē* were an important part of the Athenian identity, making it different from and in some respects, even superior to other poleis.[27] But this had certain definite limitations. Socrates would have strongly denied that he belonged to and was a product of the same culture that generated the sophists and democratic flattery that, as he believed, prevented the establishment of good laws, turned Athens into a festering ulcer, and pushed the political system to the brink of disaster. So even if he had admitted that he was a child of the Athenian *mousikē*

27 For instance, in the *Apology* Socrates compared Athens to a well-bred horse (30e4). Does this mean that Socrates believed in the essential soundness of Athenian culture embodied in *mousikē* and *gymnastikē* and that "the raw material of sound moral beliefs [was] present in Athenian *paideia*, although these nuggets of genuine insight [were] buried in the worthless heap of Athenian misapprehensions" (Mahoney 1998:14)? There is no evidence that, according to Socrates, what accounted for Athens being a well-bred horse was *paideia*, a possible reason being that education was so much influenced by sophistry that praising it would indirectly commend the sophists for their work.

and *gymnastikē*, it would never have amounted to that unqualified devotion to the Athenian commonwealth that the Laws demanded.[28]

Additionally, we can say that while the argument from education does not necessarily clash with Socrates' partial or quasi-avoidance of politics, it is certainly at odds with the concept of true politics and also with his high opinion about the regimes in Sparta and Crete. True politics implied superiority toward the polis, which resulted from Socrates having taken for himself the position of a (the?) teacher, not that of a pupil. Similarly, the apologetic remarks about Sparta and Crete could be seen—metaphorically speaking—as an attempt of a son to find better parents than those that those to whom he owed life and education.

But the argument from education was not to be totally dismissed. Although within his philosophy, Socrates could not account for the special obligation he owed to Athens, it would be unreasonable—and he never attempted it—to use this philosophy to deny any such obligation; Socrates never presented himself as a person with no fatherland, living entirely in the world of philosophy where thanks to the *elenchus* and definitions he could strive for personal excellence. On the other hand, the type of strict and even merciless obligation that the Laws postulated he could not accept because of the obvious educational defects of the Athenian system, which his philosophy detected and for which the critical diagnosis developed.

From the first argument, the Laws inferred the second—namely, that from inequality. Despite the dubious basis, the Laws came up, in the second argument, with an extremely bold claim about the state being equipped with immense power and authority. Those impressive attributes seem natural, like in a family where the parents have an unquestionably dominating position, except that in the state, they are much, much greater, stricter, and totally unaccountable.[29] It is meaningful that in the relevant passage, we

28 Strictly speaking, the parental-state argument does not require the justification of one's political loyalty in terms of the benefits one receives from the polis; in fact, taking benefits into account undermines the essence of this argument. *Mousikē* and *gymnastikē* could have been beneficial to Socrates, but this is a secondary matter. Being loyal to parents cannot depend on the calculation of the gifts and benefits the child received from them.

29 Some authors take the view that the imperative that we should "endure in silence whatever [your country] instructs you to endure" refers to all the actions,

will not find either "agreement" or "consent": the asymmetry between the citizen and the state is so imposing that these and similar words would be inadequate. The fourth *logos* concerning the "just agreement" has little relevance here.

The state's control of the citizen expresses itself in three ways. First, the state is the owner of the citizens' lives: it could inflict suffering on Socrates, beat him, imprison or send him to fight in the war where he could be wounded or killed. Second, no matter how ruthless the state can be, it is also an object of worship and reverence, being a quasi-godlike entity. And finally, at another place (51a3–4), the Laws add an additional mark of its authority: the state has the power to qualify its actions as just, including those that inflict suffering on the citizens.

The problem is, however, that we do not know anything about the nature of this inequality. Socrates, of course, was consistently supportive of hierarchy, and this support, as we know, derived directly from SCK and SBT. He argued for a hierarchy of the objects of knowledge, of experts, of

including the unjust ones, and vindicates state despotism (Weiss 2001:110). Kahn says the "true puzzle" of the *Crito* is why Socrates agreed to subjugate the citizen to the state to the extent that he was not even allowed to refuse to do unjust things; he replies that Plato allows the Laws to get carried away by the power of their own rhetoric (1989:40). This view cannot be sustained. The passage quoted above makes it clear what their expectations are: "[to] endure in silence whatever it instructs you to endure, whether blows or bonds, and if it leads you into war to be wounded or killed, you must obey." It is not a matter of committing injustice in the name and at the behest of the state but of enduring such injustice if it were to be inflicted by the state; in other words, it is a question of willingness to give one's life. Weiss argues, groundlessly, against such authors as DeFilippo (1991:257) that the distinction between committing injustice and suffering it is "alien" to the Laws. The issue of committing unworthy deeds at the behest of the state is not considered at all in the *Crito*, and it would be absurd if Socrates, waiting for his imminent death, were to deal with it, especially in the context of the proposed escape from prison. If there are true interpretative puzzles in the dialogue, they are certainly not to be found in the cited passage. Ober tries to weaken the shocking asymmetry between the citizen and the Laws by the notion of "impossibility of full reciprocity": just like the son cannot repay the debts to the parents, the citizen cannot repay the debt to the state (2011:151). The language the Laws use is much harsher to justify such an interpretation.

logoi, and in each of these, the criterion of differentiation was a degree of knowledge and virtue. The most obvious example of hierarchy for the Greeks was the one with the immortal gods at the top and the mortals at the bottom. For Socrates, this hierarchy, as we remember, looked different: the highest position was that of divine wisdom and the lowest that of human wisdom. The true craft of politics also generated a hierarchy but of a different kind: the citizens were like a gentle friendly flock to a good shepherd, not a slave to an unaccountable heavy-handed master. The hierarchy in the Laws' argument from inequality had nothing to do with wisdom or virtue, nor with *homonoia* and *philia*, and therefore does not seem to fit into Socrates' philosophy.

The problem aggravates when the Laws make another claim. On the basis of the analogy between the state and the parents, they said that whatever the state did to Socrates, he could not retaliate in kind, just as a child cannot answer back to his parents if he were reprimanded or strike back if he were struck (50e7–51a2). And the reason for this was that this highly asymmetric parentlike authority of the state over him was "just" (51b7).

This part of the Laws' argument is completely un-Socratic. Socrates could not call any practice or norm just without first reflecting on the definition of justice and, at least, before rejecting some popular versions. Socrates who started with a concrete problem immediately moved to the abstract, that is, to the logos, and then, according to EID, wanted to treat the definition as a "paradigm" to assess the concrete. The Laws reversed Socrates' standard procedure. First, they posited the overwhelming authority of the state vis-à-vis the citizen and then claimed it was just.

Why was it just? We do not know, except that it is compared to a parent, and a parent may reprimand his son, but the son is not allowed to talk back or strike back. This is the weakest possible justification for the three formidable attributes with which the Laws provided the state. It seems that the only basis for the justice of this state is its power. But then the entire argument becomes circular.

To the question why the state acquired such a power the answer is that the state is like the parents. But the parents lacked the three attributes with which the Laws equipped the state. So on what grounds did the state get these attributes? Because the state was like the parents. But—we have to repeat the objection—the parents did not have these attributes. And so we are moving in a circle. To put it somewhat differently: There is no justification of why the state had stronger authority than the parents except that it had such authority because it had more power. But to the question of why the state had more power, the answer is that it was like the parents. But the parents had less power, etc.

Of the state's three attributes specified by the Laws and mentioned above, the third one is the most disquieting from the perspective of Socrates' philosophy. The Laws said they could undertake to destroy Socrates if they considered it "just" (51a3). This, obviously, could not mean that the state has the power to define justice in the proper sense of the word. The *eidos* of the concept—as we learned from EID—is independent even of the gods' power. It could only mean that the state could decide, through its courts, what was and was not just from the point of view of the law of the land and that its interpretation was superior to that of the citizen.

If Socrates were to accept the Laws' argument, it would amount to the acceptance of the following claim. There are two legitimate senses of justice: one comes from the definition of the *eidos*, the other—from the state's courts and their decisions. There may be cases where what the courts qualify as just—for instance, sentencing a philosopher to death—will not be just in the light of the *eidos*. But—we may develop this argument—from the assumption that the immense asymmetry between the state and the citizen is "just" (51b6), one could infer a conclusion that it would be just from the point of view of the state to commit acts that, in the light of the *eidos*, were not just.

Under no circumstances could Socrates accept this claim, and the very idea that there might be two legitimate notions of justice, sometimes in conflict with each other, had no place in his philosophy. He would never say "this unjust decision of the court is just." But although Socrates should have categorically distanced himself from this consequence of the argument from inequality as well as from the argument itself, he never did. But on the other hand, he did not give it his full endorsement either.

The explanation of why Socrates refrained from an open disagreement seems to be the same as the explanation of why he did not reject the argument from education: in each, he must have found something that could not be easily dismissed. This time it is the existing asymmetry between the state and himself (or any other citizen), the asymmetry which had little to do with knowledge and virtue. Although his philosophy could not give a theoretical account of it, he himself must have found the authority of the state real and natural. If Socrates strictly followed his philosophy, he could limit himself to two of the strategies already described—avoidance of politics or envisaging true politics. But this would mean ignoring the problem, not solving it.

We know from his positive opinion about Sparta and Crete that Socrates mulled over a possible hierarchy where the criterion of virtue and knowledge did not play any significant part. The authority described by the Laws, allegedly denoting the Athenian polis, did not resemble Athens that Socrates criticized, with its democratic volatility and haphazardness. Socrates would probably prefer that the state curb these qualities and acquire more authority, whether in the Spartan or Cretan way or along the lines sketched by the Laws. But this preference could not find a satisfactory justification in his own philosophy.[30]

5.2.3 Tacit consent

(F) gives us a different kind of argumentation, this time focused on the tacit agreement. The transition from (E) to (F) occurs approximately at line 51d, although it is not well-defined. The arguments emerged gradually when the Laws ceased to speak about the commonwealth as parents, about

---

30   That the voice of the Laws of Athens might not be Socrates' *porte-parole*, but is a separate entity, is neither a standard nor a novel interpretation. A similar approach has been adopted by Young 1974, Brown 1992, Miller 1996, Harte 2005, and Weiss 2001. The most extreme interpretation was given by Weiss, who not only found the speech of the Laws to be contrary to Socrates' thought, but also spoke of the Laws with an aversion she could hardly conceal: "The Laws are oratorical bullies. Their declamations, their exaggerations, their disrespect for Socrates and their ominous threats make them unfit for the pedestal upon which many of the scholars who regard the Laws as Socrates' spokesmen seek to place them. The Laws jump from unfounded premises to wild conclusions, they fail to consider alternative explanations for phenomena they cite; and they are consumed with the single ideal of law. Their speech, analyzed without a predisposition to regard it as Socratic, is unworthy of admiration" (2001:133). After commencing with such an interpretation of the Laws, the whole issue of Socrates' duties toward his homeland, to which an important part of the *Crito* is dedicated, disappears from view.

birth, upbringing, and the godlike authority of the state and concentrated solely on the agreement or, to be precise, on Socrates' tacit consent.

The argument in this section proceeds as follows:

F_1. Athenian law provides that any citizen dissatisfied with its provisions or the state could at any time leave the city with his property and move elsewhere.

F_2. If, however, someone who was free to decide about himself and his property, "having first looked" at how the court resolved various matters and how the state was governed, then decided to stay, he accepted its political system and thus has established an agreement with the laws and the state, under which he was obliged to obey both.

F_3. There are "convincing proofs" that the laws and the state "were congenial" to him, and thereby he entered into an agreement with them; the proofs comprise the fact that he lived in the city for a long time, he was reluctant to leave it, he showed no interest in other states, and even refused the proffered penalty of exile at the trial; during his seventy years of life, he could have left a number of times if he had been unhappy and if he had considered the laws unacceptable (52c3–6).

F_4. The conclusion: escaping from prison would be a breach of Socrates' agreement with the state.

F_2 might be interpreted as a theoretical generalization of political conduct. It described a model situation in which a conscious citizen, after a careful analysis of how a given political system operates, decided to remain in the polis. By doing so, he tacitly consented to the system and its mechanisms, and thus accepted all the ensuing consequences. This should mean that Socrates understood that some actions of the state could be doubtful but he acquiesced to tolerate the system as long as those actions did not affect the overall assessment.

A lot of what the Laws say is common sense. If a citizen agrees to live in a democracy, he tacitly accepts certain procedures, for instance, that laws are passed, and decisions are made by a majority vote of eligible citizens or that he recognizes the verdicts handed down by the courts. Obviously, the citizen does not have to give his intellectual consent to every decision of the authorities or to every ruling by the court. The agreement is rather practical in nature: even though the decisions and judgments might be criticized or even rejected, the general evaluation of the principles and mechanisms of the political system continues to be positive.

It seems, however, that the Laws wanted Socrates to admit more than that. They wanted to show that Socrates' consent to the Athenian laws presupposed a particularly strong form of acceptance since he "dwelt here most consistently of all the Athenians" and, therefore, the city had to be "consistently pleasing" to him (52b3–4). The Laws might have added that not only did Socrates live in Athens and like it "consistently" (*diapherontōs*), but being a person known for his elenctic abilities and highly critical of people's views and conduct, he could not have spent his entire life in this particular polis if he did not find it ultimately acceptable.

Let us emphasize that Socrates is never quoted as saying that the Athenian state is just, nor did the Laws attribute this view to him. Their wording is cautious, either referring to emotions such as "being glad" or "congenial" or "like" (for all these using the verb *areskō*, meaning "to like"), or implying a presupposition on Socrates' part rather than an explicit admission.

But did Socrates really make an agreement with Athens in this form, and therefore with the obligations that the Laws want him to believe? Did he tacitly admit that the political system in which he lived was acceptable? The key material appears in F_3 (51e–52b), and it contains the following argument:

(a_1) whoever lives in a given state for a long time and has acquainted himself with its political system enters into an agreement with the state and undertakes to respect it;

(b_1) Socrates lived in Athens for a long time, meaning he found the Athenian state "congenial" and "consistently pleasing";

(c_1) *ergo*, Socrates agreed to enter into an agreement with Athens and to respect it.

It is easy to see that this argument (call it S_1) is seriously deficient because it does not say whether Socrates' opinion about Athens had any serious basis. Its correct version (S_2) should proceed as follows:

(a_2) whoever lives in a given state for a long time, having acquainted himself with its political system, enters into an agreement with the state and undertakes to respect it;

(b_2) Socrates, who had lived in Athens for seventy years, had enough time to acquaint himself with its political system and never intended to leave the country, which means (i) he liked it and (ii) decided that it was just;

(c_2) *ergo*, Socrates entered into an agreement with Athens and undertook to observe it.

As we can see, in (b_1), the Laws omitted an important part of the premise adopted in (a_1), which referred to a good recognition of the features of the political system in question.

A couple of lines below, the Laws formulated what looks like a correct version.

> "You are breaking the commitments and agreements that you made with us without compulsion or deceit, and under no pressure of time for deliberation. You have had seventy years during which you could have gone away if you did not like us, and if you thought our agreements unjust." (52d8–e5, Grube trans.)

This version (S_3) can be summarized as follows:

(a_3) whoever lives in a given state for a long time, having acquainted himself with its political system, enters into an agreement with the state and undertakes to respect it;

(b_3) Socrates, who had lived in Athens for seventy years, had enough time for "deliberation" and never intended to leave it, which means that (i) he liked it, and that (ii) his agreements with the polis did not appear to him unjust;

(c_3) *ergo*, Socrates entered into an agreement with Athens and undertook to respect it.

The difference between the three versions is clear. In the first version, S_1, the Laws say that because Socrates lived seventy years—"consistently"—in Athens, he must have "consistently" liked it and accepted its system. The second version, S_2, which corrects the first one, says that because Socrates lived seventy years in Athens, he had enough time to become acquainted with the system, and he must have concluded that he liked it and considered the system just. The last claim—the Athenian system was just—may be inferred from the fourth logos. The third version, S_3, differs from S_2 only in (b_3) where instead of "just," we have "not unjust." As one can see, the Laws weakened their position when they moved from (b_1) to (b_3).

If we look at the entire passage 52b1–53a7, we can see that the main verb the Laws used was *areskō*, and they used it six times, whereas the word "just" only once in the sentence quoted above. The emphasis is thus put on liking Athens, not on assuming Athens to be just. It would be, therefore, legitimate to call the tacit-consent argument an argument from liking or from being pleased. Justice did not appear until S_3 and in the very final part. But the transition from "I find x pleasing" to "I, therefore, find x just" is most dubious, no matter how "consistently" pleased I am.

"Pleasing," "liking," and "congeniality" do not and cannot be a part of Socrates' philosophy. They are even irreconcilable with the four *logoi* in the *Crito* or with any logos that would constitute the core of Socrates' theory of knowledge and virtue. And yet, the choice of point of departure of this argument—whether it be (a_1), (a_2), or (a_3)—is no trifling matter. The question is simple, and it is likely that Socrates was aware of it: did the fact that he lived his entire life in Athens have some moral significance and prove his endorsement, however qualified, of the polis, or was such a long presence in his homeland without any significance at all because he spent it by criticizing Athens and devoted his time either avoiding any involvement in Athenian politics, or theorizing the abstract concept of true politics, or complimenting Sparta and Crete for their good laws?

It seems that if Socrates was reflecting on this problem, he must have been aware that his own philosophy did not provide him with any grounds to opt for the first option. Interpreted rigorously, it could push him toward the second option, but he certainly showed no inclination to it. His attachment to Athens was real despite the fact that he could not give a theoretical account of it; after all, having good things to say about Sparta, Crete, Megara, and Thebes, he never contemplated moving to any of them.

5.2.4 Persuading the state

The Laws' speech, summarized in E and F, contains yet another way out of Socrates' predicament: to "persuade" the state. This strand appears twice in the dialogue, both in the discussion of the state as parents (point G) and of the tacit consent (point H).

The following passage comes from discussing the state as parents (G).

> "[Y]our country is to be honored more than your mother, your father and all your ancestors, that is more to be revered and more sacred, and it counts for more among the gods and sensible men, that you must worship it, yield to it and placate its anger more that your father's. You must persuade it or obey its orders and endure in silence whether it instructs you to endure, whether blows or bonds, and if it leads you into war to be wounded or killed, you must obey. To do so is right, and one must not give way or retreat or leave one's post, but both in war and in courts and everywhere else, one must obey the commands of one's city and country, or persuade it as to the nature of justice." (51a8–b7, Grube trans.)

In the passage, the possibility of persuasion is mentioned twice: first, without any qualifications, and second, with an additional piece of information—one "persuades [the state] as to the nature of justice."[31] In fact, this is the only piece of information in (G) that we have about persuading. But this information is important, and so is one particular consequence that follows from it.

31 Weiss argues that the closing sentence of the passage, "one must obey the commands of one's city and country, or persuade it as to the nature of justice" should be read differently. By changing the place of a comma we would have: "or persuade it, as is just by nature" (2001:106–07). The purpose of this modification is to emphasize the despotic nature of the Laws. To reinforce this interpretation, Weiss takes *peithein* to denote a rather peculiar way of persuasion: "entreat the fatherland by way of flattery or fawning in the hope of prevailing upon it either not to reach an unwelcome decision or to reverse that decision before it is too late" (104). This is an ingenuous interpretation, but such a caricatural view of the Laws would make Socrates' attentiveness to their arguments incomprehensible. Weiss maintains that the Laws are supposed to persuade Crito as to Socrates' decision and hence they use a language that he can understand; and the ultimate goal is to show Socrates who radically disagreed with Athens, and thus to confirm the image of the philosopher which, according to the author, is presented in the *Apology* (2001:146–69).

The phrase makes it clear that the Laws did not expect Socrates to be more active in the decision-making bodies and influence their practices through more efficient arguments or more eloquent rhetoric. The passage is quite explicit: the state should be persuaded "as to the nature of justice," not its specific manifestations. But this requirement was impossible to fulfill. Since the great asymmetry between the parental state and Socrates was just, to change the nature of justice meant to change this asymmetry by eliminating it, or making it less stringent, or replacing it with another one. This, however, would invalidate the concept of the parental state in the Laws' version.[32] Socrates arguing against its authority would be comparable to a son persuading his parents to give up their parental power.[33] The

32 In recent decades, commentators have shown the tendency to downplay the extent of obedience stipulated by Socrates in the *Crito*, which is usually justified by invoking the persuade-or-obey alternative (Woozley 1980; Kraut 1984:55–90; Reeve 1989:115–21; Vlastos 1996a; Ober 2011:148–63). Kraut's view—perhaps the most extreme—is that even in the case of unsuccessful attempts to persuade, under certain conditions the citizen may still refuse to obey the state. DeFilippo (1991) defends a slightly moderated version of this interpretation. Brickhouse and Smith represent another view: "Socrates can consistently require that the citizen never act unjustly and that the citizen never disobey the law even when the law itself is unjust and even where the citizen's actions in accordance with the law will produce injustice. The reason for this is that the responsible agent of injustice in such cases is the state, and not the citizen acting as the state's *offspring* or *slave*" (1994:153). The legalistic thesis that somebody who commits a wrongful act because his superior forced him is not only free of any responsibility for wrongdoing but can also reconcile it with his absolute obligation never to commit injustice is clearly at odds with everything Socrates ever stood for.

33 Kraut (1984:99) proposes an interesting interpretation in which the relation between children and parents concerns their adult sons rather than minors—adult children should also obey their parents, but their obedience has its limits. In the light of this interpretation, Socrates or any other citizen must obviously persuade the state, but given its inflexibility, he had the right to "justifiably disobey" it. Such an interpretation is difficult to reconcile with the text, which in no way reduces the asymmetry between the child and his father, or between the citizen and the state, since a reinforcing analogy is introduced between the slave and his master. With slavery, there can be no question of declaring disobedience. Bostock (2005:221–22) correctly argues this point against Kraut.

metaphor of strictly hierarchical family relations makes it rather implausible.[34]

There was yet another reason why persuading the parental state had no sense. Socrates could not use the main weapon that was at his disposal, that is, the *elenchus* and definitions. The parental state, as we remember, made the proviso that it had the power to define, through the courts, what counted and what did not count as justice, and demanded that these decisions be unconditionally respected. Such a stipulation—the imbrication of justice and injustice—rendered Socrates' mission impossible as it deprived the eidetic definition of any binding force and paradigmatic value. The emphasis was put on obedience to the state's justice, not to the *eidos* of justice. The power of *logoi*, in which Socrates believed, ceased to exist.

In this, the hypothetical parental state with its hyper-authority and the real Athenian democratic state with its volatility and haphazardness converged. Both resisted the *elenchus*, and both were reluctant to accept the eidetic definitions as the paradigms for human conduct. In both, the definitions were predominantly an expression of power—whether it is the power of the gods, leaders, *hoi polloi*, or the parental state. The real Athenian democracy presented itself as less monumental than the parental state. Socrates could at least argue with individual people and expect to make a difference to a small degree. Convincing the unified state, which reserved for itself the power to define justice, could never succeed.

Persuasion was mentioned again in the passage dealing with the agreement between Socrates and Athens and the former's tacit consent (point H).

> "The one who disobeys [the state] does wrong ... because, in spite of his agreement, he neither obeys us nor, if we do

34 The paramount position of the Laws also creates a problem and not a minor one. The unified homogeneous parental entity has a tremendous power, which might be benevolent, but it certainly does not have a communicative ability. It may have something like a collective mind, an internal entelechy and self-sustainable identity, but it cannot be a partner in an elenctic inquiry. If Socrates' view was that persuasion was possible only through *logos*, and *logos* presupposed the existence of a rational soul and a power of the individual intellect, then the parental state as lacking all these could not be persuaded.

something wrong, does he try to persuade us to do better. Yet we only propose things, we do not issue savage commands to do whatever we order; we give two alternatives, either to persuade us or to do what we say. He does neither." (51e4–52a3, Grube trans.)

The passage and the presuppositions of what it says are markedly different from the previous one. Previously, the Laws mentioned persuasion "as to the nature of justice," but now the Laws admit of persuasion if the state did "something wrong /mē kalōs" (51e7). While "kalōs" can mean many things, the failure to mention "justice" explicitly is significant.

When the Laws say Socrates could have persuaded the state whenever it did something wrong, they clearly meant specific problems rather than a fundamental change of law and the nature of justice. The tacit consent implied precisely that the citizen could respond to any activities that, in his view, deviated from what he believed to be the original provisions. Unlike the previous argument, where the parental godlike state did not bear much resemblance to the democratic Athens, this argument certainly applied to it. The Laws were right when they said that Athens offered Socrates a range of opportunities as it did to all its citizens, on whose involvement the shape of such a state depended. Hence, his limited concern for its affairs may be considered an aggravating circumstance, and his abstention—imprudent and unreasonable.

Did Socrates' activity count as an attempt to persuade the state whenever it did something wrong? No doubt, Socrates was more interested in the *eidos* of justice than in concrete legal or political problems. Both strategies—avoidance of politics and true politics—focused primarily on the epistemological and moral problems, and when they related to politics, for instance, in the concept of the just polis integrated by *homonoia* and *philia*, the conclusions were very general. It is true Socrates also made critical remarks about the concrete institutions, but those remarks were rather systemic than specific, for instance, about the majority rule and the role of flattery in democratic politics. It is true that occasionally he could be even more specific by reacting to very concrete decisions and regulations: he protested against the punishment of the fleet commanders returning from the naval battle of the Arginusae Islands and criticized the compensation for holding a public office. But this last type of persuasion was not typical of him.

If the Laws wanted Socrates to react to the state's wrong actions and, in this way, to persuade the polis, his philosophy was not the best tool. Socrates' distance from Athenian politics and his reluctance to be involved in the democratic (as well as oligarchic) system made this persuasion rather unlikely. This attitude, however, did not demonstrate his civic negligence but had a deeper reason that the Laws ignored.

Socrates explained this in the *Apology* when he pointed to a fundamental conflict between philosophy and politics and expressed his unwillingness to be involved in official politics. He said that if he had become involved, he would already have been killed (31d). His argument was that the man who cares for justice, as he did, is politically unacceptable because he stands in the way of political practices. The only way to survive is to adjust to those practices and behave like the rest. In the *Gorgias* (513b3–5)—it will be recalled—Socrates explained to Callicles how the latter's involvement in democratic politics serving the whims of *hoi polloi* would change him to the likeness of the Athenian demos.

From Socrates' perspective, the Laws' admonition that he should have persuaded the state whenever it did something wrong made little sense. The fact that the polis did a lot of things wrong resulted from the people's ignorance of basic moral concepts, and reacting to specific encroachments of justice did not affect the root cause and, additionally, carried the risk of adjusting to actual political practices. Socrates, therefore, was mostly pre-occupied with attacking this root cause and eschewing this risk. In both his strategies—avoiding politics and reflecting upon the true craft of politics—he engaged people in the search for the *eidē* of moral concepts and, at the same time, resisted the democratic logic of conformity, which, as he claimed, held in its grip both the leaders and the demos.

In some respects, the two kinds of persuasion—in the parental-state argument and the tacit-consent argument—converge and, in some ways, diverge. They converge because in both, persuading the state on Socrates' grounds is impossible. They diverge because each interprets the power of the state differently. In the parental-state argument, it was the Laws that attributed to the state an unusually high degree of power. In the tacit-consent argument it was Socrates who attributed a comparable degree of power to democratic politics. In both cases, the persuasion could not succeed because of this power—in the first argument, the persuasion as to the nature of justice failed; in the other, the persuasion as a corrective to specific encroachments failed. In both cases, the power made the persuasion futile, but in each for a different reason: the Laws presented this power as godlike and beneficial, Socrates—in his other dialogues—paints it as pernicious and ominous.

5.2.5 The Laws' concluding remarks and Socrates' final words

The last part of the Laws' speech (point I in the above reconstruction) seems unrelated directly to E, F, G, and H, with only marginal reference to the parental state, tacit consent, or persuasion.[35] But the overall message of their remarks is different and does not depend on this reference.

One can look at the Laws' concluding remarks in a variety of ways, but, perhaps, the best is to interpret them as justifying the inadmissibility of escape owing to its possible detrimental consequences, specifically for Socrates' friends who organized his escape; for Socrates, if he escaped to law-abiding countries; for Socrates, if he escaped to lawless countries; and for Socrates in the underworld.

What underlies the description of the first three sets of consequences is a division between law-abiding and lawless states. The division is being presented as if it were exhaustive and exclusive: Socrates was told that after he escaped, he could go to either of these.

Such a sharp division is, of course, simplistic and therefore dubious because the clear cases of each type—law-abiding and lawless—could be hard to find. Where should one put Athens, for example? The Laws, predictably, implied that Athens was a law-abiding polis. They said: "your friends will themselves be in danger of exile, disfranchisement, and loss of property" (53b1–3). Pointing out such consequences for those who broke the law by organizing the escape means that the Laws were indirectly portraying the Athenian system as effective, disciplined, and lawful.

But this is not the only indication concerning Athens in this respect.

35 There are only two such marginal references: one when the Laws call themselves Socrates' nurturers (54b2); and the other when they mention agreements and obligations (54c3).

A possible retaliation against Socrates' friends was touched upon in Crito's initial speech, but it was quickly dismissed as irrelevant. Crito mentioned the possibility that those who aided Socrates "should be compelled to lose all [their] property or pay heavy fines and suffer other punishment besides" (44e5–6) once betrayed by the sycophants (informers). But he immediately added, "Do you not see that those informers are cheap, and that not much money would be needed to deal with them?" (45a8–9, Grube trans.).

The overall impression from Crito's words would be that Athens was not a law-abiding polis. Given that such practices of dealing with the sycophants were tolerated and that it was fairly easy to avoid being charged and indicted for breaking the law, the Athenian system—in the light of the sharp division between the two types—should rather find itself together with Thessaly than with Crete and Sparta. As regards the accuracy of the description, Socrates would most certainly agree with his friend: everything he ever said about Athens suggests its closeness to the lawless rather than the law-abiding model. This obviously does not mean that he would have looked with a sympathetic eye at the behaviors that Crito condoned.

The discrepancy between the Laws' and Crito's assessments of Athens confirms Socrates' ambiguous attitude toward the Laws' arguments: while not criticizing them, he could not embrace them, either. We have another indirect indication of this ambiguity. Whatever strategies the Laws had undertaken so as to defend justice in the functioning of the state, whether in the form of a hierarchy in the parental state or as a presupposition of Socrates' tacit consent, they refrained from using the concept of justice in their final remarks about the law-abiding and lawless states. This omission seems noteworthy since one would expect this division to be a singularly suitable concept to be grounded in the idea of justice. To say that the hierarchy in the parental state is just, or that by staying in Athens Socrates made the presumption of justice is one thing, but to say explicitly that Athens was a law-abiding state and its system was based on justice is quite another. Socrates might have found some substance in the former, but under no circumstances could he have accepted the latter.

No wonder the Laws never made such a claim. What they did instead was to invoke the argument that in the preceding chapter we called traditionalist, appealing to honor, propriety and fear of disgrace. By going to the law-abiding or to the lawless states—whatever they were and regardless of how faithfully they represented either of those models—Socrates would have disgraced himself: he would have become "a laughing-stock" and "every person's toady and lackey"; he would have betrayed the ideas of virtue and goodness he had championed, and thus his entire conduct would have been ignominious (53c1–d1).

By employing this argument, the question of whether Athens was or was not a law-abiding polis or whether the organizers of Socrates' escape would have been duly punished as the law required vanish. Honor and disgrace retained their validity in every circumstance and enforced or prohibited certain types of actions, irrespective of the quality of the political system. But the use of the traditionalist argument was a new idea in the Laws' speech, and it neither grew out of the preceding parts of their speech nor in any way strengthened their arguments developed up to this point.

Justice did not appear until the very last part of the Laws' final remarks that mentioned the consequences for Socrates in the underworld, and the underworld was precisely the place where, as some of Socrates' statements indicate, he could imagine the ultimate or, at least, far more accurate assessment of his (and everybody's) conduct. The Laws excluded the possibility of any conflict between the two verdicts by expressing their kinship with the laws in Hades ("our brothers"). This alleged kinship was undoubtedly meant to increase their own importance, placing them closer to the divine and eternal, but somewhat arbitrarily. The Laws derived their authority primarily from the fourth logos, that is, from the concept of the just agreement, but what "the just" actually stood for was not and could not be in their authority. At least, this is what one can infer from Socrates' philosophy, and particularly from EID.

The Laws claimed to define justice only contextually: either in analogy to the family, or as a discretionary power of the courts, or as a presupposition of the citizen's tacit consent. What justice really meant in Socrates' terms, that is, what its *eidos* was, the Laws never explained or even tried to explain. Following the precepts of Socrates' philosophy, one can, therefore, say that since the Laws did not have a well-tested definition of justice, their use of the word "just" was not quite reliable, and, consequently, when they called the laws in Hades their brothers, they arrogated for themselves a higher status than that bestowed upon them by the fourth logos.

One can see the same tendency when the Laws admitted that Socrates was treated unjustly, but it was not themselves, but men that were to blame (54b5–c1). The distinction between the Laws, presumably guiltless, and the citizens who miscarried justice had not appeared so far, and there was no reason why it should have. For the tacit consent argument, this distinction was irrelevant. As regards the parental state argument, its logic excluded such a distinction: the parental power's control was so overwhelming that it left no room for the citizen's legitimate dissent unless, of course, this dissent was illegitimate and had to be condemned like an act of outrageous disobedience, such as Socrates' plan to escape from prison.

When in the last remark, the Laws mention justice and crown the entire speech with this concept, they invoke Socrates' philosophy rather than their own previous arguments. True, they mention "breaking compacts and agreements," but in the first place, they emphasize reacting with injustice to injustice and with wrong to wrong (54c2–3). In other words, they appeal to what is at the heart of SBT—the absolute ban on *adikein*. Socrates' escape from prison, should it happen, was definitely not an act of justice in any acceptable sense of the word. It would have been obviously a breach of the law and, as such, could clash with the principle of justice in particular because one could think of it, as Crito and then the Laws did, as an act of morally dubious retaliation against a clear act of injustice. And such a retaliation Socrates' philosophy prohibited and condemned.

So when in his final intervention, Socrates said that "these *logoi*" resounded in him and prevented him from hearing any other *logoi*, one may wonder what statements or arguments he had in mind. And the most plausible answer will be that he meant all those that presupposed or implied the absolute ban on *adikein*, those with respect to which Socrates knew no compromise and never really doubted. Therefore, the Laws' main arguments—those from the parental state and tacit consent—could not belong to that category of "these *logoi*," as their validity is limited.

As I said before, Socrates could not incorporate those arguments into his own philosophy because they blatantly contradict its main constituents. And yet he did not dismiss them, and the only reason he did not was that they touched upon certain aspects of his political life that he must have considered important and real—obligations to the state, a natural asymmetry between the state and the citizen, his attachment to the Athenian city—but which this philosophy could not justify on its own terms.

Chapter IV - Philosopher in Action

1. Philosopher and the city

One of several paradoxes that recur in Socrates' philosophy is the nature of his activity. He was an intellectual lone wolf and, at the same time, an eminent participant in public life. On the one hand, Socrates was extremely self-centered, as was congruent with his views that stressed the necessity of taking care of one's soul and following the path of justice. He was ready to defy all possible earthly (and not only earthly) authorities if they contradicted the sole authority that mattered to him—his rational soul and its elenctically tested *logoi*. On the other hand, he was ostentatiously other-directed, incessantly talking to people, occasionally annoying them, presenting himself to be on a god-given mission in the city of Athens. He could not express his philosophy but through participation in the life of the polis.

This paradox entails another concerning the relations between the philosopher and the city. What did he expect from the polis, and how did the polis receive his arguments? The question is not a sociological one but directly relates to the essence of his philosophy: it was the philosophy that sent a simple, clear, relentless, and uncompromising message about knowledge and virtue and, at the same time, left many problems undecided, open, postponed, seriously qualified, incomplete and insoluble.

Let us make a brief recapitulation to grasp the dynamics of his philosophy. It all started with the assumption that knowledge forms a system of propositions; otherwise, the *elenchus* would have made little sense. But then it turned out that Socrates focused on only a tiny part of a potentially comprehensive, almost all-encompassing system, and even that tiny part contained loopholes.

The unity of knowledge entailed the unity of the human person, which had a firm grounding in what he believed to be irrefutable truths. But to conceptualize this unity generated more problems: on the one hand, when consistently followed, it led to a model of moral perfection that was abstract and dry, turning into a sort of *eidos* incarnate, and on the other, it had to confront itself with two major obstacles—the existence of the irrational parts of human nature and the existence of evil. In both, Socrates had to make certain concessions, for instance, admitting the possibility of ineradicable evil in human nature and coupling his notion of virtue with the elements of traditionalist Homeric ethics.

Even more problems emerged with the concept of unity in politics. Theoretically, this seemed clear: the just polis was united by *homonoia* and *philia*, and good politics was true politics. But these notions were more hypothetical than real, just like the *eidos* incarnate, and the difficulties in establishing such a system seemed insurmountable—including the hegemonic anti-philosophical tendency of every political system, the democratic man with his haphazard thinking, *hoi polloi* with their volatility, bad leaders, ignorance, corruptive political practices, etc. Although Socrates thought there existed better poleis than the Athenian state, he never indicated that Sparta and Crete exemplified or approximated the true craft of politics.

And there were other complications: the Athenian state, bad as it was and with all the defects it had, required important duties and imposed loyalties that Socrates did not question. His attachment to this state—not to Sparta and Crete, not to the hypothetical good polis and true politics—was, despite severe criticism, an important political fact that did not allow him to place himself in an external position in the abstract world of the just order.

What is remarkable in Socrates is that all these criticisms, concessions, complications, admissions, and exemptions did not shake the certainty of his basic views—the validity of *elenchus*, the systemic nature of knowledge, basic moral theses (SBT), the notion of definition (EID), and true politics. How was it possible one may wonder. How could he retain his unswerving commitment to the strong—"iron and adamantine"—core of his philosophy and accept the distance between these core ideas and a vast body of aporias, counterarguments, and complications? How could he still believe in the unity, consistency and hierarchy of knowledge, human soul, and polis when what he managed to gather in his philosophical pursuits were only scraps and sketches? How could he—having only these scraps and sketches—set such incredibly high and rigorous standards for knowledge, soul, and polis that many found absurd and unnatural?

Socrates was credited with bringing philosophy closer to people and opening their minds to new and important problems that forever changed the perception of human life. Let us quote again Cicero's well-known statement that Socrates "was the first to call philosophy down from the heavens and to place it in cities, and even to introduce it into homes." Even if one feels inclined to agree with these words in a general sense, one must admit that Socrates had enormous troubles in reaching those "cities" and "homes," not only because his philosophy clashed with people's popular and allegedly self-evident opinions, but also because his philosophy was incomplete and fragmentary.

Achieving coherence in one's *logoi* with simultaneous elenctic probing was a never-ending task, generating new questions that people surrounding him were unaware of. Following those *logoi* was feasible for Socrates, though he paid for this consistency with his life, but it was hardly conceivable for people around him. One might be tempted to reverse Cicero's statement and say that Socrates' philosophy was not let into the cities and homes.

This problem started at his lifetime and culminated during the trial, which ended with the verdict of the Athenian jurors, and then the execution that followed. The debates about whether Socrates was or was not a corrupter of young men and a subverter of official religion continued after his death and persist today, although nowadays the list of Socrates' critics is conspicuously shorter. Of the two ancient writers who knew Socrates personally and left their testimonies and one who may have known him, only the latter, Aristophanes, portrayed him as a man of rather damaging influence on Athenian society. But Aristophanes' testimony should be treated with particular caution because the text is a comedy and makes lavish use of caricature and exaggeration. Xenophon's Socratic works—far more documentary or at least making this impression—give an unequivocal assessment: Socrates was innocent. He was a good loyal Athenian citizen, and both charges—corrupting the youth and not respecting the Athenian gods—were entirely unfounded.

Plato never really analyzed these charges or defended Socrates against his accusers. The only text we have is Socrates' own defense, whose genuineness is, of course, a matter of controversy. Plato was primarily interested in showing Socrates as a philosopher, but since his philosophy emerged through engaging other people in intellectual pursuits, it was essential to qualify the nature of this engagement. Was Socrates a teacher? This is the question the Athenians must have asked, and this question appears in Plato's dialogue more than once.

Obviously, the answer to this question relates to the indictment and his philosophy. If he was a teacher, did he teach the Athenians the right things or lead their minds astray? If he was not a teacher, then why all this public hyperactivity of his? When he refused to admit he was teaching, was it because he considered himself below the standards he set for human beings or because his philosophy was still incomplete and in the process of making? Or, perhaps, this peculiar mixture of uncompromising relentlessness in defending certain truths and the constant grappling with aporias made him reticent and, while undoubtedly having some educational consequences, he fell short of what his philosophy promised.

2. Irony

A part of the problem was that Socrates' *logoi* were uttered and argued for in a special atmosphere, which remains notoriously difficult to describe and employ cheekiness, uncertainty, distance, suspension of judgement, sometimes an apparent or actual change of mind, occasional ambiguity of Socrates' own position, contradictions that were difficult to unravel, and a mixture of mockery and seriousness. All this and much more is usually referred to as *eirōneia*, or "irony."[1]

1   My interpretation of Socratic irony differs from those of other scholars. Two of them, Friedländer (1973:137–53) and Vlastos (1991:21–44), are particularly well known in the literature. Friedländer identified two kinds of irony: Socratic and Platonic. The former manifests itself as simultaneous attraction and repulsion: attraction to knowledge and repulsion by demonstrating its weakness, deliberate concealment of one's own knowledge, and uncompromising disclosure of truth, whereas the latter, which grew out of the Socratic one, involves a special relationship—and Friedländer refers here to Friedrich Schlegel's distinction—between what is "unconditional" and what is "conditional," between a direct experience of the absolute and the imperfect way in which it can be expressed in words, with the imperfect and conditional words concealing the mystery of Platonic ideas. Vlastos claimed that Socratic irony differed both from the original meaning of the word, i.e., "deliberately meant to mislead," and from the later one, which is "to ridicule." The word meant,

Socrates' irony cannot be, obviously, limited to his flippant or half-serious remarks like those he made whenever he wanted to prevent his interlocutors from making long speeches (*makrologia*) and to engage them in his question-and-answer method (*Protagoras* 334e4–335c7; *Gorgias* 449b4–c8, 461d6–462b2). He explained that long speeches tired him, that he had other urgent things to do, so he could not waste his time listening to speeches, that his memory failed him, and thus he tended to forget the preceding portions of a long speech. Sometimes he threatened to end the conversation and leave if his condition was not accepted. These protestations did not sound serious. Socrates had a good memory and was able to retell long conversations full of minute details and complex arguments. Likewise, no urgent matters were likely to draw him away from his conversations, which were, after all, his main preoccupation. Indeed, Socrates himself indulged in making the odd long speech. Socrates' irony covers far more than that, and its ultimate meaning is far from obvious.

2.1 Self-deprecation

The meaning of the word "irony" has been subject to debate. The classical definition is Quintillian's formula *contrarium ei quod dicitur intelligendum est* (*Institutio Oratoria* IX.2.44). To elaborate on this, we can say that irony consists in saying things that stand in opposition to what is believed to be true while, at the same time, signaling a subtle difference between the statement explicitly made and that which is held to be true by the speaker. Irony, therefore, borders on a lie and yet is not a lie because it contains a hidden

---

or rather disguised, the kind of riddles told by Socrates, which touched upon the most important issues for man; they required his interlocutors to make an independent effort to unravel them; hence, they assumed something akin to the moral autonomy of man. These interpretations differ in many respects, but one of them seems significant to me: Friedländer perceived Socrates as someone who cognitively dominates others, whereas Vlastos emphasized a certain kind of egalitarianism in the relationships between the philosopher and his interlocutors, an anticipation of the conception of human moral autonomy. My position is closer to Friedländer's in this respect. With Vlastos, I agree that Socrates' irony may sometimes contain riddles (as in the case of Alcibiades I discuss in the subsequent pages). On the evolution of the concept of *eirōneia* see Lane (2006).

sign pointing to the truth, albeit one which is discernible to the trained ear and eye. This association of irony with truth and falsehood may have been the reason why Aristotle mentioned Socratic irony in his *Nicomachean Ethics* in a passage that deals with truthfulness. To make the picture more complete, let us add that an ironic statement does not have to represent a simple reversal of the opinion held by the speaker (for example, calling a fool a wise man)—the trail leading from one to the other may be more complex, having several referential layers.

Socrates was occasionally an ironist in the simple, straightforward sense. He good-naturedly mocked his interlocutors, famous people, and even entire nations. He generously acknowledged Euthyphro as possessing the virtue of wisdom, though the latter was a man of limited mental capacity, which was confirmed repeatedly throughout the dialogue (3d5–6). In his conversation with Meno, he delivered mock praise of Gorgias and even warmly honored the Thessalians, though it is clear that he did not hold their philosophical potential in high esteem (70a5–c3).

Why, then, did Socrates ironize? One of the answers was given by Aristotle in the mentioned passage from the *Nicomachean Ethics*:

> "Self-deprecators (*hoi eirōnes*) underestimate themselves in what they say, and so appear to have more refined characters. For they seem to be avoiding bombast, not looking for profit, in what they say; and the qualities that win reputation are the ones that these people especially disavow, as Socrates also used to do." (1127b22–26, Irwin trans.)

Aristotle said, in other words, that as an *eirōn*, Socrates demonstrated a certain nobility of character because by diminishing his position, he showed how little he cared for reputation and how much he avoided "bombast."

It should be noted, however, that sometimes "self-deprecation" may be a double-edged instrument: one may deprecate oneself by exaggerating the good qualities of one's interlocutor, and when this exaggeration goes too far, it turns into an overt mockery: the ironist then deprecates the interlocutor, not himself. This is the case in the *Greater Hippias*, where Socrates used irony to ridicule the eponymous sophist, a singularly pompous man, rather than to hide his dominant position. And since Hippias failed to notice the edge of Socrates' language and indulged in uncontrolled bragging, the dialogue can be seen as a display of spitefulness on Socrates' part.[2] The *Greater Hippias*, however, is an exception. In other dialogues, Socrates' attitude toward his interlocutors is more toned-down.

Aristotle was right to the extent that, indeed, Socrates occasionally belittled his position, but it would be wrong to claim that this was his persistent demeanor. And yet these occasional gestures, even if somewhat theatrical, were important. If it were not for them, Socrates would have presented himself—despite the dexterity of his argumentative art—in a rather unfavorable light. The question-and-answer method—let us repeat—assumed the dominance of the person who asked questions. Thus it was easy for Socrates, who was in control of conversation, to give the impression that he intended to gain an advantage from it or that he desired personal popularity. If Socrates wanted to avoid giving that impression, it was natural for him to distance himself to a certain extent from his role in the conversation and dispel the suspicion of his less-than-noble intentions. Whether this was a matter of tactics or, as Aristotle said, it stemmed from his "refined character" seems a minor point; probably both reasons mattered to some extent.

Avoiding "bombast" could also have something to do with Socrates' separating himself from the sophists, among whom self-promotion appeared to be quite common (at least according to Plato's testimony). From the available descriptions, such as a meeting at Callias' house from the *Protagoras*, we can infer that Socrates must have found the ostentatiousness of the sophists irritating and probably embarrassing too. Contrasted with their conduct, his own might look self-deprecating, but one fairly easily perceives that beneath them at the bottom, there was also a sense of superiority: he knew on the basis of his theory of knowledge that a lot of this sophistic show-off was spurious.

The self-deprecating attitude is, therefore, only a part of the story and not the most important one at that. Socrates would belittle his position by changing the language of conversation so that the interlocutors did not feel

---

2   Perhaps the most radical interpretation comes from Theophrastus who in his
     Characters defined irony as "a dissimulation with an intention to make things
     worse" (*prospoiēsis epi to cheiron*).

alienated or humiliated, and the process of questions-and-answers could continue. This did not mean that he undermined the value of what he said, even if he emphasized his lack of knowledge. And it happened that his ignorance was not really ignorance but an important insight. When in the *Apology* Socrates talked about a vast distance between human wisdom and divine wisdom and that he alone of all fellow citizens was aware of it and therefore deserved to be called a wise man, there was little self-deprecation in his words. Nor did it seem to disavow the "qualities that win reputation."

The narrative surrounding Socrates' questioning the most important groups in Athenian society can be anything but self-deprecation. When he came to the conclusion that the entire society suffers from fundamental ignorance and refuses to admit the miserable state of their knowledge, he clearly— by making such a diagnosis—not only showed no sign of humility but, on the contrary, put himself in the position of superiority. The fact that he said that the difference between the Athenians' knowledge and his own was about "this one little thing" (21d6) did not diminish his dominant position.

As regards the propositions and imperatives that constituted the core of his theory, there was no question of any self-effacement or disavowal. What the theory stated was non-negotiable and unshakable. Also, Socrates described his own position on these matters in terms that excluded any hesitancy, uncertainty, or a tactical game. He said he had never treated anyone unjustly, at least not intentionally (*Apology* 37a3–4, b2–3) and that the only authority for him were the *logoi* that, upon reflection, he found best (*Crito* 46b3–7). While it is true that he did not use the strong affirmative form— "I am a just man" and "I always follow the truth"—this resulted from epistemological precision, not from skepticism or ambivalence.

Whether Socrates' irony in the above sense derived from a tactical game or, as Aristotle maintained, was proof of his noble character, the jurors did not find any redeeming feature in his conduct and failed to notice any self-deprecation, real or pretended. On the contrary, they found him adamant and raised clamor in reaction to his words, considering them "boastful" (*mega legein*); at least, this is how Socrates interpreted their indignation (20e3–4). Moreover, it was not a passing impression they experienced during the trial, but many felt it over a long period of time (18b3–d2).

"Self-deprecation" is a good rendering of what Aristotle found in *eirōneia*, but in no way does it correspond to what Socrates was doing and saying. Socrates—let us emphasize—never used the word "irony" in relation to himself (unless quoting others' opinions of him). The term appeared solely in his interlocutors' statements but never in the Aristotelian sense. Therefore, whatever Socratic irony may have been, it resulted primarily from the way in which witnesses interpreted his conversations and his arguments. In this—let us repeat—the problem of bombast vs. self-deprecation did not play a significant role.[3]

2.2 Not speaking seriously

We have few instances of the word "irony" and its derivatives in Plato's dialogues, and in all of them it expressed the interlocutors' doubts whether Socrates was speaking seriously. They suspected his moral views were so extravagant or extreme that no person could accept them in earnest. A good example comes from the *Apology*, where Socrates explains that he was on the god's mission and could not abandon his pursuit of philosophy.

> "Now this is the most difficult point on which to convince some of you. If I say that it is impossible for me to keep quiet because that means disobeying the god, you will not believe me and will think I am being ironical (*eirōneuomenō*). On the other hand, if I say that it is the greatest good for a man to discuss virtue every day and those other things about which you hear me conversing and testing myself and others, for the unexamined life is not worth living for men, you will believe me even less. What I say is true, gentlemen, but it is not easy to convince you." (37e4–38a8, Grube trans.)

This statement is genuinely perplexing: Socrates, at the very end of his life, admitted that people did not believe in his words, even the most important ones about the divine mission and virtue because they thought he was not being serious. The word "irony" thus reflected the mistrust of the society at large or at least uncertainty as to whether Socrates actually meant what he was saying. They might have suspected that he had been distancing

3   For a different view, see Lane 2011.

himself from his words. This led to a disturbing conclusion. If irony is a deliberate aspect of Socrates' method, then in educational terms, the method would be self-defeating: instead of bolstering his own teachings, Socrates undermined them.

The problem was a chasm that separated the views of Socrates and those of *hoi polloi*. Socrates was fully aware of it and knew that his proposed path was so difficult that it was impossible to convey its significance to the vast majority of people. He explained to Crito, "For I know that only a few people hold this view or will hold it, and there is no common ground between those who hold this view and those who do not, but they inevitably despise each other's views" (49d1–5, Grube trans.).[4] It may then very well be that what the interlocutors perceived as his irony resulted from his awareness that, by and large, there was little chance his arguments would genuinely reach the minds of the people.

Whether this really affected his way of talking to people, we cannot know. What is better documented is how Socrates' *logoi* generated his interlocutors' suspicion of irony. Some of them who made such an accusation did not really free themselves from the thought that, after all, he might have meant what he said, which made their mental situation even more complicated. We have two such examples—one in the *Gorgias*, the other in the *Republic I*.

In the *Gorgias*, it was Callicles who accused Socrates of being ironic when they discussed whether the laws imposed by the "strong" were good laws, in other words, whether, in essence, "stronger" meant the same as "better." Naturally, the definition of "strong" proved to be problematic. Irritated by the inquisitive questions, Callicles retorted that a powerful man was not the same as a physically strong man: a band of strong slaves could defeat one powerful man, but that did not make them powerful. Socrates said then, "Tell me once more from the beginning, what *do* you mean by the *better*, seeing that it's not the stronger? And, my wonderful man, go easier on me in your teaching, so that I won't quit your school." Callicles responded, "You're being *ironic*, Socrates" (489d5–e3, Zeyl trans.).

Callicles was certainly irritated by Socrates' composure. The philosopher remained unmoved by his previous numerous aggressive statements.

---

4   *Cf. Gorgias* 508d6–509a7.

But the main reason was something else. Callicles believed that Socrates questioned the obvious, introduced unnecessary conceptual distinctions, exploited verbal ambiguities, and did all this in order to discredit his interlocutors' arguments. "Tell me, Socrates, aren't you ashamed, at your age, of trying to catch people's words and of making hay out of someone's tripping on a phrase? And consider it a divine gift?" (489b7–c1, Zeyl trans.). Socrates not only did so but also led his interlocutor in a direction that the latter was most reluctant to follow. In Callicles' case, it was the proposition that it is better to suffer injustice than to perpetrate it. Callicles attacked it with all his impetus, but the precision of Socrates' questions made it increasingly difficult for him to defend his position, and he probably felt that further refinements of the concept were pushing him in a direction he did not like. That is why Socrates' request for Callicles to explain the meaning of the word "better" irritated him. The accusation of "irony" was supposed to repudiate the Socratic method, but at the same time, it indirectly acknowledged its effectiveness. Callicles suggested that Socrates used frivolous tricks, but in fact, it was himself who was afraid of the power of the philosopher's reasoning.

A similar psychological context one can find in Book I of the *Republic* during the conversation on justice. At one point, Thrasymachus, upset at the course of events, accused Socrates that his method permitted one to refrain from giving an answer: by asking questions, Socrates confused people and challenged the proposed definitions but said nothing positive himself. Thrasymachus demanded that Socrates no longer asked questions but replied to the question concerning justice.

Socrates replied that if the object of the search was a gold coin, the seekers would not give up the search. But the object pursued in the discussion is much more valuable, namely justice. The interlocutors were timid not because they disregarded what was being discussed but, on the contrary, because they wanted to be as accurate and faithful as possible in conveying the essence of the concept. If that made them look awkward and insecure, they deserved compassion rather than Thrasymachus' anger. In response, Thrasymachus said gleefully, "[…] that's just Socrates' usual *irony*. I knew, and I said so to these people earlier, that you'd be unwilling to answer and that, if someone questioned you, you'd be *ironical* and do anything rather than give an answer" (337a4–7, Grube trans.).

Thrasymachus used the word "irony" to refer to Socrates' previous statement, which was supposed to disguise his unwillingness to respond, but it is not quite certain which part of the statement Thrasymachus considered ironic. The following thoughts are mentioned in the passage:

(i)   justice is more valuable than gold and cannot be searched for with selfish reasons;
(ii) the people engaged in conversation intended to find the most fundamental sense of justice;
(iii) even though they may have been clumsy in their search, they deserve sympathy, not anger, on the part of the more adept ones.

Of these three statements, the last one is ironic in Quintillian's sense. Socrates said that there were intellectually inept people, like himself and his interlocutors, and intellectually competent people, like Thrasymachus; if the former encountered problems in their reasoning, then Thrasymachus and his ilk should—as intelligent people usually do when dealing with the dull ones—demonstrate tolerance based on sympathy. In fact, Socrates did not consider himself to be dull, and neither did he consider Thrasymachus to be an eminently intelligent person. The mention of compassion should be understood as an instance of spite, showing that Thrasymachus failed to understand how important the conversation actually was.

The first two statements are definitely not ironic in Quintilian's sense. They both reflect accurately Socrates' attitude, which was profoundly serious. He believed that he was looking for the essential meaning of moral concepts and that his occupation—a selfless search of truth—was of utmost importance. It seems that both statements irritated Thrasymachus, and they irritated him because they immediately set the matter on the abstract conceptual level and thereby opened a possibility of a long series of the elenctic inquiries in which Socrates was extremely skillful.

Thrasymachus' outbreak about Socrates' irony marked his entry into the conversation. Until now, he had been a silent bystander listening to the exchange of arguments with increasing irritation, and then he burst out: "What balderdash is this that you have been talking, and why do you Simple Simons truckle and give way to one another?" (336b6–c1). And he "forbade" Socrates (337c6) to define justice by an abstract term: "don't you be telling me that it is that which ought to be, or the beneficial or the profitable or the gainful or the advantageous, but express clearly and precisely whatever you say" (336c5–d2).

For Thrasymachus, the irony did not limit itself to the mere fact that Socrates was not speaking seriously. It was precisely that kind of not speaking seriously that Thrasymachus felt compelled to "forbid." Undoubtedly, he was convinced that Socrates' theoretical ruminations on the essence of justice were "balderdash" and that they so dramatically deviated from the obvious that no sensible person could accept them. Thrasymachus considered his concept of justice so simple and self-evident—in fact, "most excellent" (338a6)—that no further examination was necessary. When he proudly came up with his own definition—"the advantage of the stronger" (338c1)—he paid no attention that he himself used the abstract term "advantageous," one of these terms he explicitly forbade Socrates to select as a *definiens*.

But Thrasymachus must have suspected that the conversation was bound to blur the obvious meaning of the concept of justice, and the subsequent distinctions would be moving the interlocutors further away from it. He seemed scornful of the Socratic method, which made the obvious obscure, yet on the other hand, he could not help but be impressed by its power over the minds of the interlocutors who had been forced to accept the arguments, often against their intentions. Indeed, in the course of the conversation, he gave up his notion of justice and started talking of justice in a more or less standard sense. His own definition, as was explained in Chapter 2 (2.1), no longer resisted the elenctic analysis as it was intrinsically flawed. Under such circumstances, he had to surrender to the philosopher and gradually give up what he thought obvious, simple, and "most excellent," while at the same time dismissing the counter-arguments as manifestations of Socratic irony.

When in the *Apology* Socrates said that the Athenians questioned his seriousness and doubted whether he really meant what he was saying and called it irony on his part, he implied that they really dismissed his teaching. It is quite probable that this was a common attitude among the Athenians, reducing Socrates to an eccentric of the type we could see in Aristophanes' *Clouds*. On the other hand, there was a strong negative reaction to Socrates, also quite common, and it resulted in the "slander" of the first accusers

(*Apology* 20d), the hatred by the politicians (21e), and probably by the poets and artisans. During the trial, the crowd reacted with anger to his words several times. Whether these were the same people who had called Socrates an ironist for not speaking seriously, we do not know. But definitely, the word "irony," which they used to describe his views, had some connection with this negative reaction.

Nowhere was it more evident than in the reactions of Callicles and Thrasymachus, who both used the word "irony" as an expression of anger toward Socrates and his *elenchus*. But the anger belied their words. If they had thought Socrates was playing with them, they would have answered in kind. But they did their best to refute Socrates' propositions.

2.3 Serious playfulness

There is another example of Socrates' alleged irony, also in the sense of not being serious, but the situation is markedly different. The example comes from Plato's *Symposium* in the passage in which the drunken Alcibiades was reminiscing about his courtship of Socrates. Alcibiades, then a handsome and promising young man, had been impressed by Socrates and thought that he could seduce him. This seduction, of course, was homosexual, although Alcibiades made it clear that his fascination with the philosopher ran much deeper. Apart from the prospect of physical gratification, Alcibiades also had other plans: he believed that by becoming Socrates' lover, he would acquire some of his wisdom, and Socrates would teach him "everything that he knew" (217a2–5).

The main point in Alcibiades' speech was that he believed himself to be the only person who had discovered the key to the enigmatic nature of Socrates and the insight he intended to reveal to other banqueteers (216c7–d1). As might be expected, this smug assertion promised more than Alcibiades could deliver. In a nutshell, this key was very simple: "things are exactly the opposite of what he [Socrates] was saying" (214d1–2). To be precise, this sentence referred to the preceding parts of the conversation but considering that Alcibiades had not been then present and could not have had any idea of what Socrates was saying, the implication must be that this was how he generally approached Socrates' words.

Later, it turned out that he had in mind only two things—Socrates' declaration of ignorance and his erotic passion for good-looking young men

(216d1–4). And Alcibiades knew better. He knew that Socrates was a man full of wisdom and that he mastered *sōphrosynē* to the degree that made him indifferent to the erotic charm of young men. "He believes"—Alcibiades continued—"that all these possessions are worth nothing and that we are nothing, I tell you, and all his life he keeps on being *ironical* and playful to human beings. And when he is in earnest and opened up, I do not know if anyone has seen the images within" (216e2–7, Benardete trans.).

Alcibiades' interpretation of irony in this statement was thus quite simple and exemplifies Quintillian's definition: when Socrates said A, he really means non-A. Socrates liked to talk about chasing good-looking young men while he was, in fact, self-disciplined, not interested in their beautiful bodies; he would often talk about not knowing anything, but he was a man full of wisdom. So, Alcibiades agreed with the Athenians that Socrates did not mean what he was saying but did not agree with them about what he was not serious about. They tended to question some of his moral teachings; Alcibiades did not (222a).

This key to understanding Socrates was obviously very imperfect, and Alcibiades, a rather conceited young man, deluded himself by making this claim. Socrates' attitude, which the Athenians called ironic, could not be reduced to a simple reversal of truth and falsehood. It would mean that Socrates hid his thoughts behind an easily deciphered rhetorical trick. But we know he was often quite explicit and unmistakably serious.

But there is another passage containing the word *irony*, more difficult to interpret, in drunken Alcibiades' reminiscences (218c7–219b1), and it refers directly to the offer Alcibiades made to Socrates. The offer consisted of three parts. First, Alcibiades would become his lover. Second, Socrates would use Alcibiades' wealth and social influence in return. Third, thanks to the philosopher's inspiration, Alcibiades would become "the best man he can be." To reduce it to the barest facts, Alcibiades offered Socrates sex, wealth, and influence in exchange for virtue. It does not take a great insight to conclude that, in Socratic terms, such an offer could not have been accepted: virtue was not a commodity to be sold or traded for profit, and whoever thought otherwise certainly did not hold much promise in terms of a prospective virtue.

Socrates' negative reply, which Alcibiades called "ironic" (218d6), contained two arguments, one clearly stated, the other implied. (1) If Alcibiades correctly perceived Socrates as possessed of great moral beauty, his offer—sex, wealth, and influence in exchange for virtue—would be grossly unfair; Alcibiades wanted to obtain something extremely valuable like virtue and truth and pay for them with something manifestly less valuable like sexual pleasure and wealth.

Then comes the beginning of the other argument, which is not finished, but starts with the possibility that Alcibiades misjudged Socrates. "I may be nothing"—said Socrates—and this "nothing" Alcibiades might have missed because in him as in every young man the sharpness of the eyesight surpassed the sharpness of the intellect: "Thought begins ... to have keen eyesight when the sight of the eyes starts to decline from its peak" (219a2–4, Benardete trans.). The other argument, when completed, would sound like this. (2) If Alcibiades, at that time an inexperienced young man easily falling into various ill-chosen fascinations, was wrong in his assessment of Socrates, then the offer was clearly disadvantageous to Alcibiades as Socrates was incapable of delivering the goods he desired.

Why Alcibiades called Socrates' reply ironic, we may guess. Probably—and this is the simplest explanation—because the reply was indirect, seemingly ambiguous, and composed of two apparently contradictory claims. All this Alcibiades interpreted as a rejection of his offer, disguised in the form of playfulness. And for this rejection, he bore Socrates a grudge for committing "an outrage" against him (*hybrisen*—222a8). He said as a rebuke that his was not an isolated case, but Socrates attracted and ultimately rejected "Charmides the son of Glaucon, Euthydemus the son of Diocles, and many, many others" (222b1–3).

What Alcibiades perceived here as irony was partly similar to and partly different from what Thrasymachus and Callicles took for irony. It is different because in the case of Thrasymachus and Callicles, the point of controversy among them is philosophical, whereas in the case of Alcibiades philosophy intermingled with a question of love and seduction. But both cases were also similar as all three men resented Socrates' playing with logic and arguments, and all three found this both repellent and enticing. But then the difference was that in Thrasymachus and Callicles, this generated anger, whereas Alcibiades treated it as a part of courtship. After being rejected, he seemingly declared the matter closed from his side, leaving the ultimate decision to Socrates, but then slipped under Socrates' blanket, threw his arms around him, and "lay down beside him the whole night" (219a–b). The erotic ruse, obviously, did not help.

If we are to believe Alcibiades, many young people treated Socrates' irony as intellectual-erotic playfulness of the kind described in the *Symposium* incident and let themselves be involved in the game. This must have also greatly increased Socrates' attraction among young men. Such a hypothesis seems quite plausible but not interesting philosophically. But what is more important—once we take Alcibiades' case as symptomatic—is that for Socrates, even if it were a game, it is a serious game, and intellectual rather than erotic.

Neither of the two supposedly ironic arguments (1) and (2) is ironic or paradoxical. Had Alcibiades been less interested in seducing Socrates and reflected more on his words, he would have found in them some truth about himself and not an ironic invitation to courtship. The mistake he made was that he assumed two pictures of Socrates—(i) a man of superb virtue and wisdom and (ii) a man whom a young, handsome, and intelligent man might seduce and then gratify him with wealth and power in reward. In argument (1), the antecedent takes (i), while in argument (2), the antecedent takes (ii). Socrates was known for his disdain not only for wealth (which Alcibiades knew very well), but for the new practice of teaching for money. If Socrates had accepted Alcibiades' offer, he would have confirmed (ii) and contradicted (i).

Socrates then used a typical elenctic device and confronted Alcibiades with the contradictory assumptions inherent in his own statements. It was a sort of puzzle, but such that with a certain amount of curiosity and inquisitiveness, Alcibiades could have discerned and solved. Had he done this—who knows?—one might speculate and imagine that this would have made him more open to Socrates' moral influence. Certainly, this would have impressed Socrates much more than slipping under the latter's blanket, putting an arm around him, and lying down beside him the whole night.

3. The educational value of the *elenchus*

Those few passages in which the word *irony* occurs give us a somewhat disturbing picture of the relations between the philosopher and the polis. What separated the two sides was not just mistrust. Those who thought that "Socrates was not speaking seriously" did not really express condescension or derision toward him as a person and toward his moral teaching. On the contrary, they intuitively felt that Socrates' *logoi* had some power that they resisted or, as in the case of Alcibiades, failed to comprehend. This showed that the *elenchus* undoubtedly had some educational value, although, eventually, it did not succeed.

It is clear that Thrasymachus and Callicles, though carried by Socrates' arguments against their will, as it were, had no intention to re-examine and revise their basic moral assumptions. Ultimately it was Socrates who seized this opportunity and continued his elenctic inquiries, as his concept of knowledge required him to do. Alcibiades, who seemed to grasp more of what Socrates represented, did not even try to reflect on the paradox that he found in Socrates' reply and therefore did not see his own moral weakness. Again, throughout it is only Socrates who has a full understanding of the situation.

All this points to a straightforward question. Did the *elenchus* educate people, or did it not? The answer is not easy, and we have conflicting testimonies on this point. In the *Theaetetus*, we find a passage that unequivocally suggests that Socrates' activity was an educational success even if Socrates himself denied being a teacher and the people around him were not disciples in the usual sense of the word. The passage in question appears in the part of the *Theaetetus* (150c–151c) where Socrates talks about his intellectual midwifery and the *daimonion*. The subject induces Socrates to identify various groups of young people according to their abilities, which he described using the metaphor of pregnancy, birth, and child rearing.

He mentioned four or five such groups. Some of those people brought forth to light "a multitude of beautiful things" and made progress that was "amazing." Others left Socrates disappointed by what he had to offer and "neglected the children" he helped them to bring forth; they wasted all the knowledge they possessed and fell into bad company with sadly predictable consequences. Some did not seem to Socrates to be pregnant at all; those people with weak intellects tended to associate themselves with the sophists. And finally, there were those who initially left Socrates but later decided to come back. And among these Socrates made a selection depending on the *daimonion*. "[T]hey come back, wanting my company again, and ready to move heaven and earth to get it. ... [I]n some cases the divine sign that visits me forbids me to associate with them; in others, it permits me, and then they begin again to make progress" (150e7–151a5, Levett, Burnyeat trans.).

The whole passage aims to prove Socrates' point that he did not teach those young men—allegedly having no knowledge himself—but only played the role of an accoucheur of the knowledge they had in themselves. As already indicated in the previous parts of the book, neither of the premises is true, at least not true literally: Socrates did have some knowledge, and not a negligible amount, and his supposed midwifery was essentially the *elenchus* that required a dominant position of the person who asked questions and steered the argumentation. In the passage, Socrates avoided using such words as "teach," "learn," "disciple," and preferred to talk about those who "associated" with him (*syneinai*) and "made progress" (*epididoasi*).

But whatever his choice of words, the passage unmistakably tells us that some kind of education was conducted and that Socrates had a leading part in it: it was around him that the young people gathered with a clear intention to learn something, and he distinguished between them and assessed their competences. He even rejected some of those young men, and while the acceptance or rejection he attributed to the decision of the *daimonion*, no supranatural force was necessary. Every good teacher can distinguish—based on his contacts with the students—between those who are likely "to make progress" and those who are not. This, obviously, does not exclude occasional bad judgments. If we trust the *Alcibiades I*, Socrates long resisted taking back Alcibiades before finally relenting. The life of this famous Athenian was, however, a series of moral failures rather than advancements; he certainly did not "make progress."

In some respects, the difference between this passage and the *Symposium* excerpt surrounding irony is not as great as it might seem. Whether Socrates refused to teach, or denied being a teacher, or was teaching only indirectly by letting young people associate with him, he rejected any suggestion that the result of his contacts with a young man would be a finished product such as a virtuous man, a true politician, or a man of wisdom. Alcibiades, in the *Symposium*, made this error and treated Socrates as if he was a sophist whom one might pay for the education on demand.

If we remember what Socrates sets forth about knowledge and virtue, it becomes clear that he could not accept such a role. It is true that knowledge is a system, but this did not mean that it could be taught like Euclid's geometry. Knowledge is also a process that requires constant activity and the training of the mind. Even such obvious concepts—at least obvious within Socrates' theory—like the unity of virtue, when subjected to the *elenchus*, did not bring an entirely satisfactory result.

Even those concepts that seemed simple and clear, such as an absolute ban on *adikein*, were difficult not only in practice, but also in theory. They derived from such a view of human nature and such an ideal of human life that presupposed a profound intellectual reorientation of anyone who intended to take this precept seriously. And this reorientation required a constant reflection on one's life, as Socrates kept reminding his interlocutors.

But there is something in the *Theaetetus* passage that is not easy to reconcile with what we read in the *Symposium* and other places. The passage clearly tells us that quite a lot of Socrates' associates "made progress," and sometimes this progress was "amazing." There are at least two problems with these statements. The first problem is that the language suggests some kind of improvement on the part of the young men. Socrates might have refused to call it teaching, but it is of no import. The facts are that Socrates admitted that those men did improve and that they improved when being exposed to his elenctic activity. Socrates could thus take some credit for this process, if only as an accoucheur. Moreover, if he could take credit for those young men who made progress, he also should have been responsible for the misdeeds of those whom he failed to turn away when appropriate.

The second problem with this passage is that no names of the successful young men are mentioned, which substantially weakens its credibility. It is striking that Socrates mentioned those who abandoned him, dissatisfied with his company,[5] but never gave names of those who could testify to his success. The truth is that hardly ever do we encounter in Plato's dialogues the persons who match the description in the *Theaetetus*. From Socrates' perspective, it would have been rational to provide some positive examples, not necessarily to defend himself against the charges raised against him but to prove the power of the *elenchus*. Even if he had been only an accoucheur, the successful delivery would have been a memorable event, especially when what those young people brought forth to light was "a multitude of beautiful things"

5   "Aristides the son of Lysimachus; and ...very many others" (151a1–2).

and their progress was "amazing." But we do not meet a single one of those beautiful things, nor hear the names of those who brought them to light.

In one of the scenes of the *Euthydemus*, Plato has Socrates converse with a young man, Clinias,[6] in order to demonstrate to the two sophists who were present his own methods of encouraging young minds to seek knowledge. In the ensuing conversation, Socrates attempted to prove that knowledge helped people to live their lives more fully and ultimately to achieve happiness. Clinias obediently followed the course of the conversation, understood the questions he was asked, agreed with the conclusion, and was praised for his earnestness along the way. We know nothing about what later became of him. But it is unlikely that this conversation put his life on a Socratic path. Was he, among others, that Socrates had in mind when he talked about the young men making progress? Certainly, Socrates did not mean Crito or Clitophon. He may have meant Chaerophon, but the latter was Socrates' contemporary and thus did not count among his young associates. None of the men present at Socrates' death had been noted by Plato for "amazing progress" in virtue or knowledge. It, therefore, seems that the information given about Socrates' educational successes in the *Theaetetus* is somewhat exaggerated.

One might, of course, dismiss this passage together with its relative educational optimism as belonging to a later dialogue and, therefore, not attributable to Socrates, but it would be a decision more convenient than justified. There is nothing improbable about Socrates selecting his companions according to their abilities and being more hopeful about some than others. Indeed, it would have been highly improbable that Socrates did not make such an evaluation and conducted his elenctic operations without any regard for their effect on the people around him. Whatever the ultimate interpretation of the *Theaetetus* passage might be, it expresses a relative optimism on the educational impact of the *elenchus* on Socrates' companions.

6   The dialogue features Clinias, the son of Axiochus. The character should not be confused with Clinias, the father of Alcibiades (*Protagoras* 309c10; *Gorgias* 481d4; *Alcibiades* 105d2, 112c4; *Alcibiades II* 141b4), or Clinias, Alcibiades' brother (*Protagoras* 320a4; *Alcibiades* 104b5–6, 118e3–5), or with Clinias of Crete, who appears in the *Laws*. The Clinias of the *Euthydemus* also appears in Xenophon's *Symposium* and in Pseudo-Plato's *Axiochus*.

But there are some statements about the *elenchus* that sound not only less optimistic but quite puzzling. In the *Apology*, Socrates again addresses the question of his alleged teaching and says: "And I cannot justly be held responsible for the good or bad conduct of these people, as I never promised to teach them anything and have not done so" (33b3–5, Grube trans.). This disclaimer sounds dissonant not only because it contradicts the *Theaetetus* passage but also because it seems somewhat undignified, not to say un-Socratic. Everyone engaged in public life, especially a man who believed himself to be conducting a god's mission, should take at least some responsibility for the effects on society.

But then Socrates makes even more astonishing statement.

"Why then do some people enjoy spending considerable time in my company? You have heard why, men of Athens; I have told you the whole truth. They enjoy hearing those being questioned who think they are wise, but are not. And this is not unpleasant." (33b8–c4, Grube trans.)

What he said amounts to the following. Young people participated in his disputes with the Athenians and with the sophists because they found it enjoyable and even entertaining to watch how other people were humiliated by having their ignorance exposed. There is no indication in the above statement that what the witnesses enjoyed was the triumph of truth over falsehood, virtue over vice, justice over injustice. The young men rather derived their enjoyment from watching those who considered themselves wise suffer setbacks and embarrass themselves.

None of the expressions from the *Theaetetus* can be applied to those young men: there is no "making progress," "amazing" or otherwise, and no "multitude of beautiful things." In this statement, Socrates seems to imply that what was happening in Athens was a clash between himself and the Athenians and that he did not really care how this clash would impact those around him who found his activity attractive. Moreover, he treated those around him condescendingly, not even allowing his *elenchus* to give their souls anything more than *Schadenfreude*.

The above is not an isolated example of the less edifying aspects of the *elenchus*. Another instance, even more dissonant, we find in Socrates' blunt remarks regarding his future followers. He makes these remarks in the final parts of his speech before the Athenian jurors after the death sentence is pronounced and directs them to those who voted in favor of the sentence. His statement sounded like a prophecy about the fate of his *elenchus* and those who will practice it:

> "I say gentlemen, to those who voted to kill me, that vengeance will come upon you immediately after my death, a vengeance much harder to bear than that which you took in killing me. You did this in the belief that you would avoid giving an account of your life, but I maintain that quite the opposite will happen to you. There will be more people to test you (*hoi elenchontes*), whom I now held back, but you did not notice it. They will be more difficult to deal with as they will be younger and you will resent them more. You are wrong if you believe that by killing people you will prevent anyone from reproaching you for not living in the right way." (39c4–d3, Grube trans.)

Socrates thus presaged the emergence of the new generation of *hoi elenchontes*, the new examiners of human wisdom, who would more acutely challenge the unfounded pretensions of the Athenians toward moral knowledge. The description of these elenctors bears a certain similarity to the young men who enjoyed watching Socrates' elenctic performances. The remarkable fact is that the new elenctors were not presented as particularly sensitive to goodness or as wise men. Socrates did not call them virtuous, just, or even interested in philosophizing about virtue and justice. There is not the slightest hint that they would continue his god-given mission. Instead, they would be proficient in *elenchus*, perhaps enjoy their skills, and embarrass the Athenians by revealing their illusions of knowledge and exposing their deplorable behavior. That was why the punishment would not only be painful but also "much harder to bear" than Socrates' sentence.

One may, of course, wonder to what extent Socrates' outburst expresses his bitterness toward the judges and to what extent it conveys the evaluation of his own role in society. If the latter is the case, then the conclusion is rather depressing. The practice of the *elenchus* would no longer be related to what Socrates valued most—virtue, justice, knowledge—but would degenerate into an ordinary technical and intellectual skill, focused on the negative part of human conduct. If those people were to represent the new élite of Athens benefiting from the new approach to knowledge introduced by Socrates, then he would have to admit that his elenctic method turns out to be a failure. Its role as a tool to punish the Athenians by mercilessly unmasking their ignorance might perhaps bring some good, but it certainly falls short of what Socrates intended it to be.[7]

4. Socrates' mission

On the basis of what has been said thus far, Socrates' situation in the polis was the following. On the side of the general public: some people were angry with Socrates for having their ignorance exposed; some felt the power of the *elenchus*, but tried to weaken it by calling it "ironic"; and many did not believe him to speak seriously and, therefore, dismissed his arguments altogether. On the side of Socrates' associates: some claimed to benefit remarkably from being in his company, but there is no evidence to support this claim; many were attracted to Socrates as a person and by his words, though this did not necessarily have a great impact on their minds; some valued the *elenchus*, but only as a negative tool and divorced it from the strong ethical message of Socrates' philosophy.

As for Socrates himself, he never doubted the validity of the *elenchus* and never suggested he would replace his elenctic pursuits with a better method. He even imagined that should there be an afterlife, he would

---

7   I consider the interpretations which treat the above passage as a reference to Plato himself as mistaken (Burnet 1991:244; Friedländer 1965:170; Stokes1997:182). Plato was not an elenctor and did not engage in probing dialogues as did Socrates. He could not, therefore, have considered himself as Socrates' elenchic successor. The passage explicitly refers to *elenchus* as specifically understood and practised. Plato could have been aware of the possible pitfalls of the elenctic practices. In the *Republic* (539b2–6) we find a following passage: "When young people get their first taste of arguments, they misuse it by treating it as a kind of game of contradiction. They imitate those who've refuted them by refuting others themselves, and, like puppies, they enjoy dragging and tearing those around them with their arguments" (Grube, Reeve trans.).

continue his elenctic work with those in the other world (*Apology* 41b4–c4). But the *elenchus* did not really touch the core of his philosophy: most of what constitutes SBT is justified by his criteria of knowledge (SCK) or by EID, that is, by the propositions that precede his more substantive moral pursuits.

This picture of Socrates' situation contains, as it is easy to see, an internal tension between the rather modest results of his activity and extremely strong claims regarding knowledge and virtue. Although he made certain concessions and exemptions while extending and developing his theory, they never referred to what is crucial—SCK, EID, and SBT. The tension seems quite perplexing, and one might wonder why Socrates never considered addressing this. He had various possibilities to do so: he could preserve the strictness of the philosophy but limit his activity; he could continue his activity but pay much less attention to theory; or he could lower the moral standards that his philosophy stipulated, and at the same time lower the expectations vis-à-vis his associates or people in general. But he did none of this.

Socrates' was not quite a new situation in Greek philosophy. Among his predecessors, it was Heraclitus who faced a similar problem. He too claimed that the logos in the sense of the objective truth that organizes the world and that we discover in our individual experiences, is accessible and common to every human being (fragments 2, 113, 116). And yet, to his dismay, he saw people indifferent to it, as if they were "deaf," "sleeping," similar to "drunks" or "cattle" (fragments 1, 29, 34, 117). Disenchanted, Heraclitus—as Diogenes Laertius tells us—turned into a misanthrope: "he became a hater of his kind and wandered on the mountains, and there he continued to live, making his diet of grass and herbs" (IX.3 Hicks trans.).

Socrates did not withdraw from the world, and the main reason was the god's command. This was a powerful incentive, and Socrates hints in the *Apology* how powerful it was: "That I am the kind of person to be a gift of the god to the city you might realize from the fact that it does not seem like human nature for me to have neglected all my own affairs and to have tolerated this neglect now for so many years while I was always concerned with you" (31a7–b3, Grube trans.). The idea of the mission was thus not an oddity of Socrates' character, something that could be dismissed as a cultural by-product of the times, but an essential component of his being a philosopher (though not of his philosophy).

The *Apology* gives us two explanations of why he thought himself on the god's mission, and both are compatible with Socrates' personality. The first is well-known. Socrates accepted the oracle's interpretation of the words of the god (Apollo). In an attempt to fathom the import of Pythia's assertion that no man is wiser than Socrates and aware of his lack of knowledge, he tried to prove the oracle wrong. Being unsuccessful, he concluded that the statement must be true. The reconstructed reasoning runs as follows:

(i)   Pythia stated that no man was wiser than Socrates;
(ii) this assertion—given the oracle's truthfulness and Socrates' inability to find falsifying examples—is true;
(iii) but it is also true that Socrates did not possess knowledge;
(iv) the only way to reconcile propositions (ii) and (iii) is to assume that Socrates' activity which the oracle prompted—examining people's knowledge—is what the god expected him to do.

This argument—it must be admitted—is not clearly stated in the text but is an accurate approximation of how Socrates might have reasoned. Needless to say, the conclusion is somewhat hasty, given the premises, but it is important that the justification of the mission is a rational interpretation of certain assumptions—what the god says must be true, Socrates was not wise, but the oracle said he was. It was not the god that spoke to Socrates, but it is Socrates himself who inferred the god's plan from a certain set of propositions.

But elsewhere in the *Apology*, Socrates gives us a somewhat different explanation. He says:

> "To do this has, as I say, been enjoined upon me by the god, by means of oracles and dreams, and in every other way that a divine manifestation has ever ordered a man to do anything. This is true, gentlemen, and can easily be established." (33c4–8, Grube trans.)

One can see that this justification is less rational in the sense that the message from the gods was more direct, through dreams and some other divine manifestations. We know little about these dreams and manifestations, but apparently the message was more straightforward, and the messenger sent clearer signals. Socrates' interpretive contribution must have been considerably smaller than in the previous case.

If we merge these two explanations, we will have the following scenario. First, inspired by the oracle, Socrates started testing people, and not being wise himself but being able to prove people's ignorance, he came to the conclusion that this activity of testing had the god's sanction. Then he began to have visions, dreams, and other signals corroborating this conclusion. The chronology might have been, of course, the reverse, but it makes no difference. In the *Phaedo* we find the relevant testimony. "Often in past life the same dream had visited me, now in one guise, now in another, but always saying the same thing: *Socrates*, it said, *make art and practice it ...* so the dream was telling me to do the very thing that I was doing, to make art, since philosophy is a very high art and that was what I was making" (60e3–61a3, Gallop transl.). In the dream, Socrates was explicitly told to practice art, which he interpreted as the art of philosophy. In the *Phaedo*, "philosophy" has a broader (Platonic) meaning, but in the *Apology*, it refers to the *elenchus*. We can therefore infer that Socrates came to the conclusion that the god ordered him to practice the *elenchus*.

That Socrates treated dreams seriously is a well-known fact. For example, in the opening scene of the *Crito*, he predicts the deferral of his death from the dream from which he had been just awakened (44a2–b6). In the dream, he saw "a beautiful comely woman dressed in white" who using a quotation from the *Iliad* (9.363) told him he would "arrive at fertile Phthia on the third day" (Grube trans.). These words could probably be interpreted in a variety of ways, and yet Socrates did not have the slightest doubt that they referred to his current situation.[8] For him, the dream's meaning was "clear" (*enarges*).

5. Mission, the god, and *elenchus*

The *Apology* gives us three clues in the three passages in which Socrates is more specific about how he understood his mission. When we look at the

---

8   Socrates was to die the after the ship from Delos arrived, and he believed the
     dream meant that the ship would arrive not on this day, but the following
     one. Hence, he would die on the third day.

three of them, we will find that they cover the three major areas of Socrates' philosophical inquiry: the first concerns knowledge, the second virtue, and the third is about the Athenian state, and thus touches upon politics. Ultimately Socrates must have come to the conclusion that the god ordered him not only to practice the *elenchus* and test people's knowledge but expound his entire philosophy and convince them as to its truth.

There are at least two questions that need to be asked. The first is: what content did Socrates claim the god ordered him to convey to the people, and on what grounds did he make such a claim? The second is: what did the god's anointment add to this content?

5.1 Wisdom and ignorance

For the first time, Socrates speaks about the mission after he finishes describing his experience with the three groups—the politicians, poets, and manufacturers—whom he proved not to be wise. And then he says:

> "The god is wise and his oracular response meant that human wisdom is worth little or nothing, and when he says this man Socrates, he is using my name as an example, as if he said: *This man among you, mortals, is wisest who, like Socrates understands that his wisdom is worthless.* So even now I continue this investigation as the god bade me—and I go round seeking out anyone, citizen or stranger, whom I think wise. Then if I do not think he is, I come to the assistance of the god and show him that he is not wise." (23a5–b7, Grube transl.)

The passage looks like the sketch of a theological-anthropological theory. We have, on the one hand, the god and, on the other, a human person, and the difference is not only that the former is immortal and the latter mortal—this much every Greek knew—but that the god had real wisdom whereas the human wisdom was exiguous. This rather sweeping statement about the mission should come as a surprise. Up to now, one would think that the god's order was only to continue the elenctic investigations and not to expound any particular theory, especially one of such magnitude.

And yet the passage unequivocally states that Socrates included this theory in the oracle and the god's message. But whatever Socrates' belief, neither the oracle nor other divine manifestations stated it explicitly, and he must have inferred this theory through some implicit argumentation. A possible argument to that effect would run as follows: (a) the god ordered Socrates to continue the elenctic investigation to expose people's ignorance and their unfounded claims to knowledge; (b) Socrates was also ignorant but still was wiser than the rest of mankind in "one little thing" (21d6), and this one little thing was his ability to distinguish what was and what was not knowledge; (c) having this ability he could discover an immense distance between the god's knowledge and human knowledge. As one can see, the conclusion, allegedly a part of the god's message, required more complicated reasoning, and only (a) Socrates could qualify as one coming more or less directly from the oracle.

To the question of what the concept of mission contributed to the argument, we can point out three such added values. The first is a transition from the testing of Pythia's concrete words to the conviction that this testing should be Socrates' main activity. The sentence "no one is wiser than Socrates" could have been treated simply as a hypothesis to be verified. And since Socrates found no one wiser than himself, he had a good reason to accept the hypothesis as true, which would end the experiment. He could, of course, continue his search for such a falsifying example, but that was unnecessary after he examined the main groups representing the Athenian society.

There is no obvious transition from this hypothesis accepted as true to a directive that Socrates had to continue his examination of his fellow Athenians—not because the hypothesis needed more corroboration, but because this examination had a larger meaning and had to be continued precisely because of this larger meaning. In fact, there is no transition at all. And this was something that Socrates' philosophy did not and could not provide. And this is where the oracle and dreams come in. When Socrates said he wanted to examine "what the oracle meant" (21e6), he had in mind not the meaning of the sentence, but the reason why the god sent such a message at all. And soon he became sure the sign was a call to action and not just a proposition about the level of knowledge among the citizens of Athens.

The second added value of the mission was the introduction of the concept of divine wisdom/knowledge. Connecting the god with wisdom is a new idea. Among the presocratic philosophers, one might find a view that the basic substance had both divine and cognitive qualities,[9] but such a substance was more of an active force than the god whom Socrates had in mind. When Socrates talked of the god, the background of his thoughts was Greek religion and its gods, including Apollo, to whom he showed particular devotion. In other words, he did not talk about the divine, *to theion*, but about the god *tout court*. And the basic quality—in fact, the only one Socrates mentions—of this god is wisdom and not power, or infinity, or timelessness.

In the *Apology*, Socrates uses both the singular and plural forms. But when he attributed wisdom to the god, only the singular was adequate. Talking about many gods having perfect wisdom seemed absurd. The whole point of polytheism was that each god had a particular character and responsibility, and the characters and responsibilities of all the gods complemented each other. Giving the god the highest status in knowledge eliminates the need to think of other lesser and assuredly not-so-wise gods. If wisdom is the attribute of divinity, a god deficient in wisdom is a contradiction in terms. Several gods, each with perfect knowledge, are collectively a redundancy.

We are not told what divine knowledge is, but if we follow Socrates' concept of the definition, we have to agree that the *eidos* of knowledge does not depend on the adjectives such as "human" or "divine." Knowledge is something that meets certain criteria (SCK), some of which—it will be recalled—emerged during Socrates' conversations with the three groups. The divine knowledge may therefore differ from human knowledge in degree, but not in the *eidos*. It also has to meet the criteria according to which Socrates assessed the opinions of the politicians, poets, and manufacturers. We might, therefore, imagine that divine knowledge encompasses all of what Socrates was looking for and found lacking among his fellow Athenians—definitions organized in a system and in a hierarchy, probably extending to cosmology (which Socrates avoided) and the questions of the afterlife (about which he professed his ignorance). In comparison to this overwhelming view of the god's knowledge, human knowledge is indeed limited and uncertain, which made people's aspirations to wisdom groundless.

9   The best-known example is Anaxagoras' *nous*, about which we read that it has "complete knowledge about everything and the greatest power" (DK 59 B12).

The claim that the god entrusted Socrates with the mission to show the groundlessness of those aspirations and to expose their hubristic nature had another far-reaching consequence. If the basic quality of the god is wisdom, and if the difference between divine wisdom and human wisdom is immense, then the use of the *elenchus* to undermine the unfounded aspirations to wisdom should help to re-establish the correct proportion between divine knowledge and human knowledge, and consequently, between the god and man. The mission that presented itself and, in fact, was epistemological, thus acquired its distinct religious and even theological aspect. The *elenchus* alone would not bring about a similar effect, and when used outside this religious and theological context, it could be used for different purposes, dubious ones included as the example of the hypothetical future elenctors illustrated.

Despite the enormous distance that separated human from divine knowledge, it is precisely the *eidos* of knowledge that humans share with the god, and no matter how small human knowledge is it has in itself the best humans could hope for. Since pursuing knowledge is doing the god's work, no wonder that for Socrates there was always something divine about this pursuit. In the *Meno*—it will be recalled—when Socrates is musing about the grand theory that encompassed everything from the soul to nature and beyond, he attributes it to "priests and priestesses" and "divinely inspired poets" (81a9–b2). But even in the realm of human knowledge, small as it is, pursuing knowledge through elenctic investigations is undoubtedly "the greatest good" (*Apology* 38a2).

There was yet another added value to the mission. It enabled Socrates to explain to himself his exceptionally superior position toward others despite his proclaimed ignorance. He must have been struck by a contrast between the negative power of the *elenchus*, which is quite considerable, and the modest amount of knowledge he attributed to himself and to other people. After all, it was rather extraordinary for a person who professed his ignorance to be a radical and effective critic of the major groups constituting the Athenian society and in fact the whole human race. It may be that the awareness of this contrast led him to a view that only the god's decision could justify it. "I continue the investigation as the god bade me," he says in the above-quoted passage, and then adds: "I come to the assistance of the god."

If one were to describe Socrates' state of mind that led him to these thoughts, it might take the form of a question. "How is it that I, a man who knows how small human wisdom is, who has not mastered any *technē* and has not been able to formulate a more comprehensive theory of virtue, not to mention other subjects, can see and prove the falseness of other people's pretensions to knowledge? The only explanation is that the god, by giving me this ability, wants me to make such use of it that no other person can."

This "one little thing" that Socrates had—to know what is and what is not knowledge—was special in kind. We remember that he dismissed the concept of *epistēmē epistēmēs* and did not consider his epistemological competence to be a form of knowledge, which made the status of SCK rather obscure. Socrates, as we remember, made use of these criteria and translated them, in a modified form, into SBT, but during his conversations with the three groups, he did not state them openly but used as an implied instrument of elenctic inquiries. If he explicitly defined this instrument as a major constituent of knowledge, then considering its significant role in his philosophy he could not call it "the one little thing" and further insist on his ignorance. The concept of mission eliminated the problem: Socrates was in a position to talk legitimately about his ignorance and, equally legitimately, to maintain his god-endorsed superiority toward his interlocutors.

5.2 Virtue and goodness

The second statement appears toward the end of the main part of Socrates' speech, before he described the immoral practices of democratic and oligarchic politicians in Athens.

> "Men of Athens, … I will obey the god rather than you, and as long as I draw breath … I shall not cease to practice philosophy, to exhort you and in my usual way to point out to any one of you whom I happen to meet: Good Sir, you are an Athenian, a citizen of the greatest city with the greatest reputation for both wisdom and power; are you not ashamed of your eagerness to possess as much wealth, reputation and honors as possible, while you do not care for nor give thought to wisdom or truth, or the best possible state of your soul? Then, if one of you disputes

this and says he does care, … I shall question him, examine him and test him, and if I do not think he has attained the goodness that he says he has, I shall reproach him because he attaches little importance to the most important things and greater importance to inferior things. I shall treat in this way anyone I happen to meet, young and old, citizen and stranger, and more so the citizens because you are more kindred to me. Be sure that this is what the god orders me to do, and I think there is no greater blessing for the city than my service to the god." (29d2–30b2, Grube transl.)

The passage gives us a different picture of Socrates' mission. The problem of an unfounded claim to wisdom is no longer there. Nor do we hear anything about the contrast between divine wisdom and human wisdom or about people's hubristic aspirations. Socrates mentions truth and wisdom only as something the Athenians did not care about, not something they groundlessly claimed to have. Thus, the problem with the Athenians was primarily not intellectual conceit but a wrong hierarchy of goods with wealth and reputation having the supreme positions.

Unfortunately, the passage does not clarify what exactly Socrates thought the god's message meant and how he arrived at this meaning. The first part of his statement resembles an *ad hominem* argument to be raised against a typical Athenian citizen. If, as we might imagine, a typical Athenian citizen was a patriot who considered Athens to be the best and noblest polis in the Hellenic world, along the lines Socrates parodied in the *Menexenus*, then Socrates was telling such a citizen that his quality should match the quality of the polis, and that he, the good citizen, should aspire to those high standards. It is, however, unlikely that Socrates could have attributed the *ad hominem* argument to the god's intervention. Such an argument is usually a matter of tactics and cannot possibly stem from any wisdom in the sense that Socrates believed the god to have.

There is not much left in the passage that might qualify as the god's message. The only candidate is the statement that in examining the Athenians, Socrates urged them to strive for virtue and for the best state of their souls. So, in a nutshell, he claimed that the god ordered him to practice *elenchus* to advance his own (that is, Socrates') view of virtue among the

Athenians and encourage them to live according to the standards that follow from it. The superiority of virtue over wealth and fame was one of the propositions of SBT, and its possible justification stemmed from SCK, which, among others, stipulated the hierarchy of the objects of cognition. At the top of this hierarchy were "the most important things" (*kalon kagathon*), which referred to the goodness of the soul, as contrasted with the satisfaction of the body.[10]

As in no way could Socrates find the god's approval of his moral philosophy in the oracle or in the dreams, he must have arrived at such a conclusion through an implicit argumentation. We do not know what this argument might have been, but it is clear that what he had to demonstrate was that the approval of the elenctic investigations necessarily implied the admission of their power to lead the soul to the greatest goods. The problem is, however, that the initial interpretation of the oracle is negative: "this one little thing" could very well serve to expose people's ignorance and their unfounded claims to knowledge as well as the chasm between human and divine wisdom, but it could hardly justify a positive statement that the

10 Socrates had two concepts of the soul—descriptive and normative. First, the soul reflected the internal orderliness of the human beings, which admits of gradation: for evil people, the degree of orderliness is low; for the virtuous, high. Whoever wanted to assess the value of a human being—one had to examine his soul which reflected his moral quality as well as the degree of his self-awareness as a moral agent. To form an opinion about human beings was always difficult in every society because it offered particularly many opportunities for them to conceal themselves behind roles, masks, rituals, social perceptions, and to play games with themselves and with others. The soul was something that existed under those many veils and was to be the proper object of evaluation both in this world and everywhere else (*Gorgias* 523c–e; *Alcibiades I* 130c3–6). On the second view, the soul was what was best in the human person, best in absolute terms. The soul was therefore contrasted with what was inferior: the body and its desires. The soul was the source of knowledge about good and evil, the source from which sprang the human desire for good expressing itself in the inculcation of virtue (*Apology* 29d7–30b4). The first sense of the soul opened the topic of justice, chiefly, punitive justice: it induced a rather dull picture of the human race where virtue was rare, and where mediocrity, selfishness, and ignorance predominated. The second sense of the soul opened the problem of the upper limits of humanity and nobler forms of existence.

greatest goods for human beings are truth, wisdom, and virtue (the best possible state of the soul).

Apparently, Socrates must have believed—though he did not state it explicitly—that the god was not only the patron of the *elenchus*, but also of the assumptions that made the *elenchus* possible and its consequences reliable. This means that the god by encouraging Socrates to pursue the elenctic inquiries awarded his approval to the criteria of knowledge within the framework of which the *elenchus* operated, including not only *a* hierarchy of the objects of cognition but *the* hierarchy of the objects of cognition, which Socrates accepted.

But this implies something more—namely the god's acceptance of the view of human nature that Socrates thought the *elenchus* presupposed. And Socrates modeled his view of human nature on himself when he was practicing the *elenchus*. And he could see that this human nature of the Socratic Man is different from and superior to those natures that were striving for wealth and reputation. The Socratic Man is concentrated on reflection and self-reflection, on the examination of his opinions and his actions. Since the rational part of his nature dominates other parts, and knowledge became the main motivation as well as the criterion of his words and deeds, the key to a virtuous life must be in a well-organized rational soul.

As one can see, quite a lot is presupposed in making a transition from the *elenchus* to virtue and virtuous life. But if in the previous interpretation, Socrates introduced an assumption about the god possessed of perfect wisdom, then it could very well be that in the second interpretation of the mission he made another assumption, this time about man being defined by his rational faculties. Since the god ordered Socrates to practice the *elenchus*, this might mean that *eo ipso* he ordered him to activate in the human beings all these cognitive properties that they had in themselves, even if dormant or insufficiently active, to achieve moral improvement.[11]

---

11 The above sheds some light on the problem pointed out while discussing SBT in Chapter I, namely, the transition from the analytical statements about the concepts to the substantive statement about the soul and virtue. The god's intervention makes it more understandable, though on the argumentative level, the problem did not disappear.

Socrates could have arrived at the positive conclusion without resorting to the concept of a mission, but the claim that the god endorsed his moral philosophy gave it an added value it would not otherwise have. Without being a part of the mission Socrates' concepts of virtue and virtuous life would have required some kind of endorsement in practice, similar to the type that Heraclitus expected from his philosophy, and who not having received it became disillusioned. Whether what Socrates did was or was not teaching, it is rational to see some confirmation of the thesis that the *elenchus* really could lead some people to the truth, wisdom, and virtue, even if or especially if this or similar theses were "iron and adamantine." Socrates' *logoi* have their power, to be sure, but how does one account for their meagre results in the human minds?

We have already pointed out that his interlocutors often confused the power of the *logoi* with the power of his personality. This was the case with Alcibiades. Another example was Nicias. In the *Laches* (187e6–188c3) he recounts his own experience of associating with Socrates. Socrates—said Nicias—was very active, asking people fundamental questions, persuading them to engage in serious self-reflection by drawing them into intellectually demanding debates. Nicias himself liked to keep him company and to be subjected to his *elenchus*. It was good—he explained—to reflect on one's own life, to reconsider the mistakes one had made and kept making, the bad things that one had done and kept doing, rather than wait for old age to bring him wisdom. In Nicias' view, Socrates was a wise and valuable man with a strong personality who did good for those around him. They became more sensible, sensitive, serious, and thoughtful.

The above might be one of the few examples where some effects were visible, yet whether they are personal, or philosophical, or both is difficult to say. But generally, the outcome of Socrates' conversations was, indeed, far from impressive. Some of his interlocutors, such as Callicles, Thrasymachus, Meletus, Polus, Anytus are the antagonists whom he could not convince. In all these conversations, Socrates had the last word in arguments, but his interlocutors knew better. Others like Protagoras and Gorgias had their own views, which they did not change after a confrontation with Socrates. Still, others like Euthyphro, or Charmides, or Laches, or Meno did not quite understand the thrust of Socrates' argument. The intellectual skirmishes he had with all of them certainly did not improve his position in Athens, and finally, the battle was lost in the sense that his life ended and the mission was terminated.

Despite these setbacks, we never hear Socrates complaining—like Heraclitus is famous for doing—that his arguments were falling on deaf ears, and the reason was precisely his conviction of being on the mission. The practical results of the mission, its success or failure, its short-term or long-term assessment, were not within Socrates' competency, just like an ordinary soldier is not expected to make authoritative comments on his commander's military strategy. Socrates had his job to do and was doing it. Whether the god intended some results, this was of secondary importance. In view of the enormous distance between human knowledge and divine knowledge, such a visible progress in virtue seemed rather unlikely, but Socrates was sure that the command included both elements—to show the weakness of human knowledge and to convince people about truth, wisdom, and virtue.

5.3 Gadfly

There is yet another passage relating to the mission, following the previous one. It is one of the best-known literary images in the *Apology*.

> "Indeed, men of Athens, I am far from making a defense now on my own behalf, as might be thought, but on yours, to prevent you from wrongdoing by mistreating the god's gift to you by condemning me; for if you kill me, you will not easily find another like me. I was attached to this city by the god ... as upon a great and noble horse which was somewhat sluggish because of its size and needed to be stirred up by a kind of gadfly. It is to fulfil some such function that I believe the god has placed me in the city. I never cease to rouse each and every one of you, to persuade and reproach you all day long and everywhere I find myself in your company." (30d5–31a1, Grube trans.)

The passage goes further than the previous two in specifying the god's alleged will. The metaphor of a horse and a gadfly surely was Socrates' invention and not the god's. Nothing in the oracle could even indirectly suggest this metaphor and had the horse and the gadfly appeared in the dreams, Socrates would not have failed to mention it.[12]

There are some puzzling aspects of the passage. The two previous versions—the distance between human and divine knowledge, and the highest position of truth, wisdom, and virtue—are general and applied to the entire human race. Socrates admitted it himself, saying that he would examine anyone he happened to meet—"citizen and foreigner" (23b4–5), "young and old, citizen and stranger" (30a2–3). In fact, many of his interlocutors were not Athenian citizens. It's true that he mentioned Athens as "the greatest city with the greatest reputation for both wisdom and power" (29d6–7), but, as I argue above, it was rather a part of an *ad hominem* argument and not the god's message.

It seems that the only ground for singling out Athens as the object of the mission was that Socrates practiced *elenchus* in this polis, his native polis, and he felt "closer kinship" with his fellow citizens than with the foreigners (30a4). And since his activity was political, that is, it extended to the polis in its entirety, he must have come to the conclusion that the *elenchus* was to affect not only his interlocutors but also the Athenian state.

Let us note that what we learn about politics from the passage does not really extend beyond the practicing of the *elenchus*. Socrates talked about "stirring up," "rousing," "persuading," and "reproaching" the Athenians, and each of these verbs could denote various forms of elenctic

12 In an engaging article, Marshall pointed out an alternative reading of *myōps* —not as a gadfly, but as a spur. To the question of why it matters whether we choose one rendering or the other, she answers as follows: the gadfly metaphor implies that "an animal stung by an insect does not move in a set direction; it merely moves"; the spur metaphor suggests "a pedagogical purpose and can be used by an intelligent agent." Then she concludes: "If Socrates' god in the *Apology* has a teaching purpose in mind for the good of the city, the spur translation makes more sense than a fly, which makes the horse move without direction" (2017:173). The argument is interesting, but I am not sure the second option was Socrates' intention. In the book, I argue that Socrates knew that the Athenian horse was not moving in the correct direction and that the sense of the mission was the god's order itself, not its justification. If the god had ascribed to Socrates his executor of the plan to improve the city, Socrates would have certainly fallen into doubt and frustration, seeing the failure of his efforts.

examinations. We will not find a single reference to true politics, *homonoia*, and *philia*, good laws, or the expert in justice. But neither do we hear the harshest words of criticism, such as "swelling and festering" of the Athenian state. One might even be tempted to say that on this view, Socrates' political role consisted in intellectually activating the Athenians, and, since the city state was—in analogy to a horse—"great and noble," one would expect that when awakened and activated, Athens had a chance to recover from its sluggishness. Such an optimistic conclusion would be, however, premature.

Most statements given above and attributed to Socrates he himself could have argued for and did not need the god's blessing. Before we answer why Socrates engaged the god in his role in Athenian politics, let us indicate another striking point. Socrates combined two tones—one slightly jocose and the other more serious. The metaphor of the horse and the gadfly has a touch of self-deprecation with Socrates belittling himself—in the form of a rhetorical device rather than for the sake of a moral manifestation—to the role of an annoying pest and mockingly dignifying Athens by comparing it to an impressive though somewhat dull animal.

The picture is remarkably vivid but can be misleading: it might associate Socrates with the features of a character that were definitely not his. He was not carried by *l'esprit de contradiction*; nor was he a social critic, a dissentient, a sparkplug, a controversialist, a faultfinder, or a gainsayer. Such roles of a gadfly fall short of the real value and scope of Socratic philosophy. In short, Socrates was primarily a philosopher, not an intellectual *provocateur*, as the gadfly metaphor might imply.

Socrates also used a serious tone as if to weaken the force of such an association. He was the god's gift to the city, and this gift the Athenians not only rejected but were likely to eliminate altogether by killing him. Killing a gadfly is dramatic enough; killing the gift from the god is far more serious. Since the god "placed" Socrates in this role (30e5) and thereby defined his position in the polis, it means that he included the possibility of Socrates' death in his plan, and Socrates, by accepting this mission, had to take into account such an end for himself.

We can now see what the god's alleged endorsement added to Socrates' interpretation of his elenctic investigations. Socrates talked about his activity of "stirring up," "rousing," "persuading," and "reproaching" the Athenians as if it were a confrontation of one person against the entire city, and it is this one person that represented and defended the good of the polis, whereas the rest of the Athenians persisted in their erroneous and harmful conduct. Socrates was telling the Athenians that what they witnessed was a major development in the city-state, in fact, a decisive development in the sense that it provided the polis with an exceptional opportunity for essential betterment. Socrates did not tell the jurors what this betterment might mean, but it was clear that he regarded himself as a unique person that might induce such changes ("you will not easily find another like me") if only the Athenians took his philosophy to heart.

Such an overbearing attitude toward the city and such a grandiose interpretation of his own role would not have been possible to justify solely on argumentative grounds: appealing to the god and his patronage seemed an obvious resort. The danger of being killed only contributed to this sense of the mission. In one of his previous remarks, he drew an analogy between his service in the army and being on the god's mission. Aborting the mission would have been an unpardonable act of disobedience toward his superior and, additionally, a morally disqualifying act of cowardice comparable to desertion from the battlefield.

> "[W]herever a man has taken a position that he believes to be best, or has been placed by his commander, there he must I think remain and face danger, without a thought for death or anything else, rather than disgrace. It would have been a dreadful way to behave, men of Athens, if, at Potidaea, Amphipolis and Delium, I had, at the risk of death, like anyone else, remained at my post where those you had elected to command had ordered me, and then, when the god ordered me, as I thought and believed, to live the life of a philosopher, to examine myself and others, I had abandoned my post for fear of death or anything else." (28d6–29a1, Grube trans.)

This remark appears earlier in the speech, not in the context of the gadfly-horse metaphor, but seems to be singularly relevant to it. Out of the three interpretations of the mission, only the third mentioned the killing of Socrates in discharging the duties bestowed on him by the god. Gadfly or not, Socrates is at the post where the god placed him, and he could not abandon it "for fear of death or anything else."

To sum up the remarks on Socrates' mission: The fact that he believed himself to be doing the god's work gave the image of his philosophy a new aspect. The Athenians could see that there was more to his elenctic arguments than just a laborious coordination of various propositions and their logical consequences. The unswerving persistence with which Socrates practiced the *elenchus* reveals not only his extraordinary intellectual capacities but also a higher motivation for his philosophizing.

Whether his remarks about the mission convinced anyone or, on the contrary, irritated the jurors and increased their hostility toward him, we do not know for sure. Judging from the final outcome of the trial, the claim about the god's work did not attract many sympathizers. It seems, however, that what in the first place motivated Socrates was not an intention to save his life but, as I have argued, to make the gap between theory and practice less acute. Each of the three versions of the mission was to provide something that the *elenchus* in itself and by itself could not deliver. They helped him to find answers to the three perplexing questions: (i) how could his being aware of ignorance contribute to knowledge?; (ii) how could he insist on the absolute character of certain moral propositions despite a striking lack of empirical corroboration?; (iii) and how could his theoretical and somewhat pedantic inquiries into definitional problems make him consider himself a major public figure in the Athenian polis?

6. Socrates' charm

There is yet another facet of Socrates's activity, independent of the *elenchus*, but important for understanding his influence on people. He was a person of unique charm, which came from his powerful personality and which some found captivating, but others also beguiling and disconcerting. People may also have seen him as a wizard who could paralyze people's minds with his *logoi* and make them unable to free themselves from the aporia.

6.1 Enchanting

This ability to enchant his interlocutors is rendered by the Greek verbs *kēleō* and *goēteuō* and denotes a compelling, pre-intellectual attraction that many felt in Socrates' presence and that was not directly the effect of his argumentative power; about the people who felt this attraction, one could say that they were inspired, possessed, or driven out of their senses (the corresponding verbs being *katechō* and *ekplessō*). For a philosopher, charm need not be an asset as it could make him similar to a wizard or charlatan rather than a man of wisdom, especially for the philosopher for whom the *logoi* were the basic tool and, at the same time, one of the principal goals.

Socrates himself made numerous derisive comments about the herd instinct exhibited by the Athenians when they yielded to the charms and wiles of the sophists. When he saw a crowd of young men around Protagoras, he said that the sophist "enchants (*kēlōn*) them with his voice like Orpheus, and they follow his voice, being enchanted (*kekēlēmenoi*)" (*Protagoras* 315a8–b1). Is it possible to say the same about Socrates? Was the reaction of his interlocutors any different from that of Protagoras' students who yielded to the latter's charm like to Orpheus' voice?

We can find some hints in the final part of the *Symposium* where Alcibiades makes his soul-searching monologue about his relationship with Socrates. We already know that this relation had a homoerotic undercurrent, which made Alcibiades confuse the attraction to Socrates with a desire to follow the Socratic ideas. But apart from homoeroticism, there is something else that Alcibiades identified in his bond with Socrates, and this is precisely the latter's enticing power. In this monologue, he compared Socrates to a legendary aulos player Marsyas, who "charmed" or "cast spells" (*ekēlei*) on human beings through instruments. Socrates—says Alcibiades—did "the same," but "with *logoi* alone." And then Alcibiades developed an analogy between the aulos-player and the philosopher. His description of Marsyas' art is the following:

(1) his charm derived not only from how he played his aulos, but from the melodies he composed;

(2) those melodies, regardless of whether played by good or by bad players, had the power to make the listeners "possessed" (*katechesthai*);

(3) and because they were divine, they could also "reveal those people who are in need of the gods and initiatory rituals"[13] (*Symposium* 215c1–6, Benardete trans.).

Alcibiades' ensuing remarks suggest that Socrates resembled Marsyas with respect to all three aspects. But it soon becomes clear that his argument is problematic. The most obvious is (1). We can assume that Socrates' *logoi* corresponded to Marsyas' melodies. Alcibiades did not specify what *logoi* he had in mind. He only said that he had "heard Pericles and other good speakers," and none of them managed to make such an impact on his soul as Socrates' *logoi* did. But it was not the speaker's rhetorical skill or the aulos player's performing artistry that was responsible for this effect. The value of these statements, like the beauty of Marsyas' melodies, was objective and inhered in the works themselves.

Alcibiades stated it explicitly in (2), where he made the following claim: just as a poor player could not destroy the beauty of Marsyas' music, a man with little talent to formulate arguments could convey the power of Socrates' *logoi* and exert a comparable influence on the listeners. "Let any anyone—man, woman, or child—listen to you or even to a poor account of what you say—and we are all overwhelmed, completely possessed" (215d3–6, Nehamas, Woodruff trans. modified).

But this is doubtful, if not plainly false. To claim that no matter how poor a player is, the beauty of a musical masterpiece will always reveal itself, is as difficult to accept as its counterpart that no matter how inept in making arguments a philosopher is, the truth in them will always enthrall the minds of the listeners. But more important is that point (2) undermines Alcibiades' view that Socrates had a singularly enchanting personality and could cast spells on people. If anyone equipped with Socrates' arguments could charm the listeners and make them feel possessed, then Socrates was simply a creator of *logoi*, but as a speaker, he was no different from anyone else, at least from the point of view of his effect on the people.

---

13 Some translate *deomenous* as "ready for," but "in need of" seems a more obvious rendering.

We cannot find any example, nor did Alcibiades provide one, of a poor speaker bewitching people by Socrates' arguments. Furthermore, since Alcibiades made so much of it, it should be natural for him to prove the power of those arguments by showing how they worked miracles when expounded by inferior speakers. There are no examples because it is most unlikely that such people existed. Indeed, it would be difficult to imagine Alcibiades, with his larger-than-life character, being possessed or under a spell cast by a poor speaker reciting Socrates' *logoi*.

Alcibiades was not consistent on this point and could not be. On the one hand, he emphasized a distinction between Socrates and his *logoi*, repeatedly claiming that it was the *logoi* rather than the person that affected him. On the other hand, he admitted—independently of Marsyas' analogy—that Socrates' personality overwhelmed him and that he was deeply impressed by the intellectual and moral power that emanated from him. It was only before Socrates that he felt shame. "In regard to this human being alone"—he says—"have I been affected in a way that no one would suspect was in me—to feel shame before anyone at all. Only before him do I feel shame" (216a7–b2, Benardete trans.).

The point (2) of the analogy is, therefore—as stated at 215d3–6—untenable: it serves only to stress what (3) will undermine—namely, that Socrates' message was simply a set of valid propositions. The core of Alcibiades' claim appears in (3), though some of it is guesswork. Alcibiades did not say explicitly what it was he found in Socrates' words. We can infer it from the analogy: Socrates did with the words "the same" what Marsyas did with the instruments, and Marsyas' music revealed the people who were in need of "the gods and initiatory rituals," so Socrates' *logoi* should likewise reveal the people who had in them the same need. And there is no doubt Alcibiades also included himself. "I am still in need of much myself," he admits.

In a generalized form, Alcibiades' statement would run like this. Certain people show peculiar propensity and desire for higher things, to be close to the gods and to grasp the divine mysteries through participation in initiatory rituals. These propensities and desires could be latent and require some impulse to come to the fore. And Socrates did precisely this: from the reactions to his *logoi*, one could identify the people who needed those higher things—the gods and the rituals. Alcibiades included himself among those people and said that this experience of higher things generated anxiety as his soul became "troubled" and "distressed" at his "slavish conditions" (215e5–6, Benardete trans.).

Whether Alcibiades' testimony was sincere, we cannot know. What we know about him indicates that he was not the best candidate to pursue higher things, such as being close to the gods and participating in religious rituals. But the fact is, he perceived Socrates as someone who exposed in people their latent religious yearnings.

Alcibiades thus presented Socrates more like a wizard or priest who leads people into a state of enthusiasm or *mania* than a philosopher who opens their minds to arguments. He ignored Socrates' philosophical side, did not mention the *elenchus*, and passed over the controversial and demanding propositions about justice and injustice. Although Alcibiades talked about Socrates' *logoi*, it seems that—despite what he claimed in (1) and (2) about the objectivity of Socrates' message—what he had in mind were not arguments, propositions, or definitions, but rather words and sentences that through their mesmerizing power generated profound emotional agitation. The emotions were so great that Alcibiades, an extremely popular public figure, could talk of his "slavish" condition, dramatically denigrating his own political activity in Athens (216a5).

In an outburst of exaltation, he says: "whenever I listen, my heart jumps far more than the Corybantes', and tears pour out under the power of his *logoi*, and I see they affect many others in the same way" (215e1–3, Benardete trans.). And a little later, he says he wanted to liberate himself from Socrates' imposing presence: "I stopped my ears and took off in flight, as if from the Sirens" (216a5–6, Benardete trans.).[14] These remarks make it clear that what Alcibiades was escaping from was not the *logoi* as arguments or propositions—after all, one cannot get rid of them by stopping one's ears— but Socrates' hypnotic influence and his enchanting personality. This is why under this influence he compared himself to the Corybantes, worshipers of the goddess Kybele, whose rhythmic music and dancing brought them to a state of near madness and complete loss of control.

14 Let it be noted that Socrates uses a similar expression in a parody of a patriotic speech in the *Menexenus*. He talks about a logos sounding like an aulos (*enaulos ho logos*) and the voice of the speaker ringing in his ears (235c1–2).

The Corybantes metaphor also appears on other occasions in the So-cratic dialogues. They were referred to in Socrates' conversation with Ion (*Ion* 533e5–534a7), in which he explained what accounted for poetry's beauty. And he asserted that the poets were "divinely inspired" (*entheoi*) and "possessed" (*katechomenoi*). In this, they resembled the Corybantes. "Just as the Corybantes are not in their right minds when they dance, lyric poets, too, are not in their right minds when they make those beautiful lyrics" (533e–534a, Nehamas, Woodruff trans.). Such a description of the poets roughly repeats what one could read in the *Apology* (22c1–2).

Another occasion was in the *Euthydemus*, and this time it was the sophists who were mockingly compared to the Corybantes. Socrates was drawing the at-tention of his young friend, Clinias, to the sophists' behavior toward him and how they employed various tricks to initiate him into their circle. The sophists— Socrates was saying—"are doing exactly what people do in the Corybantic mys-teries when they enthrone a person, they intended to initiate…. These two [sophists] are doing nothing except dancing around you and making sportive leaps with a view to initiating you presently" (277d5–e2, Sprague trans.).[15]

There is one more occasion where the Corybantes metaphor appears. Socrates must have liked this metaphor because this time he also uses it when talking about himself. In the last passage of the *Crito*, where we have a lengthy account of the Athenian Laws explaining why escaping from prison would be unjust, Socrates says,

> "Crito, my dear friend, be assured that these are the words I seem to hear, as the Corybantes seem to hear the music of their *auloi* and the echo of these *logoi* resounds in me, and makes it impossible for me to hear anything else. As far as my present beliefs go, if you speak in opposition to them, you will speak in vain." (54d2–6, Grube trans.)

What must strike the reader is the inconsistency in using the Cory-bantes metaphor. Two types of usage—opposed to each other—seem

15 Also, in the *Laws*, Plato mentioned the Corybantes when he described a mother putting her children to sleep with rocking motions and humming (790d–e).

obvious, at least from Socrates' perspective. On the one hand, we have the poets who were divinely inspired and possessed and who, precisely because of the state they were in created beautiful poems, and on the other, the sophists enticing young men with their intellectual tricks, quasi-mysteries and "sportive leaps," which looked like initiating rites and which drew those men into the sophists' circle. Socrates criticized both groups for the same reason—neither made use of nor was even interested in knowledge. But for both, the Corybantes metaphor was adequate, except that for the poets the metaphor denoted something genuine, whereas for the sophists—it is something contrived. The poets, therefore, occupied a worthier place in his eyes because they said "many fine things" and it was "natural" for them that they had little control over what they were doing, being primarily motivated by "inspiration just like seers and soothsayers" (*Apology* 22c1–3). About the sophists, Socrates could not say any of this, so he found no redeeming qualities in them and the work they did,.

The most interesting are the remaining examples, that of Alcibiades and of Socrates himself: the Corybantes metaphor applies to both but describes different states of mind. To the question of what Socrates envisioned when he compared himself to the Corybantes in the *Crito*, the only possible answer is that he saw the *logoi* about justice, not in the process of their elenctic verification, but in their final form that constituted SBT. We know that Socrates accepted these *logoi*—such as "injustice is the greatest evil" or "*adikein* is worse than *adikeisthai*"—as irrefutably true, either as self-evident in themselves or as the direct consequences of SCK or EID theory. No other justification or authority was necessary to reinforce them.

The Corybantes metaphor, therefore, did not provide an additional justification but described how the powerful impact of the *logoi* produced in Socrates an unconditional dedication to justice. The irresistibility of the *logoi* was not only intellectual, limited to a reasoning faculty, but seemed to take control of the entire person ("the echo of these *logoi* ... makes it impossible for me to hear anything else") through its unique, almost divine beauty (hence, a comparison to the music of the *auloi*). The *logoi* had for him a mysterious divine appeal, and, therefore, all the efforts to turn him away from them were futile ("if you speak in opposition to them, you will speak in vain")—as were any attempts to persuade the Corybantes to desist.

Such an interpretation of the metaphor shows how great a distance separated Socrates from his interlocutors. Having done his elenctic work, he accepted and arranged a set of basic propositions and, finally, internalized them so that they generated a state of quasi-divine inspiration in him. His interlocutors were in the early stages, grappling with the elenctic inquiries in which Socrates engaged them, and yet—as the examples of Polus, Thrasymachus, Callicles, et al. demonstrate—unable to give the basic propositions their firm endorsement.

But Alcibiades' case was different. He seems to accept the validity of Socrates' *logoi*, but although he effusively praised them, he never really reflected on them. Not once did he invoke the concept of justice, not to mention SBT and related propositions that constituted Socrates' philosophy. Instead, he jumped directly into the Corybantes metaphor and the state of quasi-divine elation that it described without really reorienting his character in accordance with Socrates' moral precepts. Hence his reaction—highly emotional, somewhat frantic, with tears pouring out and heart pounding— lacked a sense of stability and self-assurance that characterized Socrates' conduct. We know from the *Meno* that according to Socrates, the only way to integrate and stabilize the content of one's mind is through *aitias logismos*—a causal chain of arguments; otherwise, the opinions would disperse and disappear. Not bringing about any lasting results, they could not turn him away from his "slavish" life as a politician.

We do not know how many people Socrates charmed in this way, but Alcibiades' does not look like an isolated case. There is nothing unusual in a situation when a young man of great intelligence and energy, meeting an older mentor of imposing personality, impressed by his strong and exceptionally demanding moral views but being himself unable to think them through and draw serious practical consequences, becomes emotionally agitated and carried away by an upsurge of religious or quasi-religious inspiration. Whether the Corybantes metaphor might be quite adequate here is of lesser importance.

Socrates would certainly not include Alcibiades—had he believed in the sincerity of these emotions—in the same category as the poets who, as he asserted, were "by nature" possessed and could—thanks to divine inspiration—produce remarkable poetry. Nor would he put him together with those *hēgemones* he mentioned in the *Meno*, who had "many great successes in what they said and did" and "all without thought" (99d4). Alcibiades represented a category of young men whom Socrates the philosopher failed to inspire, but in whom Socrates the charmer managed to ignite some flame of deeper self-reflection, albeit short-lived and inconsequential.

6.2 Benumbing

But Socrates' charm might have a different effect—not enthusiasm, but a sort of mental paralysis resulting from the aporia that the *elenchus* generated. The conversation between Socrates and Meno provides an example of this. At a certain point, Meno admits being in a state of utter confusion, for which he makes Socrates responsible and therefore compares him to a wizard (*goēs*) who creates perplexity in himself and makes others perplexed (*aporein*).

> "I think you are bewitching and beguiling me, simply putting me under a spell, so that I am quite perplexed. Indeed, if a joke is in order, you seem, in appearance and in every other way, to be like the broad torpedo fish, for it too makes anyone who comes close and touched it feel numb, and you now seem to have had that kind of effect on me, for both my mind and my tongue are numb, and I have no answer to give you." (80a2–b1, Grube trans.)

We can see from Meno's reaction that what he felt hearing Socrates' arguments was not simply a sense of intellectual difficulty but numbness—that is, a sort of mental deadlock that was so pervasive that it seemed to him to be an effect of Socrates' sorcery: hence the comparison to the torpedo fish[16] which benumbs with an electric shock those that touch it.

Meno's reaction is partly typical and partly exceptional. It is typical in that he emphasized the state of *aporia* in which he found himself, and this was the usual effect of being exposed to Socrates' elenctic inquiries. The state of aporia became one of Socrates' trademarks, and the popular opinion hostile to him maintained that he was "ruining the younger men by reducing them to perplexity (*aporein*)" (*Gorgias* 522b6–7). In the *Theaetetus*,

16　A marbled electric ray or a marbled torpedo (*Torpedo marmorata*), Pliny, *Nat. Hist*. XXXII, 1; Aristotle, *Hist. An*. 620b19–20.

Socrates himself admits: "I am a very odd sort of person, causing people to get into difficulties (*aporein*)" (149a9, Levett, Burnyeat trans.).

But Meno's reaction to aporias was different than that of other inter-locutors. Most of them, as we remember, when they encountered loopholes in their own reasoning, came to a conclusion that Socrates was not speaking seriously but was playing games. Some of them, like Thrasymachus and Callicles, who could not totally resist his arguments, became angry and re-acted harshly toward Socrates' words. But Meno did not behave like this. Instead, he felt numbness: "Both my mind and my tongue are numb, and I have no answer to give you" (80b1, Grube trans.).[17]

Commenting on Meno's reaction, Socrates said that the aporias he en-countered affected him in the same way. He could paralyze not only other people's but also his own mind: "If the torpedo fish is itself numb and so makes others numb, then I resemble it" (80c5–6). The statement is quite unequivocal, but taking it literally creates a problem. How could a man who compared himself to the Corybantes and thereby stressed his absolute dedication to the *logoi* about justice and virtue compare himself, at the same time, to a torpedo fish and talk about the aporias paralyzing his mind? How could the *logoi's* forceful clarity and enchanting truthfulness co-exist with the numbness of the intellectual powers?

But when we look at Socrates' actual reaction to the aporias, we will dis-cover that his statement at 80c5–6 is incorrect: he was not a torpedo fish to himself. Socrates could be confused when he detected an aporia, but he was never intellectually paralyzed, and he would have never used Meno's phrase about the mind and mouth being numb. For him, the confusion and con-tradiction were the signs of an error and required the continuation of inquiry, not a capitulation or, as the sophistic enthusiasts of anti-logic would have it, the end of the inquiry. He had an incessant problem with the definition of virtue and the unity of virtues, but he never stopped delving into the

---

17 One cannot resist a conclusion that benumbing was more characteristic of Socrates' method during his conversation than midwifery. If being benumbed means being unable to respond, then one can contend that irony was not free from it. To say that Socrates was not speaking seriously could result from a sense of helplessness that his interlocutors felt when confronted with Socrates' arguments.

intricacies of the arguments that could shed light on this problem and never really doubted that virtue was supreme and that it was one.

But not being a torpedo fish or a wizard to himself, he behaved like one toward Meno. Meno, as I said above, differed from other interlocutors and what made him different was primarily his simple-mindedness. Unlike Polus, Thrasymachus and Callicles, he had neither the ambition to confront Socrates with his own set of views nor the stubbornness to defend them despite the negative results of the elenctic testing. He seemed pleased to go along with Socrates' pursuits and willingly accepted his intellectual leadership.

Another person who showed similar simple-mindedness as well as willingness to be directed by Socrates was Nicias, the famous military commander during the Peloponnesian War, one of the protagonists in the *Laches*. Nicias did not say the arguments benumbed him and never compared Socrates to a wizard or a torpedo fish. Instead, he used a quasi-military language and talked about Socrates attacking (*enpese*) his interlocutors with the inquiries, his own submission (*paschein*) to these attacks, and about his joy of being near him (187e10–188a6).

As regards Meno, Socrates awakened and drew him out of his state of numbness by launching an attack on his mind. He presented to him what I previously called the "grand theory" (81a9–b2) pertaining to the immortal souls, transmigration of souls, anamnesis and a unified theory of everything. And then he performed the experiment with the slave boy, which was undertaken to prove his own concept of recollection.

One may venture a hypothesis that without this numbness and readiness to follow Socrates, such an attack with a most daring and sweeping theory and a counter-intuitive notion of anamnesis would not have been possible. The minds attached to one view and being in the grip of received ideas, as were those of Thrasymachus et al., are certainly not ready to be engaged in the discussion of what they, most certainly, would have considered even more outlandish than other things Socrates was saying.

But Meno's mind was less dogmatic and not particularly deft in argumentation. His mind resembled in its simplicity that of the slave boy who was also "benumbed" by the geometrical problem (84c8) and became ready to profit from Socrates' intervention. It is quite remarkable to see how Meno, who a short while ago was complaining of being paralyzed by a torpedo fish, soon engaged himself in a conversation about something as controversial as anamnesis. And all this happened thanks to what Nicias would have called Socrates' attack. It is even more remarkable to see how Socrates, who had just admitted being himself touched by the same torpedo fish and unable to solve the problem of virtue, introduced into a conversation, almost immediately, a most offbeat and all-encompassing theory of nature and knowledge.

For today's reader, Socrates' ability to lead other people's minds and involve them in the peregrinations of his own mind seems perhaps more wizardly than his drawing Meno into benumbing aporia. Socrates could have enchanted Meno with the grand theory (nothing in the text indicated he did), but what is more important is that he quickly put aside this theory and reduced the problem of anamnesis to its manageable proportions, exemplified by a geometrical theorem. Socrates led Meno through the geometrical problem as much as he was leading the slave boy, passing rigorously from one statement to another. But one can imagine a person with a stronger and more disordered personality—like that of Alcibiades who would disregard the argumentative discipline of geometry and yet succumb to the breath-taking grandeur of the theory that Socrates attributed to priests and divinely inspired poets and would, similarly to the Corybantes, hear in his words only the enchanting music of the auloi.